Customer Service

Second Edition

ManageFirst
PROGRAM®

NATIONAL
RESTAURANT
ASSOCIATION®

PEARSON

Boston   Columbus   Indianapolis   New York   San Francisco   Upper Saddle River
Amsterdam   Cape Town   Dubai   London   Madrid   Milan   Munich   Paris   Montréal   Toronto
Delhi   Mexico City   São Paulo   Sydney   Hong Kong   Seoul   Singapore   Taipei   Tokyo

Pearson

Editorial Director: Vernon R. Anthony
Executive Acquisitions Editor: Alli Gentile
NRA Product Development: Randall Towns and
    Todd Schlender
Senior Managing Editor: JoEllen Gohr
Associate Managing Editor: Alexandrina B. Wolf
Senior Operations Supervisor: Pat Tonneman
Senior Operations Specialist: Deidra Skahill
Cover photo: iStockPhoto/Thinkstock

Cover design: Karen Steinberg, Element LLC
Director of Marketing: David Gesell
Marketing Coordinator: Les Roberts
Full-Service Project Management: Barbara Hawk and
    Kevin J. Gray, Element LLC
Text and Cover Printer/Binder: LSC Communications/
    Harrisonburg
Text Font: Minion Pro, Myriad Pro Semicondensed

Photography Credits

Front matter: i iStockPhoto/Thinkstock; vii (left) Suhendri Utet/Dreamstime; (right) Meryll/Dreamstime;
viii (top) Mtr/Dreamstime; (bottom) Stratum/Dreamstime; ix (bottom left) Aprescindere/Dreamstime;
xv (bottom left) Petar Neychev/Dreamstime; 24, 77, 121, 183, 209 Nikada/iStockPhoto

All other photographs owned or acquired by the National Restaurant Association Educational Foundation, NRAEF

10 2021

ISBN-10:   0-13-217932-6
ISBN-13: 978-0-13-217932-4

ISBN-10:   0-13-272454-5
ISBN-13: 978-0-13-272454-8

Contents in Brief

Contents

About the National Restaurant Association and the National Restaurant Association Educational Foundation

Founded in 1919, the National Restaurant Association (NRA) is the leading business association for the restaurant and foodservice industry, which comprises 960,000 restaurant and foodservice outlets and a workforce of nearly 13 million employees. We represent the industry in Washington, DC, and advocate on its behalf. We operate the industry's largest trade show (NRA Show, restaurant.org/show); leading food safety training and certification program (ServSafe, servsafe.com); unique career-building high school program (the NRAEF's *ProStart*, prostart.restaurant.org); as well as the *Kids LiveWell* program (restaurant.org/kidslivewell) promoting healthful kids' menu options. For more information, visit www.restaurant.org and find us on Twitter *@WeRRestaurants*, *Facebook*, and *YouTube*.

With the first job experience of one in four U.S. adults occurring in a restaurant or foodservice operation, the industry is uniquely attractive among American industries for entry-level jobs, personal development and growth, employee and manager career paths, and ownership and wealth creation. That is why the National Restaurant Association Educational Foundation (nraef.org), the philanthropic foundation of the NRA, furthers the education of tomorrow's restaurant and foodservice industry professionals and plays a key role in promoting job and career opportunities in the industry by allocating millions of dollars a year toward industry scholarships and educational programs. The NRA works to ensure the most qualified and passionate people enter the industry so that we can better meet the needs of our members and the patrons and clients they serve.

What Is the ManageFirst Program?

The ManageFirst Program is a management training certificate program that exemplifies our commitment to developing materials by the industry, for the industry. The program's

EXAM TOPICS

ManageFirst Core Credential Topics

Hospitality and Restaurant Management
Controlling Foodservice Costs
Hospitality Human Resources Management and Supervision
ServSafe® Food Safety

ManageFirst Foundation Topics

Customer Service
Principles of Food and Beverage Management
Purchasing
Hospitality Accounting
Bar and Beverage Management
Nutrition
Hospitality and Restaurant Marketing
ServSafe Alcohol® Responsible Alcohol Service

most powerful strength is that it is based on a set of competencies defined by the restaurant and foodservice industry as critical for success. The program teaches the skills truly valued by industry professionals.

ManageFirst Program Components

The ManageFirst Program includes a set of books, exams, instructor resources, certificates, a new credential, and support activities and services. By participating in the program, you are demonstrating your commitment to becoming a highly qualified professional either preparing to begin or to advance your career in the restaurant, hospitality, and foodservice industry.

These books cover the range of topics listed in the chart above. You will find the essential content for the topic as defined by industry, as well as learning activities, assessments, case studies, suggested field projects, professional profiles, and testimonials. The exam can be administered either online or in a paper-and-pencil format (see inside front cover for a listing of ISBNs), and it will be proctored. Upon successfully passing the exam, you will be furnished with a customized certificate by the National Restaurant Association. The certificate is a lasting recognition of your accomplishment and a signal to the industry that you have mastered the competencies covered within the particular topic.

To earn this credential, you will be required to pass four core exams and one foundation exam (to be chosen from the remaining program topics) and to document your work experience in the restaurant and foodservice industry. Earning the ManageFirst credential is a significant accomplishment.

We applaud you as you either begin or advance your career in the restaurant, hospitality, and foodservice industry. Visit www.nraef.org to learn about additional career-building resources offered by the NRAEF, including scholarships for college students enrolled in relevant industry programs.

MANAGEFIRST PROGRAM ORDERING INFORMATION

Review copies or support materials

FACULTY FIELD SERVICES
Tel: 800.526.0485

Domestic orders and inquiries

PEARSON CUSTOMER SERVICE
Tel: 800.922.0579
http://www.pearsonhighered.com/

International orders and inquiries

U.S. EXPORT SALES OFFICE
Pearson Education International Customer Service Group
200 Old Tappan Road
Old Tappan, NJ 07675 USA
Tel: 201.767.5021
Fax: 201.767.5625

For corporate, government, and special sales (consultants, corporations, training centers, VARs, and corporate resellers) orders and inquiries

PEARSON CORPORATE SALES
Tel: 317.428.3411
Fax: 317.428.3343
Email: *managefirst@prenhall.com*

For additional information regarding other Pearson publications, instructor and student support materials, locating your sales representative, and much more, please visit *www.pearsonhighered.com/managefirst*.

Acknowledgements

The National Restaurant Association is grateful for the significant contributions made to this book by the following individuals.

Mike Amos
Perkins & Marie Callender's Inc.

Steve Belt
Monical's Pizza

Heather Kane Haberer
Carrols Restaurant Group

Erika Hoover
Monical's Pizza Corp.

Jared Kulka
Red Robin Gourmet Burgers

Tony C. Merritt
Carrols Restaurant Group

H. George Neil
Buffalo Wild Wings

Marci Noguiera
Sodexo—Education Division

Ryan Nowicki
Dave & Busters

Penny Ann Lord Prichard
Wake Tech/NC Community College

Michael Santos
Micatrotto Restaurant Group

Heather Thitoff
Cameron Mitchell Restaurants

Features of the ManageFirst books

We have designed the ManageFirst books to enhance your ability to learn and retain important information that is critical to this restaurant and foodservice industry function. Here are the key features you will find within this book.

BEGINNING EACH BOOK

Real Manager

This is your opportunity to meet a professional who is currently working in the field associated with the book's topic. This person's story will help you gain insight into the responsibilities related to his or her position, as well as the training and educational history linked to it. You will also see the daily and cumulative impact this position has on an operation, and receive advice from a person who has successfully met the challenges of being a manager.

BEGINNING EACH CHAPTER

Inside This Chapter

Chapter content is organized under these major headings.

Learning Objectives

Learning objectives identify what you should be able to do after completing each chapter. These objectives are linked to the required tasks a manager must be able to perform in relation to the function discussed in the book.

Case Study

Each chapter begins with a brief story about the kind of situations that a manager may encounter in the course of his or her work. The story is followed by one or two questions to prompt student discussions about the topics contained within the chapter.

Key Terms

These terms are important for thorough understanding of the chapter's content. They are highlighted throughout the chapter, where they are explicitly defined or their meaning is made clear within the paragraphs in which they appear.

THROUGHOUT EACH CHAPTER

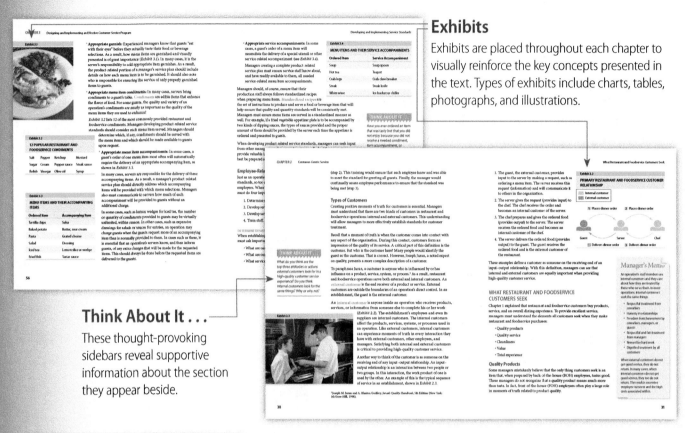

Exhibits

Exhibits are placed throughout each chapter to visually reinforce the key concepts presented in the text. Types of exhibits include charts, tables, photographs, and illustrations.

Think About It . . .

These thought-provoking sidebars reveal supportive information about the section they appear beside.

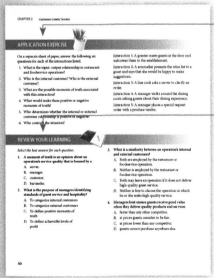

AT THE END OF EACH CHAPTER

Application Exercises and Review Your Learning

These multiple-choice or open- or close-ended questions or problems are designed to test your knowledge of the concepts presented in the chapter. These questions have been aligned with the objectives and should provide you with an opportunity to practice or apply the content that supports these objectives. If you have difficulty answering the Review Your Learning questions, you should review the content further.

AT THE END OF THE BOOK

Field Project

This real-world project gives you the valuable opportunity to apply many of the concepts you will learn in a competency guide. You will interact with industry practitioners, enhance your knowledge, and research, apply, analyze, evaluate, and report on your findings. It will provide you with an in-depth "reality check" of the policies and practices of this management function.

Tim Kirkland
CEO
Renegade Hospitality Group

REAL MANAGER

Philosophy: **Anyone can serve a hot dog . . . but no one can do it with my personality and load it with happiness like I do.**

MY BACKGROUND

I grew up in the 70s in Westminster, Colorado, a bedroom suburb of Denver. My brothers and I were raised by a single mother (still uncommon in those days) who struggled to provide for our little family. Mom worked all sorts of menial jobs, mostly laborious, like working on a roll sheet-metal assembly line or driving a bus. She worked extremely hard at two or three jobs at a time to make ends meet, and was perpetually exhausted.

In my teens, it became very clear to me that if I wanted to obtain any of the "extra" things a teenager desires (cool shoes, hip haircut, dare I even think it—a car), I was going to have to work.

My first job in hospitality was the summer after my sophomore year in high school at the local amusement park. All the cool positions, like running the mechanical rides or running the ring toss–style games, were reserved for older kids who had worked previous summers. For a rookie like me, it was the Foods Crew.

My initial assignment was in a quick-serve type hamburger and hot dog restaurant called The Burger Shack. Here, customers lined up in front of cash registers in long lines, placed their orders, and walked away with trays loaded with burgers, fries, and soft drinks (not unlike a McDonald's or Burger King). My job was to work the grill and produce an unending stream of cooked burger patties and grilled franks. I really enjoyed my one day at the cash register because I got to interact with the customers. Unfortunately, my cash-handling skills were not good, and that opportunity rarely presented itself again.

About the third week into the season, the park decided to add a satellite hot dog cart to the restaurant's operation. All of the other crew members declined the opportunity to work the cart. They saw it as banishment from the rest of the gang. They'd be stuck out there all alone, missing the horseplay and cutting up that went on in the back of the house of the restaurant itself. I saw it as a great way to get away from the greasy grill, get out in the summer sun, interact with customers all day.

I continued to work the Foods Crew during the summers, as well as several after-school jobs

during the school year—washing dishes, busing, and waiting tables. I was asked to take a management position my second summer. The reasoning was that I had been responsible for impressive sales on the hot dog cart the previous summer, and that I'd bring those types of results as a shift supervisor of The Burger Shack itself.

My first management job results were not great. I really applied myself to the tasks I thought were "important" for a manager— writing schedules, doing inventory, placing orders for supplies, counting drawers, and checking time records. In between these

important duties, I always tried to go out to the front line and interact with the customers, as this is what I thought my bosses liked about me.

I soon found that the performance of The Burger Shack was unchanged. Even though I felt that I was a terrific schedule writer and inventory manager, the store did no better. Even though I applied myself when I could to interacting with customers, I did not earn a bonus.

Then two things dawned on me. First, the reason the hot dog cart was so successful was not because I did a better job at managing the hot dogs, it was because I did a better job at connecting with the customers.

Second, as a manager I could spend all the time I wanted on the front line interacting with customers and it would make little difference, because as soon as I walked away, the team just continued to *process* the customers. The fact is, as a leader I was no longer being rewarded (bonused) on what I could do myself (as I was on the cart). I was being rewarded for the behaviors of the *team*.

It was then that I realized that the technical responsibilities of a leader in the customer service business (schedules, inventories, bookkeeping, etc.) could be done anytime, and I was wasting our most important and valuable resource—time in front of our customers. I realized that my priority had to be teaching my team to create unique, genuine, and meaningful connections with our guests while we had the opportunity, not to just be focused on hustling them along.

MY CAREER PATH

When I was in school, I had to work for every dollar I had. In fact, after the age of 18, I was responsible for supporting myself in every way. I went to school with a lot of other students who worked two or three shifts at the campus restaurant for extra beer money or just for "something to do." Those students tended to show up for their shifts, goof around, and generally "phone it in." They were always the last ones to work and the first to ask to be cut early. I couldn't do that. I knew that if I were going to give my valuable time to the restaurant, I had to make every moment pay the maximum. I devoted myself to learning how to make the most money possible in the hospitality business.

No matter what restaurant, bar, nightclub, or hotel I worked at, I noticed there always seemed to be a few servers and bartenders who made all the money. The rest of the staff stood around (usually complaining about the former). I devoted myself to studying these high performers, no matter where I went.

Soon, I had collected numerous observed behaviors that each added a little bit to the tip line. All of the tactics were slightly different, but they had at least one thing in common: None of the high-revenue servers I observed were any better or faster at serving food. For the most part, everyone pretty much "served" the customer with the same efficiency by taking orders, then moving plates from the kitchen to the dining room. What they did differently (in many small ways) was to find a way to connect with the customer on a human level. Some told jokes, some engaged kids, some asked questions about the customer, and so on.

I adopted many of these observed traits, and soon I was the highest-paid person wherever I worked. I made so much money that when I returned home from school I proudly announced to my friends and family that I wanted to be a career bartender—not a very popular announcement. For months after, whenever I'd see close friends or family they would ask that dreaded question, "When do you think you're going to get a *real job*?"

I found the question rude in the extreme. I know that what they meant was "when would I get a job where I could make some real money?" What they didn't know is that I'd discovered the secret of success in the restaurant business. It's all about customer service.

Something I always think about:

- **People don't just go to restaurants to eat; they go for their reasons, not ours.**
- **People will pay more for an experience than they will for just food.**
- **People don't want to be treated like customers; they want to be treated like human beings.**

In the end, I was able to convince my friends and family that hospitality was a real job by showing them how much money I could make. I used my tip money to buy into my first nightclub when I was 25.

My partners and I built that nightclub into a small group of bars over the years and sold the company in 2000, when I went to work for a large, national casual dining chain. I worked hard in operations there and turned around a couple of failing restaurants. Eventually, I was asked to move up to the home office and lead front-of-the-house training for the restaurant concept. In 2007, I wrote the best-seller *The Renegade Server* (with the help of all those behaviors I'd observed over my years serving). At that time, I also founded Renegade Hospitality Group, where I currently serve as CEO. We advise the restaurant, hotel, and customer service industries on service, salesmanship, leadership, and marketing. I have been a hot dog guy, server, bartender, manager, owner, trainer, author, consultant, and executive—all based on my dogged belief that customer service is not just transactional, it is experiential.

Remember: **The transactional delivery of goods and services (quickly serving food, delivering a quality product, etc.) is the *ante* into the game. It is the *basic* expectation of the customer. Just because you've served a decent product quickly and well doesn't mean you've accomplished great customer service. Ultimately, it's the *face and feeling* you attach to that transaction that people remember as service. It is a differentiator for your business and is uniquely defensible.**

WHAT DOES THE FUTURE HOLD?

In this day and age of automated service processes (ever tried to get a real person on the phone in the "customer service" department of your credit card company?), the real winners in the future of customer service are going to be those organizations that strive for customization—rather than standardization—of the customer experience.

MY ADVICE TO YOU

The best advice I ever got regarding customer service was from a fellow server when I worked at a restaurant. He was extremely successful, made a ton of tips, and had scores of regulars that always requested to sit in his section. When I asked his secret, he told me to throw out the scripts that the restaurant had trained me to deliver (you know, the same old server-speak, like "Hi, welcome to CheeseSticks, my name is Poindexter . . ."). He then said something very powerful and true—"If you look, act, and sound like every other server, you are *interchangeable* with every other server. Find a way to do these things differently, and customers will notice you and be attracted to you." Indeed. I would add that it has been my experience that this applies on a larger scale as well. If the customer service process in your business is similar or identical to that of your competitors', then you are essentially interchangeable with them. When you are considered similar or interchangeable by your customers, the only way to differentiate yourself becomes price—and no one ever got rich by discounting.

My advice to anyone interested in getting into customer service today is to resist the urge to standardize the customer experience. Every customer is different and has unique service expectations depending on their own tastes, background, and situation. If you seek a "silver bullet" customer service process, you will hit some expectations but miss most. Obviously, certain things must be standardized, like when to bring dessert or how to place plates or other technical aspects of delivering service. But again, all of these are expected by the customer to be performed flawlessly. They don't even *notice* perfection in this area. Real, lasting, and differentiating customer service experiences come from a collection of human moments. Don't stop at training your team to perfectly execute the "steps of service." But this is not the end. It is the beginning! Once the product or service can be technically delivered without flaw, teach your teams to engage the person behind the transaction. Teach them to customize the service process based on small, unique differences in each customer. Give them the empowerment to veer off script and engage in real, genuine, engaging conversations. Teach them to handle mistakes and conflict with grace—not to the customers' satisfaction, but to their *amazement*.

1

The Importance of Customer Service

INSIDE THIS CHAPTER

- What Is Quality Customer Service?
- Service: An Honorable Profession
- Commercial and Noncommercial Restaurant and Foodservice Operations
- The Importance of Exceeding Guest Expectations
- Creating a Customer Service Culture

CHAPTER LEARNING OBJECTIVES

After completing this chapter, you should be able to:

- Define high-quality customer service.

- Describe the three system components used to ensure the delivery of high-quality customer service.

- Provide examples of high-quality customer service characteristics in each restaurant or foodservice segment.

- Explain the role of managers in the development of a customer service culture.

- Explain the role of staff in the delivery of high-quality customer service.

KEY TERMS

CASE STUDY

"That isn't fair," said Leslie, a server at Brume's Petite Chateau restaurant. "That was the day Margo called in and we were shorthanded in the dining room."

"Well, it might not be fair, but it's posted anyway," replied Jack, the restaurant's manager.

Leslie and Jack were discussing a guest comment about the Petite Chateau that had recently been posted online on the *City Dining* review site.

"The reviewer says he or she was here last Thursday and the food was great, but the service was very slow," said Jack.

"Well, I remember that day," replied Leslie. "It wasn't that slow; we all picked up two extra tables when Margo called in sick."

"I remember," said Jack. "And I'm not saying you didn't do your best. I'm just saying this guest gave us a rating of only 2 on a scale of 1 to 5. And the reviewer says in the posting that he or she wouldn't likely come back."

1. Do you think most guests consider service quality to be as important as food quality when they select or recommend a restaurant or foodservice establishment? Why or why not?

2. How important do you think it would be for Jack to respond to the review posted on *City Dining*? If you were Jack, how would you reply to the online posting?

WHAT IS QUALITY CUSTOMER SERVICE?

Many people talk about providing or receiving quality customer service. But what is quality customer service? To some people in the restaurant and foodservice industry, serving hot food hot and cold food cold represents a good level of customer service. Certainly the quality of products received in an operation is associated with a good meal and with good service (see *Exhibit 1.1*).

Exhibit 1.1

But true quality service is more than that. The hot food must be the correct item ordered. It must be served promptly to the correct guest and in a pleasant manner. To achieve that goal, managers must have proper policies, procedures, systems, and employees in place. Their goal should be to deliver a high-quality service to every guest.

There are many benefits to consistently providing high-quality customer service in an operation:

- Increased customer satisfaction
- Increased customer loyalty
- Decreased marketing expense
- Enhanced business reputation
- Reduced employee turnover
- Increased revenue
- Increased profits

This book was written to help managers ensure that their guests consistently receive the highest possible level of quality customer service.

High-Quality Customer Service

The level of customer service provided is a major factor that sets apart competing restaurant and foodservice establishments. Therefore, the higher the quality of customer service, the better for the establishment and the customer. High-quality customer service means consistently exceeding customers' expectations for products and services received, as well as the level of personal attention provided during the delivery. The goal of high-quality customer service is twofold:

- Create value for the customer.
- Create profit for the operation.

The components of high-quality customer service include things such as timeliness, speed, organization, smoothness or efficiency, uniformity, correctness, convenience, and if needed, the correction of mistakes. In other words, the nature of service includes what service providers do and how they do it.

The personal attention provided during service delivery includes things such as the service provider's attitude, friendliness, sensitivity to a situation or individual needs, interest in the customer, tactfulness, discretion, avoidance of embarrassment, privacy protection, and complaint and difficult situation management. In other words, it includes how guests are treated when they receive service.

To provide high-quality customer service, managers must ensure that their staff excels at both service delivery and personal interaction. Doing just one or the other is not enough. The concept of high-quality customer service delivery will be expanded in the following chapters of this book.

Customer Service Systems, Processes, and Tasks

Experienced managers know that achieving high-quality customer service is a process that requires continuous improvement. Although the operation may be running smoothly at a given point in time, managers cannot assume there is no room for improvement. Even when things are going well, managers must ask key questions:

- How can we provide better service to our customers?
- What service-related processes can be improved?
- What systems can be made to operate even more smoothly?
- What new opportunities do we have to surprise and delight our guests with ever higher levels of customer service?

To create high-quality customer service, managers must have systems in place to make sure products and services are consistent. A system is a set of standards, processes, and tasks that work together in an organized way to achieve an end result. *Exhibit 1.2* shows an example of a high-quality customer service system. Once a system is in place, it must be managed.

Every operation should have well-defined standards for its business. A standard describes criteria for items, tasks, behaviors, practices, and other aspects of an operation that represent the norm for the business. For example, a manager may have standards for cleanliness that specify all silverware must be spot-free when placed on guest tables. Another manager's operation may have a service standard that, at all times, at least one person is available in the operation who can speak Spanish with customers.

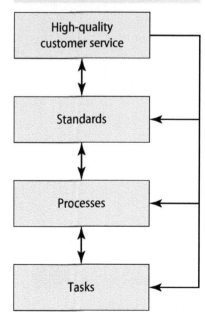

Exhibit 1.2

HIGH-QUALITY CUSTOMER SERVICE SYSTEM

High-quality customer service

↕

Standards

↕

Processes

↕

Tasks

The system consists of standards, processes, and tasks organized to achieve a result; in this case, high-quality customer service.

Remember that the activities in an operation should always meet the standards managers set for their businesses. A process is a series of operations or tasks that bring about a desired result. For example, the employee staffing system in an operation may include these processes:

- Hiring
- Training
- Coaching
- Evaluating

In a customer service system, some processes include the following:

- Identifying customers' expectations
- Satisfying customers' expectations
- Positively influencing customers' perceived value of service and products

Processes are composed of tasks. A task is a responsibility, function, or procedure that is performed as part of a process. For example, tasks that support the hiring process include the following:

- Writing an open position announcement
- Collecting completed applications
- Interviewing candidates
- Choosing candidates

Likewise, each of the customer service processes consists of tasks. For example, the process of determining customers' needs includes these tasks:

- Asking customers what their needs are for the current visit
- Surveying customer satisfaction during and after the meal
- Offering customers an incentive for their next visit, based on responses to questions or the results of surveys

This book addresses many of the processes and tasks that make up a high-quality customer service system. It also addresses how to design and implement such a system, and how these and other processes are used to create loyal customers and, ultimately, optimize profits for an operation.

SERVICE: AN HONORABLE PROFESSION

Most managers are very concerned about the quality of food they serve, and that focus is appropriate. Great food and quality beverages are a trademark of every fine restaurant and foodservice organization. But restaurants and other foodservice operations, along with hotels, are part of the hospitality industry. The hospitality industry refers primarily to those businesses that provide food and lodging services to those who are away from home. Hospitality is how services are performed and it is the feeling that customers take with them. Hospitality is an honorable profession and those professionals working in it can be proud of its history and its importance to their communities and to society at large.

THINK ABOUT IT . . .

How important is it to feel genuinely welcomed when you visit an establishment? Would you go back to an establishment that offered good food but made you feel unwelcome when you were there?

COMMERCIAL AND NONCOMMERCIAL RESTAURANT AND FOODSERVICE OPERATIONS

True hospitality, as exhibited by high-quality customer service, is important in every food and beverage operation (see *Exhibit 1.3*). Some foodservice operations are not typically considered to be restaurants because they are not open to the public. Examples include foodservice operations in hospitals, schools, and colleges. Despite the fact that they serve a select audience, managers in these operations know that they must also be concerned about delivering high-quality customer service.

There are no legally mandated ways to segment or classify restaurant or foodservice operations. One very popular method used by the restaurant and foodservice industry to categorize meals served away from home is to consider where the food is served. Is the food served in a commercial or a noncommercial setting (see *Exhibit 1.4.*)?

Commercial restaurant and foodservice operations are open to the general public. These operations most often seek to make a profit by providing food and beverages to as wide an audience of customers as possible. Examples include restaurants, mobile food carts, hotels, bars, and nightclubs.

Noncommercial foodservice operations are not typically open to the general public. The goal of these units is to provide cost-effective meals for a specially targeted audience. This segment is also commonly referred to as not-for-profit, on-site, or institutional foodservice.

Exhibit 1.5 on the following page lists some examples of foodservice operations that are commonly classified as either commercial (for-profit) or noncommercial (not-for-profit). When defined as a location serving food to those away from home, it is easy to see that managers will be found in both types of settings. It is also true that managers serving guests, clients, patients, students, employees, or other constituencies in noncommercial settings will be just as concerned about providing high-quality customer service as will managers working in commercial settings.

In some cases, the line between commercial and noncommercial operations is not always clear. For example, a coffee shop located in the student union of a college campus or a cafeteria located in a large hospital may indeed be open to the general public. The college and the hospital may even seek to operate these facilities profitably. In these examples, the two noncommercial entities have elected to operate a commercial restaurant or foodservice unit for the benefit of those they are serving.

Exhibit 1.3

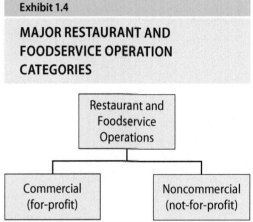

Exhibit 1.4

MAJOR RESTAURANT AND FOODSERVICE OPERATION CATEGORIES

Restaurant and Foodservice Operations

Commercial (for-profit)

Noncommercial (not-for-profit)

Exhibit 1.5	
EXAMPLES OF COMMERCIAL AND NONCOMMERCIAL RESTAURANT AND FOODSERVICE OPERATIONS	
Commercial Restaurant and Foodservice Operations	**Noncommercial Foodservice Operations**
Restaurants	Employee cafeterias (includes offices and factories)
Bars and pubs	Schools
Hotel and motel restaurants	Religious institutions
Public country clubs	Private country clubs
Casinos	Colleges and universities
Amusement parks/recreation facilities	Military bases
Stadiums/sports arenas	Hospitals, senior care, nursing homes, and assisted living communities
Vending areas and outlets	Transportation (airlines, cruise ships, trains)
Retail (e.g., food trucks, food carts, farmer's markets, grocery stores)	Correctional facilities

Regardless of the industry segment they work in, or whether their operations are considered to be commercial or noncommercial, in all settings professional restaurant and foodservice managers can use the same techniques and principles to provide outstanding customer service.

Modern Restaurant and Foodservice Operation Services

Whether they are in the commercial or noncommercial segments, restaurant and foodservice businesses are also part of the service industry. The service industry is made up of companies that primarily earn revenue by providing products and intangible services. Other service industry segments include lodging, retail, transportation, and distribution. All types of restaurant and foodservice operations are part of the service industry, regardless of their size or the type of products they offer.

Restaurants and all other classifications of foodservice operations are similar in that they usually generate most of their revenue from the sale of food and beverage products (*Exhibit 1.6*). Professionals in the industry can use a variety of criteria to group together restaurants and other foodservice operations. For example, operations could be classified as being either large or small volume in terms of revenue.

Exhibit 1.6

Other classification systems could be based on the type of menu items offered, such as subs, wraps, Italian, Chinese, Mexican, or American, or whether the food served is typically eaten in a designated dining area or is taken away from the establishment to be eaten elsewhere.

While it is easy to see that there could be many different ways to classify establishments, the most popular way is to place each operation into one of the following four commonly recognized restaurant and foodservice industry segments, based on the service levels each operation provides to its guests:

- Quick service
- Fast casual
- Casual
- Fine dining

QUICK-SERVICE RESTAURANTS

The **quick-service restaurant (QSR)** segment is one of the largest and most visible of all restaurant and foodservice groups. QSRs are characterized by their limited menus, fast service, and modest prices. QSRs are extremely popular with customers who are in a hurry and those on a budget. The menu items served in quick-service operations are limited by what people like to eat, how quickly the menu items can be prepared, the prices people expect to pay, and the time people are willing to spend eating, as well as the costs of food, equipment, and labor.

In most cases, QSRs serve simple food items with simple preparation requirements and because they do, menu prices can be kept as low as possible. While hamburgers represent the single most popular QSR type in the United States, a large group of QSRs are very successful featuring different menu items. Examples include establishments that offer Asian foods, tacos and burritos, hot dogs, sandwiches, fried chicken, gyros, salads, and fried seafood.

QSRs typically provide an indoor dining area for their customers. Many QSRs, however, sell as much or more of their food to drive-through customers as they do to those eating in their restaurants. **Drive-through customers** are those who place and receive their take-away food orders without leaving their cars. Increasingly, portable food carts and food trucks are used to make quick foodservice items available wherever large numbers of potential customers congregate.

The services offered in QSRs are limited and, of course, quick; this speed of service is one of a QSR's primary competitive points of difference. As a result, the service is very limited in nature and the customers often provide some of it for themselves. In a QSR the menu is usually posted on the wall or a signboard. Customers may order at one end of a counter and pick up their food at the other end of the counter. The food typically is served in paper or plastic containers. Customers also usually pick up their own utensils, condiments, and, often, beverages from a central station and then take everything to a table they find for themselves. When they have finished eating, it is very common for QSR customers to clear their tables of plates and utensils and place them into trash receptacles. Some QSRs provide limited table service, such as bringing the food to the table where the customer is waiting. Overall, the limited services are the least costly to provide of all restaurant and foodservice types.

Restaurant and foodservice managers working in the QSR segment are usually among the industry's most technologically advanced. Superior managers are noted for their ability to ensure consistency and cleanliness in their operations, traits that serve them well whether they stay within the QSR segment or move to other industry segments. There are several key service concerns of great importance to QSRs: cleanliness, speed of service, food quality, and consistency.

FAST-CASUAL RESTAURANTS

The fast-casual segment is a relatively new type of restaurant operation. Fast-casual restaurants do not provide their guests table service, but their food quality, overall service level, and decor is intended to be higher than that typically found in a QSR.

Characteristics of fast-casual restaurants tend to include the following:

- Limited-service or self-service format
- Average amount spent per guest between $8 and $15
- Fresh, made-to-order food with more complex flavors and dining choices than most QSRs
- Pay at the counter
- Items are brought to the table or customer is called back to the counter
- Upscale or highly developed decor

Currently, fast casual is the fastest-growing segment in the restaurant and foodservice industry. Some experts predict that it will continue to lead the industry overall in terms of growth throughout the next 10 years. The fast-casual segment's growth is based on consumers' views that, in the important areas of flavor, service, and quality, these restaurants provide excellent value. Fast-casual restaurants are especially popular with customers who are 10 to 30 years of age, as well as those 55 and older. There are key service-related concerns of great importance to customers in the fast-casual segment: cleanliness, speed of service, freshness of menu items, and taste of menu items.

CASUAL RESTAURANTS

While no universally accepted definition exists, casual restaurants are generally considered to be those that provide table service to guests and serve moderately priced food in an informal atmosphere. In many cases, casual restaurants have a full bar with separate bar staff and a large beer and wine menu. They are frequently part of a chain, but some are independently owned and operated.

Although the range of menu products may be quite extensive, many casual restaurants offer a category of cuisine, either by nationality or region of cuisine, such as Italian, French, or Chinese, or by type of entrée, such as steak or pizza. Overall, in comparison to the products offered in QSRs and fast-casual operations, casual-dining operations are more complex, the menu items more complicated to prepare, and the menu prices higher.

The services also are more extensive, and employees of the operation called servers, service staff, or waitstaff do most of the service. If the operation has a liquor license, there is typically a bartender to mix drinks. Most casual restaurants employ a greeter or host to welcome customers, show them to a table, and provide a printed menu. At the table, the server explains any specials of the day and takes beverage orders. Later, the server returns to take the meal order. There may be several courses, such as appetizer, entrée, and dessert; sometimes these courses are ordered together, but more commonly they are ordered at separate times.

The server delivers food orders to the kitchen via the establishment's point-of-sale (POS) system. The POS system is the computer used to record guest orders and payments as well as other important operating information. If no POS system is in use, servers record and submit guest orders by hand and then wait for the orders to be prepared.

When the food is ready, the server delivers the food to the guest's table (*Exhibit 1.7*). During the meal, a server or an assistant fills beverages and checks on customers' satisfaction levels. After each course, the bus staff picks up the used dishes and utensils and takes them away. When the meal is finished, the server presents the bill to the table and collects payment.

While the quality of these services and the compensation of employees who provide these services vary markedly over this category of operation, all these services cost quite a lot in comparison to the more limited services provided at QSRs and fast-casual operations. As a result, menu prices in casual restaurants are typically higher than in earlier mentioned segments. There are key service concerns of great importance in the casual segment: cleanliness, comfort, variety of menu items, and food and beverage quality.

Manager's Memo

Increasingly, casual restaurants offer a dine-in or carryout choice. When an operation offers carryout choices, the manager must consider and address key issues:

- How will carryout orders be taken? Options include walk-ins, telephone, Web site, or text message.
- Will carryout customers wait in the same line as other guests when placing or picking up orders?
- Where in the operation will customers wait if their orders are not ready when they arrive?
- Where will prepared orders be held until carryout customers arrive?
- How will food temperatures be maintained on foods held for pickup?
- How will payments be processed?

Exhibit 1.7

Exhibit 1.8

FINE-DINING RESTAURANTS

Fine-dining restaurants offer guests the highest-quality foods and full table service. Like the other segments addressed in this chapter, there is no universally accepted definition for fine dining. However, most industry professionals would likely agree that fine-dining restaurants differ from other restaurant segments in three critical areas: complexity and quality of product offerings, ambience or the feeling or mood created by an environment, and service levels. Fine-dining restaurants seek to offer their guests upscale and very memorable dining experiences (*Exhibit 1.8*).

PRODUCT OFFERINGS   The type of cuisine offered in fine-dining restaurants varies greatly; however, in all cases these operations serve masterfully prepared foods of extremely high quality. Many fine-dining restaurants are either chef-owned or employ a talented chef who develops the operation's menu. Chefs may creatively vary their menus daily, weekly, or seasonally to take advantage of locally produced fresh ingredients, and the chef's extensive skills are often a point of competitive difference.

The actual number of menu items offered in a fine-dining restaurant may be large or rather limited; however, each item must be outstanding. In most cases, fine-dining establishments also offer their guests extensive and high-quality beer, wine, and spirits menus to complement the food they serve. In short, fine-dining restaurants of all types offer the best in ingredients, food quality, and preparation methods.

AMBIENCE   Some of the most beautifully designed interiors in the world are found in fine-dining establishments. The establishment's walls, flooring, and artwork reflect the operation's upscale ambience. Even the staff's uniforms and the linens, china, glassware, and other tabletop items are carefully chosen to complement the ambience. In all cases, the job of the manager is to create a luxurious environment that is as memorable as the food and beverages served.

SERVICE LEVELS   Fine-dining establishments provide their guests with exceptionally high levels of personal service. All restaurant and foodservice operations must seek to provide good guest service; however, in most cases a fine-dining restaurant's well-trained staff perform additional tasks:

- Escort guests to the table
- Explain complex menu items in detail
- Recommend appropriate beverages to accompany menu selections
- Clean the guest's table between courses
- Replace cloth napkins and serviceware between courses

THINK ABOUT IT . . .

Where might you eat if you have only $8 to spend? Where might you eat if you have $80 to spend? What differences in service levels would you expect?

To determine the level of service appropriate for their operations, managers consider key factors:

- The customers they seek and how well their operations can meet those customers' dining preferences
- Size, décor, and cost of their facility, its equipment, and its furnishings
- The number and types of employees required, the skills they must have, and the amount of compensation they are paid
- Availability and cost of required food and nonfood supplies

In most cases, the more service provided, the more investment will be required, and the more operating expenses will be incurred. As a result, higher prices must be charged for the meals.

Finally, in addition to waitstaff, some fine-dining establishments employ sommeliers. A **sommelier** is a restaurant or foodservice staff member who is highly trained to assist customers in selecting the wines that could go well with the customer's menu choices. Other operations employ wine stewards, who may have less formal training than sommeliers but who still assist, and may serve, guests who order wine with their meals.

Additional service staff positions that may be found in fine-dining restaurants also include parking valets, coatroom attendants, and restroom attendants. There are key services concerns of great importance in the fine-dining segment: cleanliness, personal service levels, ambience, elegance, food and beverage quality, and food and beverage presentation.

THE IMPORTANCE OF EXCEEDING GUEST EXPECTATIONS

Regardless of its classification as commercial or noncommercial and regardless of its segment, when customers patronize a restaurant or foodservice operation, they purchase three distinct items, as shown in *Exhibit 1.9*:

- Products
- Service
- Dining experience

First, they purchase products to consume, such as appetizers, salads, entrées, side dishes, beverages, and desserts. To have satisfied customers, the products must meet the expectations for the type of restaurant or foodservice operation. If they do not meet the customer's expectations, the dining experience will be negative and customer perceptions of the quality of food delivered, as well as the quality of service received, will be reduced.

KEEPING IT SAFE

Cleanliness is important to every restaurant and foodservice operation regardless of its segment. Safety is just as important. Restaurant and foodservice managers who truly care about their guests and their employees know that their operations must be safe places to dine and to work.

A concern for safety is a key aspect of high-quality customer service. For that reason, managers use great care to ensure that employees take all necessary precautions to ensure guests are safe when they are greeted, seated, and served. Doing so means keeping floors clean and dry so they are safe to walk on, ensuring tables and chairs are in good repair, and making sure hot foods are delivered carefully to guest tables.

Exhibit 1.9

WHAT CUSTOMERS BUY

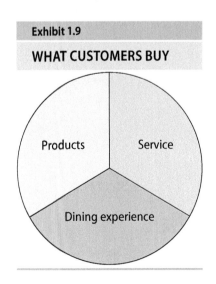

OPEN FOR BUSINESS

BY THE CUSTOMER/ FOR THE CUSTOMER

Experienced restaurant and foodservice managers know that the number one guest complaint is not poor food quality but poor service. In the past it was often said that one unhappy customer would tell 10 friends about it. Today, because of the extensive use of social network sites on the Internet, one unhappy guest can tell thousands of others about a poor dining experience. As a result, it is now more important than ever for managers to ensure their operations' quality service standards are enforced every day, and for the benefit of every guest.

THINK ABOUT IT...

Have you shared with friends a negative dining experience? What did you say? Did your comments have an effect on whether or not your friends chose to go to that operation at a later date?

Customers also purchase service when they dine out. The level and the nature of the service may vary widely from quick-service establishments to fine-dining establishments, but all customers want high-quality service because service quality influences guest perceptions of the value they receive for the money they spend.

Customers have different service expectations from each type of establishment, and they make a conscious decision to buy that type of service when they choose that type of operation. Along with products, service must always measure up to, or exceed, the customer's expectations. If service does not measure up, the dining experience will be negative, even if the products purchased were excellent.

Finally, customers also purchase a total dining experience when they visit a restaurant or other foodservice operation. This experience consists of the products and service received as well as the operation's theme, image, ambience, cleanliness, reputation, prices charged, any entertainment, and other factors. All of these factors must work together to create a positive, and hopefully an excellent, experience for the customer. When this happens, the customer is satisfied and recommends the establishment to others. When an establishment does not meet the customer's minimum expectations, the customer will not likely have positive things to say about the operation.

CREATING A CUSTOMER SERVICE CULTURE

One of a manager's most important service-related goals is to create a customer service culture. Culture refers to the attitudes, beliefs, and characteristics of a specific group. A customer service culture exists in a restaurant or foodservice operation when everyone in it considers himself or herself to be in the high-quality customer service business first, and in the food and beverage business second.

Put another way, in an organization without a true customer service culture, managers may say "we are in the food and beverage business." Managers who operate within an organization with a customer service culture may say "we are a service business that happens to sell food and beverages." The difference is significant.

Of course, managers creating a customer service culture in their organizations recognize the importance of serving quality food and beverage products. Good food and drink is important to an operation's success. But high-quality service is more important. In fact, managers seeking to create a customer service culture know that it is the single most critical thing they can do to ensure their operations' success.

A customer service culture in a business pervades everything from how it treats its customers to how it treats its employees. Creating a culture that truly values and rewards exceeding the expectation of guests requires effort from three key players on a restaurant or foodservice team:

- Managers
- Back-of-the-house staff
- Front-of-the-house staff

The Role of Managers

One good way to consider what effective restaurant and foodservice managers do is by analyzing the functions they perform. All managers' actions regarding the development of a high-quality customer service culture are interrelated and comprise an ongoing process, as illustrated in *Exhibit 1.10*.

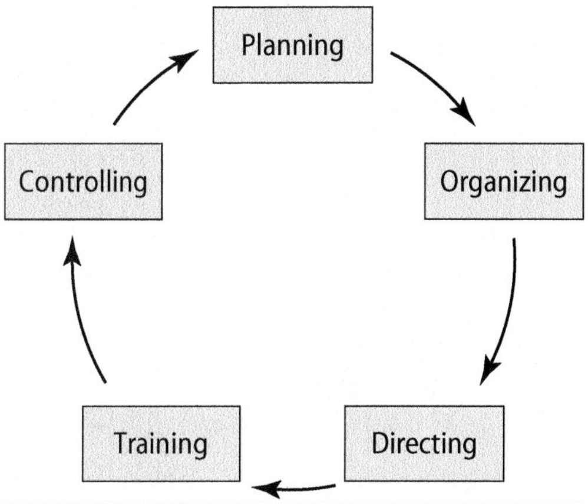

When it comes to creating a customer service culture in their organizations, managers must perform five key functions well:

- Planning
- Organizing
- Directing
- Training
- Controlling

Exhibit 1.10

KEY MANAGEMENT FUNCTIONS

PLANNING

The best managers plan their work and then work their plans. Planning is the function of management that identifies goals and the strategies that will be used to achieve the goals. Planning is the first step in the effective management of any endeavor, including the creation of a customer service culture. Managers make and adjust their plans based on the specific circumstances they encounter as they operate their businesses. As a result, planning is an ongoing process. There are several examples of the ongoing planning that must be undertaken by managers:

- Financial planning
- Marketing planning
- Production planning
- Employee development planning
- Customer service planning

All planning involves similar thought processes and actions. Managers who plan to achieve high-quality customer service define their service goals and then devise detailed plans to achieve them.

For example, assume a manager in a fast-casual restaurant establishes a customer service–related goal of filling the order of each customer within four minutes of the customer placing it. In this example, the manager has identified a specific goal and must next plan the strategies that will be used to ensure the goal is achieved.

ORGANIZING

As they seek to achieve their goals, managers have a variety of resources available to them:

- Money
- Facilities
- Inventories
- Information
- Labor

One important management role is that of organizing, or arranging available resources in a way that best helps the organization achieve its goals. Among the specific tasks managers undertake when organizing resources to achieve goals is deciding what is to be done, who will do it, and what tools must be available to workers. Employees who are asked to achieve goals must have the resources needed to achieve them. Returning to the example of the fast-casual restaurant manager who established the goal of serving guests within four minutes of their ordering, it is clear that resources must be allocated to achieve the goal:

- Adequate food supplies, so that food is available in the operation
- Needed equipment, so that menus items can be cooked properly
- Required food-production staff, so that required items are supplied to the serving line in a timely manner
- Required service staff, so that guest orders can be taken and filled quickly
- Required cashiering staff, so that guest payment–related tasks do not slow the entire line
- Required dining-room attendants, so that guests can easily seat themselves at clean tables after receiving their orders

In some cases managers may feel they do not have the facilities or financial resources needed to provide high-quality customer services. The good news, however, is that excellent customer service is more affected by service staff appearance, attitude, and skill than by an operation's physical facilities. The best managers assess the resources that are available to them, and then organize those resources in the ways that most help their organizations achieve their goals.

THINK ABOUT IT . . .

Assuming both facilities were equally clean, would you rather frequent an operation that provided excellent service but with outdated decor, or one that had just been remodeled but provided only average customer service? Why?

DIRECTING

Some managers think their jobs consist primarily of telling others what to do. Directing employees, however, means much more. Directing is a management function related to the leadership of others. Directing involves influencing and inspiring others to do their very best work. If the fast-casual restaurant manager seeking to serve guests in four minutes or less hopes to achieve that goal, every employee must be motivated to help. Most employees want to follow their leaders. As a result, managers must seek to become good leaders. That means they must create a vision for those they lead. The vision must be clear and easily understood. Most important, managers must consistently exhibit the same characteristics of high-quality customer service they seek to instill in those they are directing. By creating a positive work environment, managers can help their employees improve their own performance and achieve the organization's service-related goals (*Exhibit 1.11*).

Exhibit 1.11

TRAINING

In some cases, employees will simply not have the skills needed to help contribute their maximum effort to the achievement of their organizations' service-related goals. For example, if those employees working on the service line of a fast-casual restaurant have not been trained well enough to fill guest orders in four minutes, it will be impossible to achieve that service goal.

Training is the tool managers use to improve their employees' skills, knowledge, or attitudes. When employees are not adequately trained in guest-service methods, it is the manager's job to train them. There are several benefits to effective service-related training:

- **Improved job performance:** Trainees learn how to perform required tasks more effectively, and this improves their ability to do their job.

- **Reduced operating costs:** Improved job performance helps reduce errors and rework, which reduces costs.

- **Reduced work stress:** Employees who work correctly will feel better about doing it, and this reduces stress.

- **Increased job advancement opportunities:** Competent employees are more likely to receive promotions than are less-competent staff members.

- **Fewer operating problems:** Busy managers can focus on priorities and not spend time on routine problems caused by a lack of training.

RESTAURANT TECHNOLOGY

When some managers think of training they envision a formal classroom with "lecture-style" presentation of information. But today's managers know that employee training is one area in which advanced technology has made a big impact. Today's managers can choose from a variety of service-related training tools that include reading materials, instructional videos, and interactive activities and games. Desktop and laptop computers, as well as notepads, electronic readers, tablet computers, and cell phones, can all be used to deliver service-related training at a time and place most convenient to employees.

- **Higher levels of work quality:** Effective training identifies quality standards and helps employees work at levels that meet quality requirements.

- **More satisfied customers:** Training can help make employees more confident in their skills and that helps make them more able to be customer-oriented.

CONTROLLING

Controlling is the term used to describe a manager's efforts to monitor performance and take corrective actions as needed. Control consists of measuring "what is" and comparing it with "what ought to be" and then addressing the planning, organizing, directing, or training needed to meet established goals and standards.

It is critical that managers know what *should* take place so that they have a tool to measure current performance. In the example of the fast-casual manager with a goal of serving guests in four minutes, control consists of measuring actual service times and then, if the standard has not been met, addressing key issues:

- Would better planning help the operation reach its goal?

- Would better organization including processes help the operation reach its goal?

- Would better leadership help the operation reach its goal?

- Would better service training help the operation reach its goal?

- Is the goal or standard realistic?

Accounting and financial management is a portion of, but not the entire job of, controlling a business. Accounting information and other data often provide managers with measures of "what is happening now," but most often do not provide complete answers about what *should* be done in the future. That is the manager's control-related task. The degree to which a manager controls the achievement of service-related goals and takes corrective action is one good indicator of his or her ability to create a culture that results in outstanding customer service.

Despite the importance of their own role, experienced managers know that providing high-quality guest service is truly a team effort. Managers play a critical role on the team, but so does every other staff member in an operation.

The Role of Back-of-the-House Staff

The **back of the house (BOH)** in a restaurant or foodservice business refers to those areas of the operation that are not typically entered into, or seen, by guests. BOH staff includes employees working as chefs, cooks, and dish washers. BOH employees are primarily responsible for an operation's products (see *Exhibit 1.12*).

These positions are critically important to the delivery of the dining experience. While employees holding these positions do not typically have direct contact with guests, their work in filling guests' food orders safely, quickly, and accurately has a direct impact on those guests' perceptions of service quality. Similarly, perfectly cleaned dishware, glassware, and eating utensils provided by dish-washing personnel all contribute to a customer's feeling that high-quality service has been delivered.

Exhibit 1.12

Additionally, when all BOH staff members interact in positive and pleasant ways with those servers who are in direct contact with guests, the attitudes of the servers will remain positive about their work, their coworkers, and their customers. That positive attitude will be directly reflected in the way servers treat each of the operation's guests.

The Role of Front-of-the-House Staff

The **front of the house (FOH)** is the area of a restaurant or foodservice operation in which guests can see and enter. These include a variety of locations:

- Parking areas
- Reception areas
- Waiting areas
- Bars and lounges
- Dining rooms
- Restrooms
- Patios

In some operations that allow it, even selected areas of the kitchen may be designated as FOH areas. FOH employees such as reservationists (*Exhibit 1.13*) are primarily responsible for an operation's service, and are critically important to the delivery of the dining experience. A variety of staff members are employed in FOH areas:

- Reservationists
- Valets or parking attendants
- Receptionists
- Hosts
- Bartenders
- Food and beverage waitstaff
- Sommeliers
- Wine stewards
- Bus staff

Exhibit 1.13

Employees in FOH positions are critically important to the delivery of quality service because these employees have direct contact with guests. Regardless of the tasks to which they are assigned, to consistently exceed guest expectations all FOH service personnel must project an image of high-quality customer service in three key areas:

- Personal appearance
- Attitude
- Skills

The personal interactions between guests and FOH staff members define how guests will feel about their treatment in an establishment.

Working together, managers, BOH staff, and FOH staff can help ensure that all guests receive high-quality customer service. In the chapters of this book that follow, you will learn how to ensure each customer receives that level of service. You will also see how ensuring high-quality customer service will lead to satisfied guests and to a very profitable operation. The information is important because exceptional service companies will be the ones that will continue to increase their profits, retain the best employees, and win the loyalty of their customers.

SUMMARY

1. **Define high-quality customer service.**

   High-quality customer service includes all processes used and actions taken by managers to consistently exceed their customers' expectations. This includes the guests' expectations for products, service, and the overall dining experience, including personal attention. The goal of high-quality customer service is to create exceptional value for the customer and profits for the operation. High-quality customer service most often includes a high level of personal service. The personal attention provided during service delivery includes friendliness, sensitivity, interest in customers, and the ability to manage difficult situations. High-quality customer service also includes timeliness, speed of service, consistency, and, as needed, correction of service errors.

2. **Describe the three system components used to ensure the delivery of high-quality customer service.**

   The three key components of a high-quality customer service system are standards, processes, and tasks designed to ensure high-quality customer service. Standards are the items, tasks, behaviors, and practices of an operation that represent the desired norm for the business.

A process is a series of operations or tasks to be completed to bring about a desired result. A task is a responsibility, function, or procedure that is performed as part of a process. To achieve high-quality customer service managers identify standards, develop processes, and ensure that needed task are completed.

3. **Provide examples of high-quality customer service characteristics in each restaurant or foodservice segment.**

Operations in each segment of the restaurant and foodservice industry strive to deliver high-quality customer service. For QSR operations the emphasis is on cleanliness, speed, food quality, and consistency. In the fast-casual segment, the emphasis is on cleanliness, speed, freshness of menu items, and taste. In the casual restaurant segment cleanliness, comfort, variety of menu items, and food and beverage quality are of the utmost concern. Fine-dining restaurants seek to offer the best in food and beverages in very attractive settings, and with a high degree of personal service. In these operations, high-quality customer service means an emphasis on cleanliness, personal service levels, ambience, elegance, food and beverage quality, and food and beverage presentation.

4. **Explain the role of managers in the development of a customer service culture.**

To develop customer service cultures in their operations, managers perform five critical functions: planning, organizing, directing, training, and controlling. Planning is the activity that identifies goals and the strategies that will be used to achieve goals. Organizing is the function involved in arranging the resources available for reaching goals. This task involves deciding what is to be done, who will do it, and the tools required to reach the goals.

Directing is the function of leading others to do their very best work. Training is a tool managers use to improve their employees' skills, knowledge, or attitudes. *Controlling* is the term used to describe a manager's efforts to monitor performance and take corrective action as needed. Control consists of measuring current performance, comparing it with desired results, and then readdressing the planning, organizing, directing, or training actions needed to achieve organizational goals.

5. **Explain the role of staff in the delivery of high-quality customer service.**

Each member of a restaurant or foodservice operation's staff plays an important role in achieving high levels of guest service. Customers making purchases in a restaurant or foodservice operation buy three things: products, service, and an overall dining experience. Back-of-the-house (BOH) staff such as chefs, cooks, and dish washers are primarily responsible for creating high-quality food and beverage products ordered by an operation's guests. Front-of-the-house (FOH) staff such as reservationists, parking attendants, hosts and greeters, bartenders, waitstaff, and bus staff are primarily responsible for the delivery of service. Both BOH and FOH staff must perform well if the guests' overall dining experiences are to consistently exceed their expectations.

APPLICATION EXERCISE

Imagine that you are the dining-room manager for a fine-dining establishment. You observe two employees seating guests on the same evening and in the same time period. The following is a description of what you observe:

Employee #1: "Good evening. How many? Follow me." The employee races to the table, leaving the guests to catch up. When they do, the employee says, "Here you go. Your server will be with you shortly." The employee then leaves the table.

Employee #2: "Good evening, Mr. and Mrs. Thompson. Will there be the two of you tonight or do you have guests joining you?" The employee notices that the guests are dressed more formally than normally and says, "Are you celebrating a special occasion? Well, happy anniversary! I'll try to find you a quiet table. Would you follow me please?" The employee carefully leads the couple to a table and then says: "Here we are. I think you will like this table. Allisha will be your server tonight. She's one of our very best and she will be with you shortly. Happy anniversary and enjoy your dinner!"

Employee #1 and Employee #2 both did their jobs. The guests were greeted and seated. Answer the following questions to determine which employee provided better customer service:

1. What do you think were the customer service perceptions left with the guests seated by Employee #1?

2. What do you think were the customer service perceptions left with the guests seated by Employee #2?

3. Which of these employees provided the better customer service?

4. If you were the dining-room manager, which employee would you prefer to be a role model for your other employees? Why?

REVIEW YOUR LEARNING

Select the best answer for each question.

1. **What is a characteristic of a high-quality customer service operation?**

   A. Its customers' expectations are most often met.

   B. Its customers' expectations are most often exceeded.

   C. Its customers' expectations are consistently met.

   D. Its customers' expectations are consistently exceeded.

2. **An example of an objective standard within a high-quality customer service system is ensuring that all drive-through customers**

   A. are served quickly.

   B. are happy with their service.

   C. are served in 90 seconds or less.

   D. receive excellent guest service.

3. An owner purchases a fast-casual restaurant open to the public. That restaurant would be classified as

    A. a not-for-profit operation.

    B. an institutional operation.

    C. a commercial operation.

    D. a noncommercial operation.

4. In which restaurant and foodservice industry segment will personal service levels likely be the most minimal?

    A. Quick service

    B. Casual

    C. Fast casual

    D. Fine dining

5. In which segment of the restaurant and foodservice industry would an organization most likely employ a sommelier?

    A. Quick service

    B. Casual

    C. Fast casual

    D. Fine dining

6. What service characteristic is a top priority in every segment of the restaurant and foodservice industry?

    A. Speed

    B. Elegance

    C. Cleanliness

    D. Ambience

7. *Directing* is the term used to describe the management function related to

    A. the leadership of staff.

    B. the establishment of organizational goals.

    C. the arrangement of resources to meet organizational goals.

    D. the comparison of actual performance to planned performance.

8. What is the first management function that must be performed to achieve an organization's service-related goals?

    A. Controlling

    B. Organizing

    C. Directing

    D. Planning

9. Which situation describes a service failure by a BOH employee?

    A. Dirty menu

    B. Dirty tabletop

    C. Dirty glassware

    D. Dirty dining-room floor

10. Which situation describes a service failure by an FOH employee?

    A. Overcooked steak

    B. Inadequate portion sizes

    C. Lack of variety on menu

    D. Wrong order delivered to guest

FIELD PROJECT

Observe a dining experience for yourself or someone else. You may observe any dining establishment—high-quality customer service is not limited to full-service or fine-dining establishments. However, remember that customer service expectations are influenced by the type of establishment. Complete the following form. Know the content of the form well enough so you can make observations without the staff's awareness. After you have completed the observation, write a brief analysis of what you have learned. You can discuss product knowledge, communication skills, employees' attitudes, employees' appearances, and how your expectations and decision making were influenced.

Rate the following on a scale from 1 to 5:

1 = Not acceptable   4 = Exceeds expectation
2 = Below expectation   5 = Outstanding
3 = Meets expectation

Please include comments if you give a rating of "1" or "5" on this form. Comments for other scores are also helpful. You may add questions or points of observation to this list.

1 Overall appearance of the facility from the outside   ① ② ③ ④ ⑤
Comments:

2 Greeting by the staff   ① ② ③ ④ ⑤
Comments:

3 Overall appearance of the facility from the inside   ① ② ③ ④ ⑤
Comments:

4 Appearance of the staff   ① ② ③ ④ ⑤
Comments:

5 Cleanliness of the facility   ① ② ③ ④ ⑤
Comments:

6 Professionalism of the staff   ① ② ③ ④ ⑤
Comments:

7 Product knowledge of the staff   ① ② ③ ④ ⑤
Comments:

8 Quality of the service   ① ② ③ ④ ⑤
Comments:

9 Promptness of the staff   ① ② ③ ④ ⑤
Comments:

10 Professional appearance   ① ② ③ ④ ⑤
Comments:

11 Management visibility   ① ② ③ ④ ⑤
Comments:

12 Adequate staffing   ① ② ③ ④ ⑤
Comments:

13 Staff pleasantness   ① ② ③ ④ ⑤
Comments:

14 Problems solved effectively   ① ② ③ ④ ⑤
Comments:

15 Your experience made you feel like a valued customer   ① ② ③ ④ ⑤
Comments:

16 Overall evaluation of customer service   ① ② ③ ④ ⑤
Comments:

2

Customer-Centric Service

CHAPTER LEARNING OBJECTIVES

After completing this chapter, you should be able to:

- Describe the "moment of truth" concept.

- Explain the three steps managers take to develop employee customer service expectations.

- Discuss the differences and similarities between internal and external restaurant and foodservice customers.

- Identify the elements customers seek when making a restaurant or foodservice purchase.

- List the areas of a restaurant or foodservice operation directly affected by the delivery of high-quality customer-centric service.

- Describe the challenges faced by managers in providing high-quality service to all guests.

- Identify categories of guests with special needs that create unique service-related challenges for managers.

KEY TERMS

allergen, p. 45

capacity, p. 40

competitive point
of difference, p. 36

consistency, p. 39

cross-contact, p. 46

customer-centric
service, p. 32

customer loyalty, p. 35

customer with a disability,
p. 42

employee turnover, p. 36

external customer, p. 30

food allergies, p. 45

inseparability, p. 40

intangible, p. 39

internal customer, p. 30

moment of truth, p. 28

suggestive selling, p. 38

value, p. 33

CASE STUDY

"Look, you two simply have to start getting along better," said Elizabeth, the manager at the Creek Bend Buffet. Elizabeth was addressing Anthony, the operation's kitchen production supervisor, and Amanda, the dining-room supervisor.

"Then tell him that when I ask for additional food, it's because the pans in the dining room are empty. It's the guests who eat the food, not me. He acts like it's a personal insult to him if I tell him we're out of fried chicken or any other item. All I'm doing is telling him we're out. That's my job—to let the kitchen know when we need more items on the line," said Amanda.

"And you can tell her that we make things as quickly as we can. It doesn't help when she keeps coming back every two minutes to ask when it will be ready," replied Anthony.

"That's exactly what I'm talking about. You two need to improve your attitudes toward each other. And that's probably why I had a customer say that they overheard your last argument all the way out in the dining room," said Elizabeth. "Everyone has to start working together."

1. In what areas can front-of-the-house (FOH) and back-of-the-house (BOH) employees get into conflict as each seeks to serve guests?

2. How do you think that obvious service-related conflicts between FOH and BOH employees affect guests?

3. What would you suggest Elizabeth do in this case to help ensure all of her staff members understand the importance of working together to provide excellent customer service?

THINK ABOUT IT . . .

Some customers may not do business with an organization because of the way they were treated when they called for information. Has this happened to you? How can managers help prevent such negative customer experiences?

MOMENTS OF TRUTH

Karl Albrecht, in his book *At America's Service*, discusses the term *moment of truth*. A **moment of truth** is "any episode in which the customer comes into contact with any aspect of the organization and gets an impression of the quality of its service."[1] Whenever a customer has an opportunity to form an opinion about an operation, it is a moment of truth.

There can be hundreds of moments of truth in a customer's dining experience. The following experiences can be moments of truth:

- Customer sees a billboard promoting a business
- Customer reads a Web page
- Customer hears from a friend about a business
- Customer drives into the parking lot
- Customer is greeted at the front door
- Customer observes spots on the silverware
- Customer feels too hot or too cold in the dining room

Exhibit 2.1

Managers know that critical moments of truth can begin to occur even before customers physically enter a restaurant or foodservice operation; for example, when customers call for reservations (see *Exhibit 2.1*). Moments of truth can be positive. In these cases, the guest forms a favorable impression of service. Moments of truth can also be negative, and the guest forms an unfavorable impression of service.

For restaurant and foodservice managers, creating positive moments of truth has several benefits:

- Contributes to customer loyalty
- Helps customers be more forgiving of minor mistakes
- Provides an opportunity for positive word-of-mouth advertising
- Allows customers to feel comfortable providing feedback

Effective managers want to manage moments of truth to ensure their operations consistently provide high-quality customer service. They do so by developing standards of service and establishing expectations of the

[1] Karl Albrecht, *At America's Service: How Corporations Can Revolutionize the Way They Treat Their Customers* (Homewood, IL: Dow Jones-Irwin, 1988).

service levels employees will provide. To do so managers take three important steps:

Step 1. Identify appropriate standards of guest service and hospitality that define positive moments of truth.

When managers undertake step 1 of the process, they can refer to industry documentation or standards, and their company's mission statement. To do so they ask specific questions:

- What are the company's expectations in regard to customer service?
- What are the demographics of the operation's customer base?
- What are the customers' expectations?
- What do employees need to know?
- Where can they obtain information about industry standards?

Step 2. Develop or acquire training materials designed to teach employees the operation's standards.

When addressing step 2, managers consider specific questions to ensure that training materials and the training procedures to be used are clear, concise, and accurate:

- What training will be effective?
- How detailed should training materials be?
- What is the best medium to train employees?
- What should the training materials look like?
- What type of training materials should be used?

Step 3. Conduct ongoing training and assessment to ensure employees can meet management's standards-related expectations.

When addressing step 3, managers also consider specific questions:

- Which training methods will be used for various staff?
- How often should the training be provided?
- How is the importance of the material best explained?
- How will the effectiveness of the training be assessed on an ongoing basis?

To illustrate, a manager may want to help ensure that a moment of truth first experienced by arriving guests is a positive one. As a result, the manager establishes a service standard for how all guests will be greeted (step 1). The manager would then prepare training materials and conduct employee training designed to teach workers how the service standard can be achieved (step 2). This training would ensure that each employee knew and was able to meet the standard for greeting all guests. Finally, the manager would continually assess employee performance to ensure that the standard was being met (step 3).

Types of Customers

Creating positive moments of truth for customers is essential. Managers must understand that there are two kinds of customers in restaurant and foodservice operations: internal and external customers. This understanding will allow managers to more effectively establish standards for customer treatment.

Recall that a moment of truth is when the customer comes into contact with any aspect of the organization. During this contact, customers form an impression of the quality of its service. A critical part of this definition is the customer. But who is the customer here? Many people would identify the guest as the customer. That is correct. However, Joseph Juran, a noted expert on quality, presents a more complex description of a customer.

To paraphrase Juran, a customer is anyone who is influenced by or has influence on a product, service, system, or process.[2] As a result, restaurant and foodservice operations serve both external and internal customers. An **external customer** is the end receiver of a product or service. External customers are outside the boundaries of an operation's direct control. In an establishment, the guest is the external customer.

An **internal customer** is anyone inside an operation who receives products, services, or information from someone else to complete his or her work (*Exhibit 2.2*). The establishment's employees and even its suppliers are internal customers. The internal customers affect the products, services, systems, or processes used in an operation. Like external customers, internal customers can experience moments of truth in every interaction they have with external customers, other employees, and managers. Satisfying both internal and external customers is critical to providing high-quality customer service.

Another way to think of the customer is as someone on the receiving end of any input–output relationship. An input–output relationship is an interaction between two people or two groups. In this interaction, the work product of one is used by the other. An example of this is the typical sequence of service in an establishment, shown in *Exhibit 2.3*.

Exhibit 2.2

[2] Joseph M. Juran and A. Blanton Godfrey, *Juran's Quality Handbook*, 5th Edition (New York: McGraw-Hill, 1998).

1. The guest, the external customer, provides input to the server by making a request, such as ordering a menu item. The server receives this request (information) and will communicate it to others in the organization.

2. The server gives the request (provides input) to the chef. The chef receives the order and becomes an internal customer of the server.

3. The chef prepares and gives the ordered food (provides output) to the server. The server receives the ordered food and becomes an internal customer of the chef.

4. The server delivers the ordered food (provides output) to the guest. The guest receives the ordered food and is the external customer of the restaurant.

Exhibit 2.3

PRIMARY RESTAURANT AND FOODSERVICE CUSTOMER RELATIONSHIP

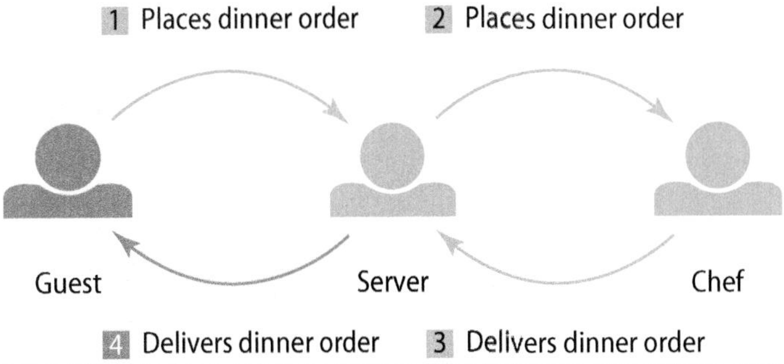

These examples define a customer as someone on the receiving end of an input–output relationship. With this definition, managers can see that internal and external customers are equally important when providing high-quality customer service.

WHAT RESTAURANT AND FOODSERVICE CUSTOMERS SEEK

Chapter 1 explained that restaurant and foodservice customers buy products, service, and an overall dining experience. To provide excellent service, managers must understand the elements all customers seek when they make restaurant and foodservice purchases:

- Quality products
- Quality service
- Cleanliness
- Value
- Total experience

Quality Products

Some managers mistakenly believe that the only thing customers seek is an item that, when prepared by back-of-the-house (BOH) employees, tastes good. These managers do not recognize that a quality product means much more than taste. In fact, front-of-the-house (FOH) employees often play a large role in moments of truth related to product quality.

Manager's Memo

An operation's staff members are internal customers and they care about how they are treated by those who serve them. In most operations, internal customers seek the same things:

- Respectful treatment from coworkers
- Honesty in relationships
- Freedom from harassment by coworkers, managers, or guests
- Respectful and fair treatment from managers
- Reward for hard work
- Dignified treatment by all customers

When external customers do not get good service, they do not return. In many cases, when internal customers do not get good service, they too do not return. The result is excessive employee turnover and the high costs associated with it.

For example, consider an operation that makes an excellent soup. A customer orders the soup. The customer's server does not deliver the soup in a timely manner. As a result, the soup gets cold. The customer believes the quality of the product received was poor. In this example and many others, the actions of FOH service personnel directly affect moments of truth related to product quality.

Quality Service

Customers who make a purchase expect to buy service. In the restaurant and foodservice industry, however, the word *service* is almost never used alone. It is most often combined with other words to express a specific type of service:

- Friendly service
- Fast service
- Elegant service
- Courteous service
- Attentive service
- High-quality service

Regardless of the specific type of service desired by guests, all guests seek customer-centric service. Customer-centric service is service that is centered, or focused, on guests and their unique needs and desires. All customers seek customer-centric service regardless of the segment of the restaurant and foodservice industry in which they are making a purchase; all customers want their own needs met. When their needs are met, customers' views of an operation's service levels will be positive.

Cleanliness

Every restaurant and foodservice customer making a purchase wants to do so from an operation that is clean and that provides safe and wholesome food. For many guests, cleanliness is one of the major reasons they would, or would not, return to an operation. Experienced managers know that dining areas are just as important as kitchens when it comes to keeping a restaurant or foodservice operation clean (see *Exhibit 2.4*).

To determine just how important cleanliness is to some customers, researchers from San Diego State University studied the conditions that influence restaurant choices in families with young children. The mothers of the families were chosen to represent their family and rated 19 restaurant-related items in terms of importance in selecting restaurants.

Exhibit 2.4

The 19 factors included items such as taste of food, atmosphere, price, nutritional content, coupons, language, ethnic specialty, and cleanliness. The most highly valued aspect of restaurant selection was cleanliness. This was true among almost all respondents.[3]

Value

Value has been defined as the difference between what customers get when they buy a product or service and what they pay to get it. The more customers get for their money, the more value they receive. All customers desire good value. But good value is *not* the same as low price. In fact, when products or services are sold at prices so low that it is not possible to deliver good quality products or service, it is usually not possible to deliver good value. For restaurant and foodservice managers, ensuring good value means consistently delivering high-quality products and services at prices guests consider to be fair.

Total Experience

Moments of truth related to quality products, quality service, cleanliness, and value all combine to create a total dining experience. It is the manager's responsibility to manage those moments of truth in a way that consistently results in a positive total guest experience.

Each manager must assess his or her own operation on a continuous basis if all of the many moments of truth experienced by customers are to lead to a positive overall experience. Doing so leads to satisfied guests, repeat business, and increased profits.

PROVIDING CUSTOMER-CENTRIC QUALITY SERVICE

Customer-centric high-quality service is a commitment to service that is focused on guests. Customer-centric quality service, to the utmost possible degree, places satisfying the needs of guests first and foremost in the mind of each restaurant and foodservice employee.

Can a business survive and be profitable while not providing customer-centric quality service? Sometimes a business has a unique product, is in a market with little or no competition, or just happens to be in the right place at the right time. Such a business can get away with ignoring the desires of their customers and provide low levels of customer service, at least for a while. However, in a competitive business environment, the competition will quickly offer better service alternatives to customers.

KEEPING IT SAFE

Managers must do all they can to make sure that the facilities they operate are kept clean and that the food they serve is safe to eat. There are key factors that increase the risk of serving unsafe food products:

- Purchasing food from unsafe sources
- Failing to cook food properly
- Holding food at incorrect temperatures
- Using contaminated equipment
- Practicing poor personal hygiene

Service personnel may be directly involved with many of these risk areas. For that reason, it is essential that managers do all they can to keep service and production areas clean and their staff well-trained in safe food and beverage handling techniques, including personal hygiene.

THINK ABOUT IT . . .

Consider an establishment that does a poor job of providing value to customers. Who would be most responsible for ensuring the operation resolves the issues that are preventing it from delivering real value to its guests?

---

[3] John Elder, James Sallis, Michell M. Zive, et al., "Factors Affecting Selection of Restaurants by Anglo- and Mexican-American Families," *Journal of the American Dietetic Association* 99, no. 7 (July 1999): 856–858.

The quality of customer service strongly impacts a customer's overall dining experience. High-quality customer service leads to customer satisfaction and a good dining experience. It also adds to the already good food, decor, and value to make the overall experience positive.

A few poor customer service experiences can cancel out any good impressions of food, decor, and other values, and can quickly turn the overall experience into a negative one. When other dining choices are available, a number of things can happen when customers are dissatisfied with an operation's service:

- Customer loyalty and repeat business decreases.
- Additional marketing expense is needed to maintain a profitable business.
- Top-quality employees may leave for better places of employment.
- Profits can decline.

However, high-quality customer service can positively impact the establishment with many benefits (see *Exhibit 2.5*):

- Leads to repeat business
- Distinguishes the establishment from its competition

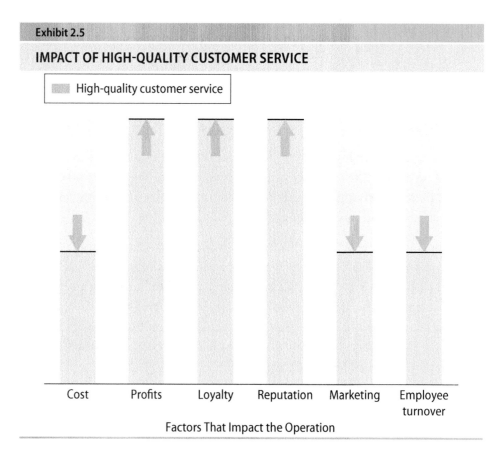

Exhibit 2.5

IMPACT OF HIGH-QUALITY CUSTOMER SERVICE

High-quality customer service

Cost   Profits   Loyalty   Reputation   Marketing   Employee turnover

Factors That Impact the Operation

- Allows customers to make a personal connection to the establishment

- Contributes to increased revenue and increases profits when costs are controlled

- Supports marketing efforts

- Enhances the establishment's overall image and reputation

- Provides increased interaction with customers so staff can determine their needs and satisfaction

- Contributes to employee pride and satisfaction

Customer-centric quality service also impacts other areas of a business:

- Customer loyalty

- Marketing success

- Reputation and image

- Employee turnover

- Costs

- Profits

Effect on Customer Loyalty

One impact of customer-centric quality service is its effect on customer loyalty. Customer loyalty means that customers prefer one establishment to all similar establishments. Some managers think that customer loyalty means that their establishments are the only operations where their customers dine. This is not realistic since most people do not eat at the same establishments every time. There are many legitimate reasons why customers will visit many establishments:

- They want different types of service.

- They want different types of food.

- They want to experience variety.

- They are traveling in that direction.

Nevertheless, when an establishment offers what they want, loyal customers will make that establishment their first choice.

For example, if a manager operates a seafood establishment, his or her customers have certain expectations of the operation. If the manager successfully identifies and consistently satisfies those expectations, the customers will identify that seafood operation as the one of their choice. If a customer consistently chooses that establishment, he or she has become one of its loyal customers.

CUSTOMER-CENTRIC SERVICE

People don't just go to restaurants to eat. While working at an amusement park, I had shifted my position from working at a hamburger restaurant to running my own hot dog cart. People had to go out of their way to come to my cart, while the Burger Shack was centrally located in the park. Add to that, they had to wait longer for my hot dogs because I had to grill each one to order, as I didn't have a steady stream of customers and the constant production method used at the 'Shack would have resulted in a ton of waste. As a result, I had the opportunity to chat people up while they waited. I talked to them about their scariest ride, told jokes, and talked to kids. I asked them how they liked their hot dog grilled (some people like 'em a little bit burned!). As a result, I had created an "experience" around my hot dogs that people were willing to go out of their way for and wait longer for.

Effect on Marketing Success

Customers expect and accept different levels of service between a QSR and a full-service restaurant. However, if there is a perceived or actual difference in the service level between similar types of establishments, it is called a competitive point of difference. A competitive point of difference is a perceived or actual difference between any two things that can be used to influence a customer's buying decision.

An operation can have many competitive points of difference. A competitive point of difference can be part of a marketing strategy to separate one operation from its competition. The customer service an operation provides can be a competitive point of difference in its business marketing strategy. If the operation's marketing strategy emphasizes speed, as in QSRs, then customers will expect speedy guest service. If the operation markets professional and courteous staff, then that becomes the expectation of its customers. If managers' marketing strategies create service expectations for their customers, those expectations must be met every time and at each moment of truth.

Effect on Reputation and Image

Another impact of customer-centric service is its effect on business reputation or image. Word of mouth is one of the most effective forms of advertising for a business. It can enhance the business's reputation and image, or it can hurt it. It is not difficult to get people to talk about a business.

The benefit of a good word-of-mouth reputation is that it promotes a business at no additional marketing cost. The challenge for managers is to make sure that customers say positive things about their businesses. For example, managers want customers to say things such as the following:

- "You want great seafood? Go to Jack's Seafood on Williamson Street."
- "Jordan's over by the stadium has the best service in town."

Managers want to avoid customers saying things such as the following:

- "Are you sure you want to eat at the College Grill? I had a terrible experience the last time I was there."
- "I am never going back to that bistro; the servers are so arrogant."

Effect on Employee Turnover

Employee turnover occurs when an employee leaves a job and must be replaced. Turnover in the restaurant and foodservice industry has been reported to be from 25 to 100 percent or higher. Reasons for this turnover include poor training, personality conflicts, poor management, and moving out of the area. However, another reason for employee turnover is poor customer service. The environment in which a person works has a lot to do with that person's job satisfaction. Employees who have the ability and desire to provide exceptional customer service want to work in pleasant environments. Such environments have minimal levels of complaints, chaos, uneasiness, ambiguity, stress, and lack of focus. Employee satisfaction can help reduce turnover because satisfied employees are more likely to stay at their jobs (see *Exhibit 2.6*).

Effect on Costs

Achieving high-quality customer service has an effect on costs. When establishments do a great job of giving their guests positive experiences, the guests share their experiences and recommendations with others. As a result, the establishment gains new customers by word of mouth rather than by spending money for marketing. The story in *Exhibit 2.7* is an example of this.

Exhibit 2.6

Exhibit 2.7
ALEX'S BIRTHDAY PARTY

A family of four went to a local establishment to celebrate their four-year-old son Alex's birthday. Alex's father spoke to the host privately and asked for a slice of cake with candles for Alex's dessert.

The host pleasantly and enthusiastically replied, "We would love to do this for your son. We like birthdays here. What is your son's name, and how old is he?"

Alex and his family ordered, received, and ate their meals. Everyone enjoyed the food and ambience. Then it was time for dessert. Without being told to, several servers brought out Alex's birthday cake with four candles on top. They all sang "Happy Birthday" and clapped their hands.

They presented the cake to Alex and everyone could see that the icing said, "Happy Birthday Alex." The server asked Alex how old he was. When he told them, the server said, "You are so-o-o big now. I'll bet you can ride a two-wheeler," and held a short conversation with Alex. Everyone could see that the four-year-old was happy and proud. It was a magical moment for Alex.

In the story of Alex's birthday dinner, what did it cost the establishment to provide that magical moment for Alex? There were costs in hiring the right person, training costs, costs in creating the culture where the servers felt empowered to act, and the labor costs of having those servers on duty.

Now, balance those costs with the benefits and the potential revenue that the experience may generate. What would it cost the establishment to successfully influence Alex's family, friends, relatives, neighbors, the people who observed that experience, and the people those witnesses told about it? Managers' must determine what they are willing to invest in high-quality customer service to ensure that their businesses consistently exceed their customers' expectations.

Effect on Profits

Customer service can also affect an operation's profits. It is important to recognize that revenue does not equal profit. There are many operations that generate high revenue but are not profitable. In this situation, some operations cut services to increase profits. In the short run, providing less training, hiring fewer staff members, and taking shortcuts can reduce costs and increase profits. However, those cuts will result in poor service and customers will perceive less value for their dollar; eventually, they will go somewhere else.

But, improving customer service can increase profits. Managers can do this by both taking a personal interest in their customers and by training their employees in suggestive selling techniques. Suggestive selling means recommending additional or different items to a customer. For example, a server could ask a customer, "Would you like a pastry with your coffee?"

Suggestive selling can actually be a way of providing high-quality customer service. It should be approached as enhancing the guest experience and not as a way of increasing the check or tip. If done correctly, suggesting a side dish that will enhance an entrée, a wine or beer that complements the main course, or a dessert to complete the meal will influence the guest's perception of value. If a suggestion results in a higher tip, a higher average check, or more profit, all the better. Suggestive selling is discussed in detail in chapter 4 of this book.

QUALITY SERVICE CHALLENGES

Experienced managers know that providing high-quality customer service that consistently meets the needs of guests is a continual challenge. This is true for all guests, but some guests with special needs pose additional quality service challenges.

Challenges for All Guests

The assessment of service levels, and particularly the assessment of high-quality service levels, can be difficult. To illustrate, consider the following six service characteristics that guests may indicate they would like to experience when dining out:

- Friendly service
- Attentive service
- Professional service
- Quick service
- Responsive service
- Courteous service

Experienced managers know that they face several challenges related to the delivery of these six service characteristics:

- Intangibility
- Consistency
- Inseparability
- Capacity

INTANGIBILITY

The characteristics that define quality service conditions are most often intangible. The characteristics are intangible because they *cannot* be seen, touched, or held before or after they are experienced. As a result, they cannot always be easily evaluated. In some cases, an identical service level can result in two very different assessments of that service. For example, two different guests may have very different views of what actually constitutes friendly or quick service.

In fact, because of its intangibility, some managers believe delivering quality service is more like delivering a theatrical performance than a product. Employees are actors on stage, with each seeking to give his or her best performance to their audience of guests!

CONSISTENCY

Consistency refers to providing the same level of service every time the guest visits the establishment. However, in the restaurant and foodservice industry, a guest's view of the service quality he or she has received depends, to a large degree, on the person delivering it. Thus, consistency in the delivery of service is much harder to achieve than consistency in the delivery of products when standardized recipes are used.

To illustrate, consider a group of office workers. After work, the group visits an establishment whose lounge has large TV screens for playing interactive trivia games. If all the members of the group order bottles of a popular beer while playing the games, the operation's manager can be certain there will be consistency in the product served.

However, the manager also knows that the attentiveness, skill level, appearance, dress, and even the attitude of the server will have an impact on this group's satisfaction level. The manager also knows these same service characteristics can vary between servers and have a direct impact on the quality of the group's overall experience. It is for that reason managers responsible for ensuring high-quality customer service in their operations should make certain all employees are well-trained in all the service standards identified for the operation.

Exhibit 2.8

INSEPARABILITY

Inseparability is another service-related challenge. **Inseparability** refers to the tendency of restaurant and foodservice customers to connect the quality of service provided with the personal characteristics of the individual staff member who delivers it. Thus, a guest's view of service quality and his or her view of the individual employee providing the service are inseparable.

To illustrate, consider two guest experiences. In the first, a neat, well-dressed, and smiling member of the waitstaff took the guest's order promptly (*Exhibit 2.8*). The order is quickly delivered 10 minutes later.

In the second guest's case, the order is also taken promptly but this time by an employee dressed sloppily and in a dirty uniform. While taking the order, the employee never smiled and appeared to be quite distracted with issues other than the guest's order. The order is also delivered 10 minutes later.

Most guests will feel they received quality service during the first visit, but not during the second visit. Even though the order was delivered in the same time during each visit, in the second example the server forgot several key characteristics of quality service:

- Making guests feel welcome
- Making guests feel special
- Making guests feel good about their dining-out choice
- Dressing and grooming professionally
- Cheerfully addressing any service shortcomings and correcting them promptly

Understanding the customer's common inability to separate service quality from those who actually deliver it is important. It is one reason why many managers hire workers with positive attitudes and train them to do their jobs, rather than hire well-trained employees without a positive and customer-centric attitude toward guests.

CAPACITY

Finally, service capacity is an important factor related to the consistent delivery of high-quality service. **Capacity** refers to the different service-related situations and outcomes that exist when establishments are busy and when they are slow. To illustrate, consider that two guests arrived at an establishment on a very busy Saturday night. They placed their name on a waiting list, were directed to a comfortable lounge area, and in 10 minutes were escorted to their table. In this example, their view of the operation's commitment to high-quality customer service would likely be very positive.

Assume further that on the next Saturday night the same guests arrived at an establishment that was nearly empty. They waited near the host stand for five minutes before a host finally arrived to escort them to their table. In this scenario, the guests were seated in five minutes. Their wait time in this example was only half of the wait time they experienced at the prior establishment. Their view of this operation's commitment to attentive quality service, however, will most likely be *lower* than that of the operation that took twice as long to seat them!

All restaurant and foodservice operations with a fixed number of seats face the service-related challenge of matching service levels with seating capacity. In every operation offering dine-in service, unused seating capacity means the operation's managers must make decisions about scheduling the optimal number of service staff. For those operations offering drive-through service, similar volume-related challenges exist in staffing drive-through windows properly when the operation is extremely busy or extremely slow.

If too many service employees are scheduled to work when business is slow, labor costs may be too high to make the operation's desired profits. If too few service staff members are scheduled to work when the establishment is busy, however, the result may be poor levels of customer service.

In many establishments, one example of unused capacity is the time period between lunch and dinner. Service levels during this period must remain high despite the lowered number of guests likely to be served. To ensure high-quality customer service managers must also staff properly during those time periods when the operation is running at, or near, its maximum capacity. It is important that managers realize poor staffing decisions most often result in poor customer service.

PUTTING IT TOGETHER

Despite the challenges associated with delivering quality service, experienced managers know that service is as important and sometimes more important than product quality for ensuring positive guest dining experiences. *Exhibit 2.9* summarizes some important service-related challenges and key methods for addressing them.

Exhibit 2.9

SERVICE CHALLENGES AND SOLUTIONS

Challenge	Solution
Intangibility	Establish and enforce service standards with all employees.
Consistency	Enforce standards and ensure quality employee training to maximize reliable and consistent service delivery.
Inseparability	Hire for positive attitude; train to ensure adequate skill.
Capacity	Make thoughtful employee scheduling decisions that reflect the realities of changing business volume levels and desired service levels.

Challenges for Guests with Special Needs

While managers face service challenges related to all guests, some guests have special needs that must be addressed. These guests include a variety of guest types:

- Families with small children
- Customers with disabilities
- Customers with communication barriers
- Customers with dietary restrictions
- Customers who are elderly

FAMILIES

Those operations that serve large numbers of families with small children face special service challenges. For example, if families are to be served in an operation, special seating for small children will likely be required. Managers must ensure there are a sufficient number of clean and solidly constructed high chairs and booster seats available. Servers should be helpful in securing proper seating for small children. However, it is best to instruct servers that parents are to be the ones placing the child in the special seating. Allowing parents to seat their children minimizes the potential liability for an operation.

Exhibit 2.10

Some operations have special children's menus or sections of the regular menu devoted to menu items commonly preferred by children. Parents appreciate this. Also, some operations provide paper placemats and crayons or other items to keep small children busy during meal periods (*Exhibit 2.10*). Most parents also appreciate the availability of bibs and extra napkins when small children are served. Some operations also provide chairs or benches in bathrooms for breastfeeding mothers and changing areas for children in diapers.

In some cases, children may be allowed by parents to leave their table and wander, or run around, in dining areas. If that occurs, servers should be instructed to politely inform the parents that, for their child's own safety, the child should remain seated at the parent's table.

CUSTOMERS WITH DISABILITIES

A **customer with a disability** is a person who has a physical or mental disability that could have been acquired for a number of other reasons, including heredity, illness, accident or injury, or advancing age. Understanding disabilities and helping guests discreetly and appropriately is essential to these guests enjoying their meals and receiving high-quality service. Disabilities can be classified in several ways:

- Physical disability
- Vision impairment
- Hearing impairment

There are a variety of types and different degrees of physical disabilities. Not every physical disability relates to mobility and not all require wheelchairs. For example, people who have arthritis, heart or lung conditions, or amputated limbs may also have difficulty with moving, standing, or sitting.

In some cases, it may be difficult to identify a person with a physical disability; in other cases, guests with physical impairments may arrive at a restaurant or foodservice operation using crutches, a cane, a walker, or a wheelchair. Managers who train servers to deal with guests with disabilities of all types should emphasize key points:

- Servers should smile, relax, and keep in mind that people with disabilities are people who may need extra help.
- Servers should exercise patience. People with some kinds of disabilities may take a little longer to understand and respond than will other guests.
- Servers should always ask before they offer to help. Customers with disabilities know if they need help and will inform servers how they can provide it.
- Servers should look directly at their customers when speaking to them, but should not stare.
- When taking orders, servers should speak directly to people with disabilities, and not defer to their dining companions, unless specifically asked to do so.
- Servers should always ask permission before touching a guide animal, wheelchair, or other piece of a guest's equipment.
- Servers should be informed about any special emergency procedures related to customers with disabilities.

Some guests with vision impairments will arrive at an operation using guide animals. It is important that managers let all servers know that guide animals are allowed in restaurant and foodservice establishments. The animals will usually follow servers to tables, guiding their owners. Guests are then seated and the server may offer to hold the animal's leash while the guest sits. The dog should then be placed at the feet of the guest if it is possible to do so, or at a place near the table where it is out of the way, but can see its owner. Servers should not allow anyone to pet, feed, or disturb the dog while the guest is seated.

Manager's Memo

The Americans with Disabilities Act (ADA) defines a service animal as *any* guide dog, signal dog, or other animal individually trained to provide assistance to an individual with a disability. These types of animals are considered service animals under the ADA. Service animals perform some of the functions and tasks that the individual with a disability cannot perform for himself or herself:

- Alerting persons with hearing impairments to sounds
- Pulling wheelchairs or carrying and picking up things for persons with mobility impairments
- Assisting persons with mobility impairments with balance

A service animal is *not* a pet. The ADA requires operations to modify any "no pets" policy to allow the use of a service animal by a person with a disability. This does not mean managers must abandon their "no pets" policy altogether, but simply that they must make an exception to their general rule for service animals.

Guests with vision impairments may need help reading menus. Some operations provide these guests with menus in Braille. Others make flashlights and/or magnifying glasses available to help people with visual impairments read menus. Still others offer reading glasses of various strengths for customers who may have left their glasses at home.

When presenting a check to a guest with a visual impairment, the server should clearly state the total amount due, and if requested, go over the individual menu item prices. If the guest is paying using a credit card, the server should restate the amount due before the person signs the slip. If the guest pays with cash, the server should state the bill denominations and the coins used to give change.

Going to a busy and noisy establishment can be difficult for customers with hearing impairments. Hearing loss is a medical condition affecting many guests. Those guests with hearing impairments can be best served when the employee taking the guest's order faces the guest and speaks clearly and slowly—not necessarily more loudly.

CUSTOMERS WITH COMMUNICATION BARRIERS

Customers with communication-related barriers include those who speak a different language and those whose speech is difficult to understand. Foreign language speakers can be assisted when servers attempt to identify similarity of menu terms or by hand gestures. In some cases, these guests can communicate best by pointing to pictures of items or descriptions on the menu rather than by speaking. In operations serving large numbers of foreign language speakers, some managers seek to hire employees who speak other languages, an advantage of diversity in staffing.

Guests with speech impairments may be difficult to understand. In these cases, servers should courteously ask, "Did I understand that you asked for . . . ?" or a similar statement. They can then restate the customer's order or request. In those cases, the guest may respond with a nod yes or no. In all cases, servers should be very careful not to embarrass or to make these guests feel uncomfortable.

CUSTOMERS WITH DIETARY RESTRICTIONS

The dietary restrictions of guests may be self-imposed or may be required by a guest's medical condition. Common examples of self-imposed dietary restrictions include those related to religion or other strongly held beliefs such as vegetarianism. In most cases, these guests simply need accurate information about the ingredients contained in a menu item, or how the item was prepared, to make informed menu selections. In those cases where guests' dietary restrictions are medically related, however, managers and their staff must be especially vigilant and knowledgeable.

One reason for this is that about 4 percent of people in the United States have food allergies. Food allergies occur when the body mistakes an ingredient in food, usually a protein and referred to as an allergen, as harmful and creates a defense system (antibodies) to fight it. There is no known cure. The only way to prevent an allergic reaction is to avoid the food that causes it.

When a person eats a food to which he or she is allergic, reactions can begin quickly. Reactions include swelling of the lips, tongue, and throat; difficulty breathing; hives; and abdominal cramps, vomiting, and diarrhea. Symptoms can range from mild to severe and even death in the worse cases, and reactions can occur a few minutes to up to two hours after eating the offending food.

Many customers do not mention their food allergies to servers. Instead, they rely on the menu for ingredient information. To help prevent food allergy incidents, managers may add a menu caution statement or post a sign prompting customers with food allergies to talk with the manager about ingredient information.*

When persons with food allergies dine away from home, they rely on service staff to provide accurate ingredient information so they can make informed decisions. Inaccurate or incomplete information puts these customers at risk for a reaction, can end their dining experience, and may require ambulance transport to the hospital. Education, cooperation, and teamwork are keys to safely serving a customer with food allergies. All employees must know about the issues surrounding food allergies. Managers must also let them know what to do if an allergic reaction occurs.

Peanuts and other nuts are among the most common food allergens in the United States (see *Exhibit 2.11*). Although an individual can be allergic to any food, these eight food items account for approximately 90 percent of all food allergy reactions: peanuts, tree nuts, milk, eggs, wheat, soy, fish, and shellfish.

Allergic reactions can occur in some persons when they consume even invisible amounts of an allergen. This can happen, for example, by indirect contact with hands or

Exhibit 2.11

COMMON FOOD ALLERGENS

- Peanuts
- Tree nuts

- Fish
- Shellfish

- Milk

- Soy

- Eggs

- Wheat

*The preceding section is adapted from: The Food Allergy & Anaphylaxis Network. Welcoming Guests with Food Allergies. Fairfax, VA 2001.

Exhibit 2.12

utensils, such as when a measuring tool comes into contact with an item that causes reactions and then, before it is properly cleaned, it is used to measure out another food that is not thought to typically cause reactions. Or there might be **cross-contact**, which is the result when one food comes into direct contact with another, causing proteins in the two food items to combine. When cross-contact occurs, each of the food products contains small and often invisible amounts of the other food. For example, if a knife is used to spread peanut butter but is only wiped clean with a cloth before being used to spread jam, there could be enough peanut protein remaining on the knife to cause a reaction in a peanut-allergic person.

There are several areas of importance to managers and servers as they seek to prevent the inadvertent introduction of allergens into guests' food:

- **Unclean hands or gloves:** Something as simple as picking up a cookie containing nuts and then picking up a nut-free muffin may cause cross-contact (*Exhibit 2.12*). Wash hands thoroughly and put on a fresh pair of gloves before serving an allergen-free meal. Soap and warm water are effective for removing allergens from hands, but hand sanitizers are not.

- **Splashed or spilled food:** It is possible for allergens to come into contact if a customer's food, drinks, or utensils are carried on a tray with other items containing allergens. For example, milk or cream can spill, or butter can come in contact with a food item that is otherwise milk-free. Servers should use a small plate or saucer when carrying cream or butter to catch any spills. Ideally, the allergen-free meal should be carried by itself directly from the kitchen to the customer.

- **Trays:** Trays used to carry allergen-free meals should first be cleaned thoroughly with hot, soapy water or other appropriate cleaning compounds and procedures. Wiping a tray with a damp towel is insufficient.

- **Garnishes:** To minimize the chance for mistakes, only the chef, manager, or other designated employee should garnish the plate of a guest who has stated that he or she is allergic. Ingredients on the production line can easily spill into containers of other ingredients. For example, it is easy for shredded cheese, croutons, or nuts to become mixed with prepared vegetables, garnishes, or herbs.

- **Pockets:** Servers should not carry cheese graters, pepper mills, or other similar tools in their apron pockets as these may result in allergens inadvertently coming into contact with food products that will be served to allergic guests.

If servers are not certain about all of the ingredients used in a menu item, they should be trained to say so. Customers will appreciate the honesty. Servers can then speak to the chef or manager to learn needed details and provide guests with accurate information about potential allergens. Managers can print notes on their menus and Web sites for customers with food allergies:

- "For those with food allergies, please inform your server, who will be happy to discuss any necessary changes."
- "Please alert your server to any food allergies before ordering."

CUSTOMERS WHO ARE ELDERLY

Guests who are elderly may require assistance parking, entering and leaving an operation, walking to their seats, seeing the menu clearly, and hearing voices at typical speaking levels. Also, in some cases, elderly guests may prefer to be seated in areas that have ample lighting and that are relatively quiet. They may also have special requests regarding areas of the dining room that are less drafty, or warmer or cooler than other areas.

In some cases it is helpful for the employee seating elderly guests to walk ahead to ensure the way to the table is clear and no obstructions are in the way. When assisting elderly guests with crutches, canes, or walkers, these should be stored near the guest's table, but not under it, nor in the way of other guests. Elderly guests in wheelchairs may wish to sit in establishments' chairs, in which case the wheelchair needs to be stored out of the way. Many guests in wheelchairs prefer to remain in their chairs, in which case extra room at a table may be a necessary accommodation. When the customer is ready to leave the operation, the walking aids should be promptly returned to the guests.

RESTAURANT TECHNOLOGY

Managers should keep all printed materials and the information about menu ingredients posted on the operation's Web site accurate and current. If recipe ingredient information is posted on the Web site, managers must make sure that the same information is then included on printed material available in the operation.

Posting information for customers with food allergies is worth considering because many potential customers view an operation's Web site before deciding to visit an operation. Some establishments have even added a link from their site to the informational Food Allergy & Anaphylaxis Network Web site (*www.foodallergy.org*).

SUMMARY

1. **Describe the "moment of truth" concept.**

   A moment of truth occurs each time a customer comes into contact with any aspect of the organization and gets an impression of the quality of its service. When guests have an opportunity to form an opinion about an operation, it results in a moment of truth. Moments of truth can be positive, and when they are customers will form a favorable impression of an operation and its service. Moments of truth can also be negative, and when they are customers will form an unfavorable impression of the operation. Moments of truth can occur before a customer arrives at an operation and in some cases can even occur after the customer has left an operation. Managers seek to manage moments of truth to ensure that their operations consistently offer customers high-quality service levels.

2. **Explain the three steps managers take to develop employee customer service expectations.**

Three steps are needed to develop employee expectations related to high-quality service. In the first step, managers establish exactly what they want all their guests to experience. Because managers seek to provide customers positive moments of truth, the standards developed are designed to ensure these positive moments occur. In the second step, managers communicate the standards to employees and provide workers with the tools and information needed to achieve the operation's identified standards. In the third and final step, managers assess their workers' performance and provide additional training, information, or tools if these are needed to ensure customer service expectations are consistently met.

3. **Discuss the differences and similarities between internal and external restaurant and foodservice customers.**

Managers who want to manage moments of truth and thus ensure their operations consistently provide high-quality customer service recognize that they actually have two types of customers. Managers must meet the expectations of both their external and internal customers. External customers are the buyers of products or services who are outside the manager's direct control. In most cases, guests are external customers. By contrast, internal customers are those within an organization who serve each other. Employees are internal customers if their work results in them directly serving other employees. External and internal customers are similar in that managers must satisfy both to provide high-quality customer service and to minimize unnecessary employee turnover.

4. **Identify the elements customers seek when making a restaurant or foodservice purchase.**

Customers who make a restaurant or foodservice purchase seek quality products, quality service, cleanliness, value, and a total dining experience. Quality products mean more than good taste. The products must also be served properly. Customers expect to buy excellent service, which may be classified in many ways including friendly service, fast service, elegant service, courteous service, or attentive service. In all cases, the service must be of high quality and be customer-centric. Customers also want to buy products and services from an operation that is clean. For many guests, cleanliness is one of the major reasons they would, or would not, return to an operation. Customers also seek good value in their purchases. Good value means consistently receiving high-quality products and services at fair prices. Last, customers buy a total dining experience. It is the responsibility of restaurant and foodservice managers to manage their customers' moments of truth in a way that consistently results in a positive total guest experience.

5. **List the areas of a restaurant or foodservice operation directly affected by the delivery of high-quality customer-centric service.**

Customer-centric quality service impacts customer loyalty, marketing success, reputation and image, employee turnover, costs, and profits. When an operation offers high-quality customer-centric service, loyal customers will make that operation their first choice when selecting among their dining alternatives. As a result, marketing costs are reduced. Customer-centric service also directly affects the reputation of a business. When service quality is high, guests say good things about the operation, and that promotes the business at no additional marketing cost. Employee turnover is affected by customer service quality, because one reason for high employee turnover is poor customer service.

The environment in which a person works affects that person's job satisfaction. Employees who have the ability and desire to provide exceptional customer service want to work in operations that have those organizational goals, and they will often leave if it does not. Customer service levels directly affect an operation's costs and profits. When service is high, costs are reduced and profits increase.

6. **Describe the challenges faced by managers in providing high-quality service to all guests.**

Because service is intangible, managers face that unique service challenge, as well as the additional challenges of consistency, inseparability, and capacity. The characteristics of good service are intangible because they cannot be seen, touched, or held. As a result, they cannot always be easily evaluated.

Consistency refers to the delivery of the same level of service every time the guest visits the establishment. Because a guest's view of the service quality depends upon the person delivering it, consistency in the delivery of service is more challenging than consistency in the delivery of products.

Inseparability refers to the fact that customers associate the quality of service provided with the personal characteristics of the staff member who delivers it. Thus, a guest's positive or negative view of a server directly affects the guest's assessment of service quality delivered. Capacity refers to staffing an operation to ensure service excellence both when it is busy and when it is slow.

7. **Identify categories of guests with special needs that create unique service-related challenges for managers.**

Guests who have special needs can include families, customers with disabilities, customers with communication barriers, customers with dietary restrictions, and customers who are elderly. Families with small children have special needs related to seating, smaller portion sizes, and keeping children occupied during mealtime. Customers with disabilities include those with physical disabilities and vision and hearing impairment. Managers must train servers to address these guests' special needs.

Some guests restrict their diets due to religion or other strongly held beliefs. In other cases, guests face dietary restrictions because they are allergic to specific food items. In these cases, managers and staff must take all precautions to prevent guests' allergic reactions. Elderly guests often have special needs because they may prefer to be seated in specific areas that have good lighting, are quiet, are less drafty, are warmer, or are cooler than other areas.

APPLICATION EXERCISE

On a separate sheet of paper, answer the following six questions for each of the interactions listed.

1. What is the input–output relationship in restaurant and foodservice operations?

2. Who is the internal customer? Who is the external customer?

3. What are the possible moments of truth associated with this interaction?

4. What would make these positive or negative moments of truth?

5. Who determines whether the internal or external customer relationship is positive or negative?

6. Who controls the situation?

Interaction 1: A greeter meets guests at the door and welcomes them to the establishment.

Interaction 2: A sommelier presents the wine list to a guest and says that she would be happy to make suggestions.

Interaction 3: A line cook asks a server to clarify an order.

Interaction 4: A manager walks around the dining room asking guests about their dining experience.

Interaction 5: A manager places a special request order with a produce vendor.

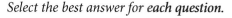

REVIEW YOUR LEARNING

Select the best answer for each question.

1. **A moment of truth is an opinion about an operation's service quality that is formed by a**
   A. server.
   B. manager.
   C. customer.
   D. bartender.

2. **What is the purpose of managers identifying standards of guest service and hospitality?**
   A. To categorize internal customers
   B. To categorize external customers
   C. To define positive moments of truth
   D. To define achievable levels of profit

3. **What is a similarity between an operation's internal and external customers?**
   A. Both are employed by the restaurant or foodservice operation.
   B. Neither is employed by the restaurant or foodservice operation.
   C. Both may leave an operation if it does not deliver high-quality guest service.
   D. Neither is free to choose the operation in which he or she seeks high-quality service.

4. **Managers best ensure guests receive good value when they deliver quality products and services**
   A. faster than any other competitor.
   B. at prices guests consider to be fair.
   C. at prices lower than any competitor.
   D. guests cannot purchase anywhere else.

5. In a survey of mothers, what factor was most important to their establishment selection decisions?
   A. Price
   B. Cleanliness
   C. Food quality
   D. Service quality

6. High-quality levels of customer service most often result in
   A. lower profits.
   B. lower revenue levels.
   C. greater customer loyalty.
   D. greater employee turnover.

7. Which comment made by a server to a guest is an example of suggestive selling?
   A. "Thank you for coming in tonight!"
   B. "Would you like ice cream on your pie?"
   C. "Would you like me to bring your check now?"
   D. "I'm sorry. I'll bring you a clean fork right away."

8. A server in an operation is competent but is never friendly with guests. Which challenge is most likely negatively affecting this employee's service delivery?
   A. Capacity
   B. Consistency
   C. Intangibility
   D. Inseparability

9. What is the service challenge related to staffing an operation at appropriate levels?
   A. Capacity
   B. Consistency
   C. Intangibility
   D. Inseparability

10. Which food product is among the leading causes of severe allergic food reactions in the United States?
    A. Rice
    B. Apples
    C. Lettuce
    D. Peanuts

3 Designing and Implementing an Effective Customer Service Program

INSIDE THIS CHAPTER

- The Importance of a Customer Service Plan
- Developing and Implementing Service Standards
- Staffing to Achieve Service Standards
- Monitoring Service Standards

CHAPTER LEARNING OBJECTIVES

After completing this chapter, you should be able to:

- Explain the importance of creating a formal customer service plan.
- Describe the four main areas for which service standards must be established.
- Summarize the steps managers take when implementing customer service standards.
- Identify the staffing-related procedures managers use to achieve their service standards.
- Explain the process managers use to monitor service standards.

KEY TERMS

CASE STUDY

"So tell me what happened with Mrs. Luciano," said Ralph, the claims manager for the Hoshburt Insurance Company.

Ralph was talking to Sonya, the manager of the Red Door Family Restaurant, about a guest who had fallen at the Red Door and had sprained her ankle. Hoshburt Insurance was the restaurant's liability insurance company.

"Well," said Sonya. "It was last Friday night. We were really busy when a customer came up to me and said the sink had overflowed in the ladies' restroom. I checked my watch and it was almost exactly 7:00 p.m. I immediately told Tommy, our buser, to go check it out while I went to help ring out some guests in a long line at the register."

"OK," said Ralph, "what happened next?"

"Well, Tommy came back and told me there was water all over the floor. I instructed him to get a mop and clean it up," said Sonya.

"When I talked to Tommy he said it took him about 10 minutes to find the mop, rinse it out, grab the mop bucket, and head back to the ladies' room. Does that sound right?" asked Ralph.

"Yes, that sounds about right," said Sonya. "When he went back to the ladies' room, he told me he found Mrs. Luciano lying on the floor. She had slipped, fallen, and was unable to stand up. I looked at my watch and it was about 7:10 p.m. Mrs. Luciano must have fallen between the time Tommy saw the water on the floor and the time he got back with the mop bucket."

1. In his report, do you think Ralph will state that Tommy was partially responsible for this accident? Do you think Ralph will report that Sonya was partially responsible?

2. Assume you were the restaurant's owner. What would you want the managers of your operation to do to prevent such incidents in the future?

THE IMPORTANCE OF A CUSTOMER SERVICE PLAN

Chapter 1 defined planning as the function of management that identifies goals and the strategies used to achieve the goals. Planning is the first step in the effective management of any process. That includes the process of providing high-quality customer service. Just as they plan for food production, marketing efforts, and the management of their operations' finances, managers should create a customer service plan. A customer service plan is the well-thought-out and systematic identification and recording of exactly what must be done to provide high-quality customer service.

Managers create customer service plans designed to address key service-related questions:

- What will be the product-related service standards in our operation?
- What will be the employee-related service standards in our operation?
- What will be the facility-related service standards in our operation?
- What will be the safety- and security-related service standards in our operation?
- How will we implement our service standards?
- How will we staff to achieve our service standards?
- How will we monitor our success in achieving our service standards?

Customer service planning is an ongoing process. It consists of establishing standards of service and the methods for ensuring those standards are met. If an operation does not establish standards, there will be no way to compare what actually happens with what the manager wants to happen.

For example, assume it takes a fast-casual operation four minutes to serve the average guest. Is that good or bad? This question cannot be answered unless the manager knows the goal was five minutes. With this knowledge, the manager will likely be very pleased. If the goal had been three minutes, the manager would not likely be pleased. Successful quality service planners define desired results. Then they take the steps needed to ensure that the results are achieved. There are specific reasons why managers develop plans that focus on service-related standards (see chapter 1):

- Standards provide direction.
- Standards provide a means to determine how much more progress is needed to achieve service goals.
- Standards can be assigned to specific departments, teams, or employees.
- Standards clarify employees' roles and responsibilities.
- Standards can be used to motivate and challenge employees.
- Standards help ensure a business's long-term profitability.

THINK ABOUT IT . . .

Some managers think long-range service quality planning is a good idea, but they do not have time to do it because they are dealing with current service-related problems. What advice would you give these managers?

DEVELOPING AND IMPLEMENTING SERVICE STANDARDS

While there are a variety of planning approaches that could be used to develop quality service standards and plans, one good way to do so is to consider desired service standards in several key operational areas:

- Product-related standards
- Employee-related standards
- Facility-related standards
- Safety- and security-related standards

Product-Related Standards

Some managers make a distinction between the products they serve and how those products are served. The best managers understand that, in the eyes of the guest, product quality and service quality are directly related. For example, assume an establishment is famous for the quality of its French fries. When the fries leave the kitchen they are hot, crispy, and flavorful. Assume further, however, that service staff does not regularly provide guests with ketchup to accompany the fries. When guests do ask for ketchup they invariably have to wait a long time to get it and, when they do, the portions served are very small and insufficient for most guests. In this example, many guests will not likely leave the establishment with a favorable impression of its French fries. As a result, managers who develop customer service plans must assess each menu item they sell and establish product-related standards of service related to several key areas:

- **Serving size:** In some cases, service staff may be responsible for the amount of a menu item received by guests. Common examples include glasses of milk, soups, salads, bread and rolls with butter patties, and ice cream. In each of these examples and more, managers must establish the precise amount of a menu item to be served and then communicate that information to service staff. Managers' plans in this area must also include ensuring service staff have the proper portioning tools and proper-sized serving dishes to make this important part of a server's job easy to complete.

- **Serving temperature:** Just as some service staff may be responsible for the amount served to guest, they may also have an influence over the temperature at which menu items are served. When menu items are prepared but remain in the server pickup area, hot food items can get cold and cold food items can become warmer than they should be. Managers must establish appropriate service temperatures for all menu items. They must also ensure that servers are well trained to deliver prepared items to guests at each menu item's optimal temperature.

THINK ABOUT IT . . .

Some managers consistently understaff the number of servers needed during busy times. What are some specific examples of what could happen to hurt product-related standards in an operation when managers use this practice?

Exhibit 3.1

- **Appropriate garnish:** Experienced managers know that guests "eat with their eyes" before they actually taste their food or beverage selections. As a result, how menu items are garnished and visually presented is of great importance (*Exhibit 3.1*). In many cases, it is the server's responsibility to add appropriate item garnishes. As a result, the product-related portion of a manager's service plan should include details on how each menu item is to be garnished. It should also note who is responsible for ensuring the service of only properly garnished items to guests.

- **Appropriate menu item condiments:** In many cases, servers bring condiments to a guest's table. Condiments are edible items that enhance the flavor of food. For some guests, the quality and variety of an operation's condiments are nearly as important as the quality of the menu items they are used to enhance!

Exhibit 3.2 lists 12 of the most commonly provided restaurant and foodservice condiments. Managers developing product-related service standards should consider each menu item served. Managers should determine which, if any, condiments should be served with the menu item and which should be made available to guests upon request.

Exhibit 3.2

12 POPULAR RESTAURANT AND FOODSERVICE CONDIMENTS

Salt	Pepper	Ketchup	Mustard
Sugar	Cream	Pepper sauce	Steak sauce
Relish	Vinegar	Olive oil	Syrup

- **Appropriate menu item accompaniments:** In some cases, a guest's order of one menu item most often will automatically require the delivery of an appropriate accompanying item, as shown in *Exhibit 3.3*.

In many cases, servers are responsible for the delivery of these accompanying items. As a result, a manager's product-related service plan should directly address which accompanying items will be provided with which menu selections. Managers also must communicate to servers how much of each accompaniment will be provided to guests without an additional charge.

In some cases, such as lemon wedges for iced tea, the number or quantity of condiments provided to guests may be virtually unlimited, within reason. In other cases, such as expensive dressings for salads or sauces for entrées, an operation may charge guests when the guests request more of an accompanying item than is normally provided to them. In cases such as these, it is essential that an operation's servers know, and then inform guests, of any extra charges that will be made for the requested items. This should always be done before the requested items are delivered to the guests.

Exhibit 3.3

MENU ITEMS AND THEIR ACCOMPANYING ITEMS

Ordered Item	Accompanying Item
Tortilla chips	Salsa
Baked potato	Butter, sour cream
Pasta	Grated cheese
Salad	Dressing
Iced tea	Lemon slice or wedge
Fried fish	Tartar sauce

- **Appropriate service accompaniments:** In some cases, a guest's order of a menu item will necessitate the delivery of a special utensil or other service-related accompaniment (see *Exhibit 3.4*).

Managers creating a complete product-related service plan must ensure service staff know about, and have readily available to them, all needed service-related menu item accompaniments.

Exhibit 3.4	
MENU ITEMS AND THEIR SERVICE ACCOMPANIMENTS	
Ordered Item	**Service Accompaniment**
Soup	Soup spoon
Hot tea	Teapot
Crab legs	Crab claw breaker
Steak	Steak knife
White wine	Ice bucket or chiller

Managers should, of course, ensure that their production staff always follows standardized recipes when preparing menu items. Standardized recipes are the set of instructions to produce and serve a food or beverage item that will help ensure that quality and quantity standards will be consistently met. Managers must ensure menu items are served in a standardized manner as well. For example, if a fried vegetable appetizer plate is to be accompanied by two kinds of dipping sauces, the types of sauces provided and the proper amount of them should be provided by the server each time the appetizer is ordered and presented to guests.

When developing product-related service standards, managers can seek input from other managers, employees, and customers. Each of these groups can provide valuable input about an operation's menu items and how they can best be prepared and served.

Employee-Related Standards

Just as an operation's products must be assessed to establish service-related standards, so too must managers develop service standards related to employees. When managers develop employee-related service standards, they must do four important things:

1. Determine desired service standards.
2. Develop service standard expectations.
3. Develop service standard training materials.
4. Train staff.

DETERMINE DESIRED SERVICE STANDARDS

When establishing desired service standards related to employees, managers must ask important questions:

- What are our company's goals and objectives?
- What are our company's service standards?
- What service standards are important in the operation?

THINK ABOUT IT . . .

Have you ever ordered an item that was tasty but that you did not enjoy because you did not receive a needed condiment, item accompaniment, or proper eating utensil? What did you do?

- What are our customers' expectations?
- What are my personal expectations?
- What are my staff's abilities?

Managers establishing service standards may focus their attention on different operational areas, depending on the type of operation managed. However, all managers share some concerns:

- How should guests be greeted upon pre-arrival (when making reservations) or upon arrival?
- How should guests' orders be taken?
- How should guests be treated while in the operation or in its drive-through areas?
- How will guest payments be processed?

Each of these areas should be addressed properly. Otherwise, the result can be confusion among staff, guest complaints, and reduced operational profitability.

DEVELOP SERVICE STANDARD EXPECTATIONS

Managers can use their operation's **mission statement**, a written reminder to employees about the purpose and goals of a company, to develop their service standard expectations. Managers also consider their own expectations. For example, assume a fine-dining establishment wishes to be known as one that provides the very highest levels of personal service. In this case, managers must consider their personal view of exactly what that means. In some cases, industry standards or norms can also be very valuable in helping managers establish their own operation's service standards.

If service standards are not carefully identified and documented for future reference, the standards may not be known and followed by all. If that happens, the result can be the misuse of employee time, a waste of resources, and decreased profits. Managers can document their specific service standards related to several periods of time:

- Guest pre-arrival
- Guest arrival
- Guest ordering and service
- Guest payment
- Guest departure

DEVELOP SERVICE STANDARD TRAINING MATERIALS

Identifying employee-related service standards is important. After completing that task, those standards must be properly communicated to the appropriate employees. To do that, managers must consider and acquire the employee training tools they will need. As they do so, managers must ask key questions:

- What are the training abilities and characteristics of my staff?
- What types of training will be most effective?
- How detailed should the training materials be?
- What method(s) of information delivery should be used?
- How can employee interest be maintained?

TRAIN STAFF

The training of new service staff is a critical management task (see *Exhibit 3.5*). This is so because effective employee training is a key to providing excellent guest service.

Managers may use a variety of approaches and materials when delivering effective training sessions. Possible training styles include one-on-one training, small-group training, and large-group or all-staff training. Depending on the situation, managers may choose to use training aids such as handouts, videos, and role-playing activities.

Exhibit 3.5

There are additional areas of training-related concern that managers must address:

- When will the training occur?
- How long should the training last?
- Where will the training occur?
- Who will conduct the training?
- How will trainee learning be assessed?
- How often should the training session be repeated?

In all cases, the information provided to employees during training should be clear, concise, and accurate. If it is not, the result can be a lack of understanding by employees, and a long-term inability to meet the operation's desired service standards.

THINK ABOUT IT...

Have you ever attended a training session that was poorly planned or delivered? What could the trainer have done to improve your training session?

Facility-Related Standards

An operation's physical facilities affect guests' perceptions of service quality. Facilities include the grounds, building, equipment, and furnishings that combine to make up an operation's physical environment. Facilities and some nonfacility-related characteristics, such as employee uniforms and style of meal service (see chapter 6), all combine to form an operation's ambience. Ambience is the atmosphere or mood that a particular environment creates. A variety of facility-related factors directly influence a restaurant or foodservice operation's ambience:

- Design
- Décor
- Lighting
- Sound
- Temperature

In most cases the design and décor of an operation's building cannot be easily changed or modified by managers. This is because improving these may require the significant expenditure of funds which may need to be approved by the operation's owner. Managers do, however, have direct control over lighting levels, sound, and temperature. These three critical facility-related factors affect an operation's ambience and, as a result, directly affect guests' perceptions of quality service.

LIGHTING

Lighting levels are one of the biggest contributors to the ambience of an operation. The lighting in a restaurant or foodservice operation affects guest comfort and worker efficiency, as well as guest and worker safety and security. When lighting levels are too low, guests may have difficulty reading menus. Guest and employee safety also may be threatened due to possible trips and falls. When lighting levels are too high, guests may become uncomfortable due to the harshness of the lighting levels. In addition, the operation's energy costs may be higher than they need to be.

Lighting is also referred to as illumination, and light levels are measured in **foot-candles**. Generally, the greater the number of foot-candles present, the greater the level of illumination. Restaurant and foodservice operations often require varying degrees of illumination in different locations. Therefore managers may be responsible for ensuring that lighting levels are appropriate to the needs of different areas. To maintain proper lighting levels managers ensure that specific activities are undertaken:

- Establish and enforce appropriate lighting levels for each area of the operation.
- Keep lighting fixtures in good repair.
- Examine light bulbs in lighting fixtures daily and replace as needed.
- Clean light bulbs and fixtures (after being turned off) on a regularly scheduled basis.

WHAT'S THE FOOTPRINT?

In many restaurant and foodservice operations, artificial light is produced to supplement natural sunlight. Because it is free, sunlight is a cost-effective source of lighting. When it is used to its maximum effect, it can have a very positive impact on utility costs by limiting the amount of artificial light that must be produced. The result is lower operating costs, increased profits, and a lessened impact on the natural resources used to create the energy that powers the artificial lighting. In very sunny climates, letting in too much sunlight may increase an operation's air-conditioning costs, but in colder climates it can decrease heating costs. In nearly all cases, however, when natural lighting can be used cost-effectively in a estaurant or foodservice operation, everybody wins.

SOUND

Some sounds in a restaurant or foodservice operation, including background music, are introduced and directly controlled by a manager. Sound also includes noise from the conversations of guests and employees, as well as the normal noises made in the operation of a food facility. In all cases, however, managers must seek to maintain sound levels appropriate for their operations.

Exhibit 3.6

Different customers have different expectations of the sound levels preferred when they eat out. Some like relaxing and soothing sounds, whereas others prefer sounds that project a higher energy level. As a result, a sports bar may determine that the sounds of many televisions and loud customer conversations make it attractive to guests. Similarly, a high-energy, after-work spot may also encourage a higher level of sound (*Exhibit 3.6*). A fine-dining operation, however, will likely have customers that seek a sophisticated or romantic atmosphere. As a result, managers of these establishments will want to keep the sound levels low enough for quiet conversation.

Sound is measured in **decibels**. The higher the decibel level of both wanted and unwanted sounds, the higher the volume level. While managers do not routinely have a way to measure the changing decibel levels of their operations, there are specific steps they can take to ensure sound levels in their operations are appropriate:

- Establish appropriate volume level standards for overhead music, radios, or television sets during slow and busy serving periods. Strictly enforce the standards.

- Request staff to speak in clearly audible but quiet voices when communicating with other employees or guests.

- Require staff to wear soft rubber soles to reduce footstep noise and protect from slip and fall injuries.

- Use window treatments, such as blinds, valances, and curtains. These window treatments can absorb sound.

- Ensure the proper location of machines that have constant noises, such as ice machines and machines with condensers that cycle on and off.

TEMPERATURE

Temperatures in a dining room are critical aspects of a guest's dining experience. Room temperatures that are too warm or too cold can seriously detract from the enjoyment of a meal. The temperature in a restaurant or foodservice operation is controlled by its HVAC system. **HVAC** is an industry

WHAT'S THE FOOTPRINT?

HVAC systems can be fairly straightforward or very complex, but all consist of components responsible for heating, venting, and cooling a building and all require regular attention to operate most efficiently.

Managers can make their HVAC systems more efficient, save on energy costs, and help conserve natural resources when they implement effective preventive maintenance programs for their HVAC systems. These programs include regular inspection and cleaning of motors, belts, gaskets, and filters—all HVAC components that will directly affect the system's efficiency and energy consumption, because when they are in good repair the systems operate more efficiently.

term for an operation's heating, ventilating, and air-conditioning system. Heating, ventilation, and air-conditioning are considered together because each uses the operation's air treatment, thermostats, duct, and air handler systems. Air treatment can involve either the heating or the cooling of air. Thermostats control air temperatures in rooms. Ducts are the passageways, usually built of sheet metal, that allow fresh, cold, or warm air to be directed to different parts of a building. Air handler systems are the fans and mechanical systems used to move treated air through ducts and expel it into rooms through heating and cooling vents.

A properly operating HVAC system delivers treated air to rooms at a preestablished temperature determined by the manager. The efficiency of an HVAC system and the comfort of a building are affected by several factors:

- The temperature of the air delivered to the room
- The original temperature of the room
- The relative humidity, or amount of moisture, of the air delivered to the room
- The air movement in the room
- The temperature-absorbing surfaces in the room
- The number of people in the room

It is a manager's job to establish the desired temperatures for all areas within an operation. Then, the manager trains employees to help ensure those temperatures are maintained. There are several things employees can do that directly affect a room's temperature, such as opening or closing doors or windows, and adjusting thermostats.

It is the manager's job to ensure guests are always comfortable in dining areas, regardless of the time of day, time of year, or the number of guests being served.

Unlike some other areas, facility-related service standards in restaurant and foodservice operations can vary widely. A music level that is too loud in one operation may be just right for another. Similarly, a low lighting level may fit the ambience for one operation but be wrong for a different operation. The ambience of an operation must appeal to the guests it seeks to attract (see *Exhibit 3.7*). As a result, managers must consider a variety of factors when they develop facility-related service standards:

- What do customers prefer?
- What is appropriate for the facility?
- What are industry standards?

Exhibit 3.7

- What are applicable governmental laws or codes?

- What is the competition doing?

- What will support the operation's mission statement?

- What do the employees think?

After considering each important factor, managers take specific steps to ensure facility-related standards are developed:

- Determine what type of ambience is appropriate for the facility.

- Develop specific standards partially based on customer input.

- Train applicable employees on ambience standards.

- Implement the standards.

- Ensure that the standards are met.

Safety- and Security-Related Standards

All managers are concerned about the safety of their guests and employees. Managers also have security concerns. Safety is related to the protection of an individual's physical well-being and health. Security involves the protection of a guest's, an employee's, or the operation's property.

Safety and security are important service-related issues. Guests and employees have a legal right to expect managers to protect their health, well-being, and property to the greatest degree possible. The laws related to protecting guests and employees, however, do not mean that managers will be held responsible for everything that can happen in their operations.

For example, a guest may slip and fall on a sidewalk leading up to the operation. The operation would be held responsible only if it could be determined that the operation did not exercise reasonable care in the maintenance of its sidewalks. Reasonable care is a legal concept that identifies the amount of care a reasonably prudent person would exercise in a specific situation. The legal standard of reasonable care means that managers must operate their businesses with the degree of care equal to that of other reasonable managers.

A concern for guest and employee safety and property security and the use of reasonable care is an important part of every manager's job. In fact, the emphasis placed on safety and security by a manager is a good indicator of that manager's professionalism and commitment to high-quality guest service. Managers developing safety- and security-related service standards consider four key areas:

- Personal safety

- Public health concerns

- Facility safety

- Security

RESTAURANT TECHNOLOGY

Increasingly, operations use computerized energy control systems to manage energy use in public spaces. These spaces include restaurant and foodservice dining rooms. These systems can monitor and control energy usage automatically by adjusting thermostat settings to reflect changes in outside air temperatures and the number of people eating in a dining room. Manufacturers of such systems point to reduced operating costs and improved guest comfort as advantages of their products. Managers benefit directly because the key area of temperature control is addressed on a continual and highly controlled basis.

KEEPING IT SAFE

A safety audit is a systematic examination of any area in an operation that could pose a threat to guest or employee safety. The areas to be inspected during an audit include a variety of locations:

- **Building exterior:** sidewalks and entrances
- **Parking lot:** lighting and signage
- **Back-of-the-house:** flooring, lighting, and equipment
- **Front-of-the-house:** tables, seating, flooring, and lighting
- **Restrooms:** flooring, fixtures, and lighting
- **Fire and life safety:** emergency exit lighting, fire suppression (sprinkler) systems, smoke alarms, and fire extinguishers

In a safety audit, needed repairs and maintenance should be noted a well as target dates for their completion.

Exhibit 3.8

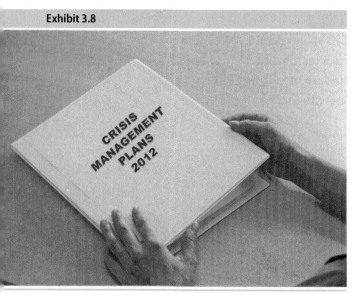

PERSONAL SAFETY

To provide truly excellent service, employees must know what to do if guest or another employee's safety is threatened. The personal safety of guests and employees can be threatened for several reasons:

- Medical crisis
- Fire
- Power outage
- Severely inclement weather
- Natural disasters
- Robbery

To address issues of this type, managers prepare written emergency plans. Emergency plans identify a threat to the safety or security of a property as well as the property's planned response to it (*Exhibit 3.8*). For example, an emergency plan for an establishment located in a heavily wooded area might include an evacuation plan that should be implemented in case of a forest fire. In a similar manner, an operation located on the coast of the ocean may include in its emergency plan a method of evacuating the operation in the event of an approaching hurricane.

To ensure guest as well as employee safety in their operations, managers can take specific steps:

- Review the operation's historical records related to guest safety including accident reports, internal incident reports, police reports, and insurance claims.
- Conduct a safety audit, which is a formal and detailed examination of an operation's areas of potential threats to guest safety.
- Request external audits as needed, including those to be conducted by fire departments, police departments, or insurance carriers.
- Develop an action plan to correct deficiencies that includes:
  - Formation of safety teams
  - Scheduling of regular inspections
  - Communication of inspection results to affected employees
- Implement corrective action plans
- Retrain employees as needed

Managers must take great care to ensure guest safety and to address potential public health concerns. In some cases, events will occur that can cause guests to have concerns related to their well-being such as foodborne illness outbreaks or the presence of known food contaminants or allergens. For each of these issues, guests rely on managers to take the appropriate steps to protect against threats to public health. To help ensure public health concerns are addressed, managers take specific steps:

1. Determine those public health concerns affecting their operations.

2. Create a plan for addressing each important area of concern.

3. Train employees in their specific roles for each area addressed in the plan.

4. Implement the plan.

5. Stay current on public health–related issues and revise the plan as needed.

6. Communicate important parts of the plan to guests via effective communication channels:
   a. Web site
   b. On-premise signage
   c. Handouts or fliers
   d. Newspaper
   e. Social media

7. Update the plan as needed and as conditions change.

FACILITY SAFETY

Most restaurant and foodservice facilities are safe, but events can occur that threaten guest safety. When they do, it is essential that managers have written emergency plans in place. Written emergency plans are important because they identify precisely what is expected of management and employees in times of crisis. In addition, if the operation becomes subject to a lawsuit as a result of a crisis, a written emergency plan can help show the operation exercised reasonable care in preparing for the crisis.

Emergency plans should be kept simple because they will be implemented only in a time of elevated stress. For each potential threat, such as medical crisis, fire, or power outage, the emergency plan would include:

• Type of crisis

• Who should be told when the crisis occurs; include telephone or pager numbers

• What should be done and who should do it

The actual emergency plan should be reviewed often and shared with employees so they too know what they should do in the event of an emergency.

SECURITY

Threats to the security of property can come from guests or employees. In either case, these individuals seek to steal or damage property that belongs to other guests, employees, or the owners of a business. It is the manager's job to identify and minimize internal and external property threats.

Sometimes employees steal property owned by guests, other employees, or the operation. Some operations specifically inform employees when they are hired that theft is grounds for immediate dismissal. If the theft involves significant amounts of property or cash a manager may even elect to file criminal charges against the individual employee. Regardless of what managers do when they encounter employee theft, they should use the same approach for all employees at all levels.

In many cases, when managers think of internal security threats, they think of employees stealing money from guests, other employees, or the operation. Theft is indeed a potential problem in foodservice operations, but using procedures and policies designed to prevent it can minimize its occurrence. Good financial controls, based on solid management principles, go a long way toward reducing the potential for employee theft of money.

Money is not the only thing of value that can be stolen by dishonest employees. Guests' property and property owned by the operation are subject to theft. Also, company property can disappear through the actions of guests.

There are several approaches that are effective for minimizing the potential for theft of property:

- Carefully screen employees prior to hiring.
- Ensure that managers, as well as employees, are aware of the penalty for theft.
- Treat all proven cases of similar theft in a similar manner.

It is unlikely that 100 percent of employee theft can be eliminated. In most cases, there are simply too many opportunities for dishonest employees to take advantage of their access to an operation's food, beverage, and supply inventories. However, management's creation of an atmosphere that discourages stealing and that consistently disciplines, terminates, or prosecutes for known cases of theft can go a long way toward reducing employee-related theft.

Restaurant and foodservice operations that are open around the clock are susceptible to property theft any time of the day or night. Managers must protect property from the illegal activities of those not employed or served by the business, and must guard cash and noncash items owned by guests and employees. It is good business practice to take precautions to reduce theft by training all employees to be alert regarding the loss of property and to report any suspicious activity they encounter.

Putting It All Together

Managers who complete their customer service plans will have addressed four key areas:

- Product-related standards

- Employee-related standards

- Facility-related standards

- Safety- and security-related standards

They will have referred to their budgets to determine the financial resources available to them as they implement their plans. They then consider how best to implement their plans as well as whom in their organizations can help them do so. Finally, they consider the best timetable for plan implementation.

The proper implementation of the standards is a process that includes several key steps:

- Documentation of the standards in writing

- Communication of the standards to affected employees

- Staffing to ensure service standards achievement

Documentation of service standards makes it easy to communicate them to those employees who must help ensure the standards are met. Managers, however, must take extra special care as they staff their organizations to ensure that guests consistently receive high-quality customer service.

STAFFING TO ACHIEVE SERVICE STANDARDS

Staffing is the management task that addresses recruiting and selecting employees, then training and coaching them. Managers must train employees to know and maintain the operation's standards. Managers then consistently schedule the number of trained employees needed to ensure that the operations' service standards are met.

Employee Selection

Recruitment is the first step in the staffing process. Recruiting involves the search for persons who are potentially interested in an operation's vacant positions. Effective recruiting is a series of activities designed to influence the largest number of qualified persons to apply for a job. Screening is the process of reviewing the skills, experience, attitudes, and backgrounds of applicants to make a selection decision.

Managers employ a variety of activities in their recruitment efforts:

- Identify and advertise the best features of the job and the restaurant or foodservice organization.
- Advertise openings effectively.
- Explain job requirements to applicants clearly.
- Ensure that the wages and salaries to be offered are competitive.

Experienced managers use both internal and external sources when recruiting. Internal sources of potential employees include persons referred by employees and the employees themselves. Even customers may have suggestions about potential employees. An advantage of internal recruiting sources is that job applicants are more familiar with the operation than those recruited through external sources. Potential problems can occur if a manager advertises internally for a position but then does not seriously consider the internal applicants. If this occurs, employees will likely be suspicious of any further internal promotions. Other employees also may lose faith in the system of internal recruiting and may stop applying or encouraging people outside the operation to apply.

In addition to internal recruitment efforts, managers use effective external efforts. External recruitment methods for service staff are varied:

- **Sponsoring school, community, and professional programs:** Possibilities vary widely depending on the type of organization. Managers can sponsor a meeting for a professional or community organization, and they can offer an internship program or sponsor a joint school–industry program.
- **Marketing to professional and community organizations:** Ongoing and general marketing to professional and community organizations increases the establishment's name recognition as a place to visit and a place to work.
- **Advertising through traditional media:** Job openings can be advertised through traditional media such as radio, television, newspapers, and magazines. Advertisements in local newspapers and other publications are commonly used by some restaurant or foodservice operations.
- **Advertising through other media:** Signs and postings in and around the establishment, on public bulletin boards, and Web sites are ways to advertise job openings. Public bulletin boards include those found in stores, coffee shops, and laundry facilities.

Good internal and external recruitment efforts will most often result in a number of job applicants. When screening and then selecting service-oriented employees, managers look for specific personal characteristics:

- Friendly, outgoing personality
- Positive attitude
- Ability to speak clearly
- Ability to speak a foreign language, if applicable
- Ability to listen carefully
- Attention to detail
- High standards of personal grooming (see chapter 4)

In small operations, the general manager, dining-room manager, chef, or other manager often does recruiting and screening (*Exhibit 3.9*). In larger organizations, human resources staff may complete some of these tasks.

Recruitment tasks range from considering the number of new employees needed for each position to deciding how, when, and where to encourage good applicants to seek employment with the establishment. Recruitment activities include the following:

- Deciding what vacancies exist based on the future staffing levels
- Determining the skills and backgrounds new employees will need
- Clarifying what the establishment can offer to potential employees
- Identifying sources of applicants
- Effectively communicating the vacancies to identify a pool of qualified people

While communicating the need for new service employees is the most visible part of the recruiting process, recruiting actually starts when the manager identifies the need for additional employees.

Exhibit 3.9

Employee Service Training and Coaching

After selecting the best employees, managers turn their attention to training. Training is the process of helping employees meet, and then continually achieve, an operation's performance standards. The benefits of effective employee training are well documented and include improved job performance, less workplace stress, better customer service, and more satisfied guests. Additional benefits of training include reduced operating costs and increased profits.

In addition to formal training, employees also benefit from coaching. Coaching occurs when managers praise and encourage those employees who are achieving the operation's service standards. Coaching also occurs when managers point out those times when service standards are not being achieved. Coaching most often takes place simply by talking to employees one-on-one.

Coaching can occur when a manager observes an employee doing something correctly. In these cases, a manager's encouraging words can help ensure that the employee achieves the same level of service standards in the future:

- "Tasha, you did a great job with that large table!"
- "Ahmed, thanks for helping Bess when she got so busy yesterday. I appreciate it and I know she did, too!"
- "Marin, you handled that guest's complaint about slow service really well. Great job!"

Coaching can also occur when a manager observes an employee doing something incorrectly. In these cases, a manager's words can help employees improve service to guests:

- "Enrique, if you get behind on a large table again, let me know so I can get some help for you."
- "Tom, Elias could really have used your help yesterday when he got so busy. I know if you pitch in with him when he needs help, he will do the same for you when you get busy."
- "Gabriel, I know that guest's complaint upset you, but let's talk about how you can handle similar complaints that might happen in the future."

Almost all employees like coaching because most employees truly want to do a good job. And since coaching costs no money, it is one of the best things managers can do to continually improve service to guests.

Coaching can correct many minor service-related problems when managers use the following effective practices and techniques:

- Be tactful.
- Explain what is wrong.
- Explain why it is wrong.
- Allow employees a chance to explain their actions.
- Demonstrate the proper behavior or techniques.
- End on a positive note.

Most managers agree that corrective coaching is best done in private, while coaching that praises an employee's effort can be done in public or in private.

THINK ABOUT IT . . .

Did you ever have a supervisor who praised you for your good work and helped you improve in areas where you needed help? How did that make you feel about doing your best?

Employee Scheduling

Managers cannot operate their businesses without the help of knowledgeable and skilled employees. Managers need employees who are motivated and service-oriented, and who enjoy working with people. To provide excellent guest service, managers must schedule the proper number of these employees at the proper times. Scheduling employees is an important management task. A properly prepared schedule has two primary purposes:

1. To ensure that the correct number of employees are available to provide guests with prompt, efficient service, and properly prepared products

2. To ensure labor costs meet management's preestablished budget goals

How well managers schedule their employees affects a variety of crucial operational areas:

- The quality of products and services provided to guests

- The employees' level of job satisfaction

- The operation's profitability

- The perception that the manager's own boss has of his or her ability to manage effectively

The process of scheduling staff has come a long way in the past 20 years. Today, managers can choose from a variety of inexpensive software tools to create the actual employee schedule. The advantages of using these programs are many and include the ability to preload important employee data such as requested days off, prearranged vacations, maximum allowable hours to be worked, restrictions on when those hours can be worked, employee time preferences, and numerous additional factors identified as important by management.

The manner in which the manager presents and distributes the work schedule to service staff will vary according to the individual needs of the operation. However, all completed employee schedules should include key information:

- The dates and days of the week covered by the schedule

- Employees' first and last names

- Scheduled days to work and scheduled days off

- Scheduled start and stop time, designated by a.m. and p.m.

- Total schedule period hours to be worked

- On and off days for salaried personnel

- The date the schedule was prepared

- The individual who has prepared and approved the schedule

Regardless of whether managers develop the employee schedule manually or use available software, there are several principles that should be used:

1. Begin with an estimate of the number of guests to be served.

2. Determine the optimal number of needed employees.

3. Compare the cost of the number of optimal employees needed with preestablished labor budgets. Adjust staffing levels or budget as appropriate.

4. Schedule for the needs of guests first and employees second. Never let an operation be understaffed or overstaffed because of employee preferences.

5. Avoid scheduling overtime whenever possible, because overtime pay is expensive.

6. Where possible, use part-time employees for peak service periods.

7. Be fair to all employees when scheduling preferred time periods.

8. Distribute the schedule in a timely manner.

In most restaurant and foodservice operations, there are peak periods of volume and slower periods. For example, in some operations the hours between 11:00 a.m. and 1:00 p.m. may be very busy as guests come in for lunch. As a result, additional service staff may be needed in this time period, but only in this time period. Regardless of the volume levels anticipated, managers must schedule enough workers to ensure that they can achieve their operations' desired guest service standards (*Exhibit 3.10*).

Historically, managers have increased their staff members during peak periods with part-time employees. This is a sound idea for most managers. However, it is important to recognize that the total number of hours worked per week is important for many employees seeking to meet their personal financial goals. Good managers are sensitive to this, and they hire only as many part-time employees as can be reasonably assured sufficient hours to make their part-time jobs desirable.

Exhibit 3.10

THINK ABOUT IT . . .

Some managers like to schedule as few employees as necessary based on the estimated customer count. Others prefer to slightly overschedule to ensure that customer demand is met. Which method do you prefer? Why?

MONITORING SERVICE STANDARDS

After managers have identified and implemented the service standards appropriate for their operations, they must monitor how well they are achieving the standards. For example, assume a manager has identified hourly cleaning of restrooms as an important service standard. Even if the standard is communicated to well-trained staff, if the manager does not regularly monitor the restroom cleanliness, the service standard may not consistently be achieved. If it is not consistently achieved, the manager must determine the cause and take appropriate corrective action to ensure future compliance with the standard.

When monitoring product-related service standards, managers perform a number of important activities:

- Ensure standardized recipes are in place and in use.
- Hold regularly scheduled tasting sessions to ensure food quality standards are being met and so that employees can discuss the menu items from personal experience.
- Regularly inspect menu items as they are plated and delivered to guests.
- Circulate in the dining room during meal periods to ask guests about the quality of the products they have received.
- Monitor guest feedback on social media sites and on comment cards provided to guests and returned by them (see chapter 7).
- Revise production-related procedures as needed to correct any identified deficiencies.

When monitoring employee-related service standards, managers also perform a number of important activities:

- Observe staff performance in meeting service standards.
- Identify staff deficiencies in meeting service standards.
- Identify solutions to staff deficiencies.
- Provide solutions to staff deficiencies.
- Monitor effectiveness of solutions.
- Revise solutions as needed.

When monitoring facility-related service standards, managers undertake a similar number of important activities:

- Observe ambience in the operation, such as lighting, sound, and temperature, to determine if ambience standards are being met.
- If ambience standards are not met, identify why the standards are not being met.
- Identify solutions to ambience problems.
- Implement solutions to ambience problems.
- Revise and improve the solutions as needed.

To illustrate, assume a manager has established a standard for the volume level of background music in an operation. When walking through the dining room, the manager observes that the music level exceeds the desired standard.

OPEN FOR BUSINESS

RESTAURANT TECHNOLOGY

Technology has changed the options available for managers who wish to distribute employee schedules. Managers may want to inform employees about changes made to the schedule due to changes in estimated sales forecasts, employee illnesses, or employee terminations. Increasingly, tech-savvy managers create and distribute employee work schedules via e-mail.

Because e-mails can be retrieved via computer, tablet, or smartphone, employees can easily retrieve real-time updated schedules. This communication approach allows employers to make schedule changes as needed and send key information to scheduled employees as quickly as possible.

BY THE CUSTOMER/ FOR THE CUSTOMER

Many of the negative comments about restaurant and foodservice establishments that are posted on social media sites relate to service quality deficiencies rather than problems with product quality. Therefore, the continual monitoring of social media sites is an activity managers can undertake to ensure any reoccurring problems are addressed and corrected as quickly as possible.

When they are in an establishment, some guests may feel uncomfortable complaining about a rude server or sloppy server even if a manager asks, "So how was everything?" These same customers may not hesitate to share their negative dining experiences online. For that reason, some managers may pay even more attention to customers' online postings than they do to the guests they speak with directly.

When asked about it, the operation's host states: "Some guests asked me to turn it up. They said it wasn't loud enough. So I turned it up." In this case, the manager has determined why the standard was not met and must take corrective action to ensure it is met in the future. This could involve several alternative courses of action:

- Revise the sound standard.
- Provide the host with additional customer service training so he or she could better respond to similar guest requests in the future.
- Disable the volume control mechanism on the music system to prevent staff from adjusting volume levels.

After the manager has made the decision about how to respond, the solution should be implemented to ensure attainment of the sound standard in the future.

When monitoring safety- and security-related service standards, managers continually inspect their operations, make needed repairs, or change operating procedures. Then they ensure all employees follow all rules and procedures related to the safe operation of their businesses.

SUMMARY

1. **Explain the importance of creating a formal customer service plan.**

   A formal customer service plan is essential if managers are to achieve the service goals that they set for their operations. Managers develop effective customer service plans when they identify the standards they wish to achieve in the key areas of products, employees, facilities, and safety and security. After standards have been identified, managers' customer service plans address how proper staffing will impact their operations' ability to achieve the standards. Finally, an effective customer service plan addresses the important issue of how managers can monitor their success in achieving the service standards they have established, and the steps they will take if the operation falls short of meeting its service standards goals.

2. **Describe the four main areas for which service standards must be established.**

   Managers establishing service standards do so in four key areas: products, employees, facilities, and safety and security. Product-related standards address the use of standardized recipes as well as tasks and accompaniments such as condiments and utensils related to serving menu items. Employee-related standards address how employees will treat guests from their pre-arrival through departure. Facility-related standards focus primarily on those areas managers can control, including lighting and sound levels and room temperatures. Safety- and security-related standards concentrate on guests' and employees' personal safety and property security, and are first addressed by the use of safety audits that identify threats to safety. Managers also establish standards related to public health concerns and facility safety using emergency planning. Finally, managers establish security standards to safeguard the property of guests, employees, and the business against theft.

3. **Summarize the steps managers take when implementing customer service standards.**

   Managers who have completed customer service plans that establish their service-related standards will have addressed the key areas of product, employee, facility, and safety- and security-related standards. The effective implementation of these standards is a multistep process that begins with committing the standards to writing. Next, the standards must be communicated to all affected employees. Finally, managers must take great care to staff their operations in a way that permits employees the time needed to achieve the identified standards.

4. **Identify the staffing-related procedures managers use to achieve their service standards.**

   Staffing is the management task that addresses recruiting and selecting employees, training and coaching them to know and maintain the operation's standards, and then scheduling the correct number of employees needed to ensure service standards are met. Employee selection begins with the effective recruiting of job candidates. After they are hired, employees must be trained in all of the service standards applicable to their jobs. Managers ensure service standards are consistently met by continually coaching employees in the ways their jobs are to be done. Finally, managers must schedule the number of employees needed to stay within their budgets while still achieving all the service-related standards needed to ensure high-quality customer service.

5. **Explain the process managers use to monitor service standards.**

   When monitoring product-related service standards, managers perform a number of important tasks. To meet product-related standards, managers ensure that standardized recipes are in use, hold regularly scheduled tasting sessions, and inspect menu items as they are plated and delivered to guests. They also circulate in the dining room during meal periods to ask guests about the quality of their menu selections and respond to feedback as it is received. Managers monitor employee-related standards by observing staff performance, identifying any staff deficiencies, and making corrections as needed. When monitoring facility-related service standards, managers observe ambience including lighting, sound, and temperature. Then they identify if standards are met, and implement solutions when they are not. When monitoring safety- and security-related service standards, managers continually inspect their operations, authorize needed facility repairs, and ensure all employees follow the rules and procedures related to the safe operation of their businesses.

APPLICATION EXERCISE

Assume you are a restaurant or foodservice manager who has been given the responsibility of updating employee-related service standards related to how guests will be treated when they come to your establishment. The specific items to be addressed are:

- How should guests be greeted upon pre-arrival (when making reservations) or upon arrival?

- How should guests' orders be taken?

- How should guests be treated while in the operation or in its drive-through areas?

- How will guest complaints be addressed?

- How will guest payments be processed?

1. What guest expectation-related issues might you consider as you update your standards?

2. How will employee input be obtained before you make your recommendations?

3. How will your approved new standards be communicated to employees?

4. What training will you provide employees to help them achieve the new standards?

REVIEW YOUR LEARNING

Select the best answer for each question.

1. **What is the purpose of a customer service plan?**
   A. To eliminate the need for employee service training
   B. To tell what must be done to provide high-quality customer service
   C. To ensure facility-related service standards do not vary throughout the day
   D. To substitute for the service-related information included in a mission statement

2. **Customer service planning is**
   A. best done annually.
   B. an ongoing process.
   C. best done without staff input.
   D. required only in poorly managed operations.

3. **What is a customer service standard that relates to an operation's ambience?**
   A. Food presentation
   B. Speed of service
   C. Customer greetings
   D. Room temperatures

4. **What is the purpose of a mission statement?**
   A. To establish the methods used for employee service training
   B. To help remind employees about the purpose and goals of a company
   C. To inform guests about pricing and service standards in place in an operation
   D. To lay out the steps used to implement safety- and security-related service standards

5. What are three areas of facility-related service standards that most managers can establish and enforce?

   A. Décor, lighting, and sound

   B. Design, sound, and lighting

   C. Temperature, décor, and design

   D. Lighting, sound, and temperature

6. What management tool identifies who employees should notify in case of a threat to guest or employee safety?

   A. Safety audit

   B. Incident report

   C. Emergency plan

   D. Facility inspection report

7. What is the first key step managers take when implementing a service standard?

   A. Communicate the standard to staff.

   B. Document the standard in writing.

   C. Train staff in the implementation of the standard.

   D. Staff properly to ensure achievement of the standard.

8. Coaching to correct deficient employee performance is best done in

   A. public.

   B. private.

   C. group training sessions.

   D. pre-shift employee meetings.

9. What is one purpose of a properly prepared employee schedule?

   A. Ensure labor costs meet the manager's preestablished budget goals.

   B. Identify the number of guests to be served during the schedule period.

   C. Identify the amount of revenue to be achieved during the schedule period.

   D. Ensure each part-time worker is scheduled for a predetermined number of hours.

10. What type of skills are managers using as they walk thought their operations to monitor facility-related service standards?

   A. Planning skills

   B. Coaching skills

   C. Observation skills

   D. Safety auditing skills

FIELD PROJECT

Get permission to visit a restaurant or foodservice establishment in your area and complete a facilities inspection sheet like the one that follows. Then answer the questions.

Outside signage:

Lighted at time of arrival? *Yes or No (circle one)*

Easily readable? *Yes or No (circle one)*

In need of repair? *Yes or No (circle one)*

Parking lot:

Littered? *Yes or No (circle one)*

Well lighted? *Yes or No (circle one)*

In need of repair? *Yes or No (circle one)*

Landscaping/sidewalks:

Grass trimmed? *Yes or No (circle one)*

Bushes located properly to ensure guest safety? *Yes or No (circle one)*

Sidewalks in need of repair? *Yes or No (circle one)*

Service staff:

Well groomed? *Yes or No (circle one)*

Properly attired? *Yes or No (circle one)*

Offer a friendly greeting upon your arrival? *Yes or No (circle one)*

Dining area:

Proper temperature? *Yes or No (circle one)*

Proper lighting? *Yes or No (circle one)*

Sound at appropriate level? *Yes or No (circle one)*

Restrooms:

Clean and well stocked? *Yes or No (circle one)*

Proper lighting? *Yes or No (circle one)*

Fixtures in need of repair? *Yes or No (circle one)*

Flooring dry and nonslip? *Yes or No (circle one)*

1. Do you think this operation's facilities help its managers and employees in the delivery of high-quality customer service?

   _____

   _____

   _____

   _____

2. What recommendations would you make for service-related improvements that could be undertaken by this operation in the specific areas you inspected?

   _____

   _____

   _____

   _____

4

The Professional Server

CHAPTER LEARNING OBJECTIVES

After completing this chapter, you should be able to:

- List and describe the two factors that most affect a server's ability to deliver high-quality service.

- Explain the importance of server appearance to service quality.

- List and describe the personal attributes all professional servers must possess.

- Describe the relationship between servers' product knowledge and effective suggestive selling programs.

- Explain how an employee suggestive selling program is implemented.

- Explain the importance of teamwork to the effective delivery of high-quality customer service.

KEY TERMS

average sale per guest, p. 92

check average, p. 92

dress code, p. 85

empowerment, p. 83

foodborne illness, p. 87

pathogen, p. 86

pre-shift team meeting, p. 97

reasonable accommodation provision, p. 85

skill set, p. 82

teamwork, p. 96

uniform, p. 85

upselling, p. 91

CASE STUDY

"You did it again," said Anthony.

Anthony was a server at the La Louisa establishment. He was talking to Pauline, a server who had been with the operation for nearly a decade.

Anthony and Pauline were looking at the employee bulletin board where Mr. Larson, the establishment's manager, had just posted the employee incentive awards for the month of June. As she had in four of the previous five months, Pauline had received the Best Seller award. That meant that Pauline's guests tended to spend more, on average, than guests of other servers.

"How do you keep doing that?" asked Anthony. "Doesn't it make you uncomfortable pushing guests to buy things they don't really want? It makes me so uncomfortable to do it."

"If I was pushing guests to buy things they didn't want, I guess that would make me uncomfortable, too," said Pauline. "But I never do that. You can't make people buy menu items they don't want."

"But you are always getting the Best Seller award," said Anthony. "How do you do it?"

"Well, I know our menu, listen carefully, and then help guests make their own decisions about what they want to order to make their meals really special for them," replied Pauline.

1. Why do you think Pauline's guests often spend more, on average, than those guests served by other members of the operation's waitstaff?

2. Do you think teamwork at the establishment is affected when one server receives the award so often?

THE IMPORTANCE OF SERVERS

Service is critical in a food and beverage operation. Therefore, servers are important. Industry professionals know that qualified servers are as essential to success in noncommercial operations as in for-profit businesses.

The finest building and the most modern or elegant décor cannot provide guests with memorable experiences if service quality is lacking. Physical facilities do not provide a welcoming smile or a sincere greeting. An organization can offer its guests true hospitality only through personal contact with another human. Only those operations that hire and train outstanding individuals consistently deliver outstanding guest service.

Well-trained servers possess skills, attributes, and knowledge. These characteristics make them key players in an operation's ability to deliver high-quality service and to reach its financial goals. In all restaurant and foodservice operations, two factors most impact a server's ability to deliver high-quality guest service: skills and empowerment.

Skills

A qualified server is a highly skilled professional. This is true of servers in all segments of the restaurant and foodservice industry. For quick-service, fast-casual, casual, and fine-dining operations, managing the pace and flow of service is all about timing. Servers must possess the skills to do their jobs properly and promptly.

In a quick-service environment, it is important to get the guest through the ordering process as quickly as possible while being friendly and accommodating. In a fine-dining environment, the objective is to create a smooth and elegant culinary experience that leaves the guest with a pleasurable memory.

All restaurant and foodservice operations have a service system that involves timing of various tasks such as these:

- Greet guests
- Take orders (*Exhibit 4.1*)
- Produce menu items
- Serve menu items
- Process guest payments

The system used to complete these tasks will vary by operation. Some systems may be simple, and others very complex. As a result, the skill set needed by servers may be easily acquired or may be fully gained only after years of experience. A skill set consists of the skills needed to properly perform a task or to complete a job.

Exhibit 4.1

> **THINK ABOUT IT...**
>
> Think about a dining experience in which you received excellent service. What characteristics did the servers possess that made your dining experience so memorable?

Unless servers possess the entire skill set required to do their jobs well, it is impossible to provide high-quality guest service. It is the manager's job to train servers.

The training required for a particular server's skill set varies. Much of it depends on the type of operation and the specific tasks included in the server's job. However, in most cases managers will need to provide some level of skills training that addresses key server tasks performed prior to taking guest orders:

- Taking of reservations
- Dining-room arrangement and setup
- Table and place settings setup
- Greeting and seating procedures

In addition, managers will most often need to provide skills training that addresses key server tasks performed after guests have been seated:

- Order taking
- Preparation and presentation of menu items
- Food and drink delivery and placement
- Ongoing attention to guests' needs
- Beverage replenishment
- Guest check presentation
- Payment acceptance and processing
- Goodbyes

Empowerment

Even well-trained staff members will be constrained in their ability to give excellent guest service if they are not empowered to do so. Empowerment is the act of giving authority, or power, to employees to make decisions within their areas of responsibility. Empowering staff simply means letting service employees use their own good judgment in meeting the needs of guests.

For example, assume a guest on a diet wants to substitute cottage cheese for mashed potatoes and gravy that normally accompany a dinner entrée, and asks a server if this can be done. Can the server make this decision? An empowered worker could give the guest an answer and not be forced to reply to the guest "let me go ask my manager."

THINK ABOUT IT . . .

Have you ever been asked to complete a task for which you did not have the proper skills? How did that make you feel about yourself and the person who asked you to complete the task?

THINK ABOUT IT . . .

Have you ever made a special but reasonable request to a server only to be told he or she was not allowed to grant your request? How did you feel about the customer service you received?

Servers make so many service-related decisions. For this reason, they must be empowered to react appropriately to guests' reasonable requests for personalized service. Some managers are afraid to empower their workers for fear the employees will use poor judgment when making decisions.

It is true that decision-making authority should be granted only to those qualified to make good decisions. However, managers can help ensure the success of empowered workers by understanding the conditions under which empowerment works best:

- **When managers respect the potential of empowered workers:** Empowered workers increase their skills and decision-making abilities when allowed to make decisions on their own. When they do, guests benefit. Managers must have real faith in the "power of empowerment."

- **When managers understand what empowerment means:** Empowerment means more than asking employees their opinions or seeking employee input before management makes decisions. True empowerment means enabling people to make their own decisions about how to best do their jobs.

- **When managers establish clear boundaries:** Employees should know very clearly where their decision-making authority begins and ends. In what specific situations can employees make their own decisions? In what situations must they first seek management approval? Employees will be just as uncomfortable making decisions in murky areas as will their managers.

- **When managers resist second-guessing employees' decisions:** If managers continually undermine and overturn the decisions of their employees, the workers will not feel empowered. Instead, they will likely feel embarrassed and reluctant to make any decisions in the future. Managers can aid their staff by training and coaching. They can also model good decision making. But they should avoid overturning an employee's decision unless the decision made by an employee would result in very serious and negative consequences. Most will not.

- **When managers ensure fairness:** Empowerment does not mean asking employees to do the work of managers instead of the managers doing their own work. Likewise, empowerment does not relieve the manager of responsibility for results. Rather, empowerment is a way for managers and employees to work together to best meet the needs of guests. Most workers seek empowerment, but most also do not want to be taken advantage of by doing work for which they feel they are not being paid.

SERVER APPEARANCE

Servers must be skilled and empowered. However, when guests first encounter service personnel, these are not factors that can be seen with the guest's eyes. Instead, guests' visual first impressions are often based on a server's uniform and his or her personal hygiene. As a result, the personal appearance of servers is critical to making a positive impact on guests' first impressions of service quality (see *Exhibit 4.2*).

Exhibit 4.2

Uniforms

Uniforms are any garments worn to identify the wearer as an employee. All employees should wear well-fitting and clean uniforms each day. Ideally, employees should keep an extra uniform at work in case of an emergency. Employee uniforms are important for two very significant reasons: server appearance and food and service safety.

SERVER APPEARANCE

Employees wear uniforms to comply with an operation's dress code. A dress code contains an operation's rules regarding attire and other aspects of employees' personal appearance. Items typically addressed in dress codes include appropriate clothing and hairstyles as well as jewelry that are considered suitable for a work setting and reflect the service standards of the operation.

Uniforms must be well made and fit the employee properly. If uniforms are too small, they may restrict the movement of a worker. If they are too large, they may cause safety hazards and will look unprofessional.

In most operations, wedding and engagement rings are allowable parts of the dress code. However, excessive jewelry such as bracelets and neck chains, dangling earrings, lapel pins, and any type of clothing that might be considered offensive are not. Most often, managers are free to make any reasonable requirements or prohibitions regarding employee dress and hairstyles at work. There are, however, some exceptions.

Under Title VII of the Civil Rights Act of 1964 as amended, employers must make adjustments to an employee's dress code that will allow him or her to observe a sincerely held religious practice. This is known as the reasonable accommodation provision.

An employee who seeks a religious accommodation must make the employer aware of the following:

1. There is a need for an accommodation.
2. The accommodation is requested due to a conflict between religion and work.

The reasonable accommodation requirement extends to religious practices concerning dress and other personal grooming habits. Religious dress may include clothes, head or face coverings, jewelry, or other items. For example, an employer may be required to accommodate a Muslim employee's request to wear a headscarf. Similarly, a Hindu employee may request to wear a bindi: a religious marking on the forehead between the eyebrows. An Orthodox Jewish employee may request to wear a beard. It is not true, however, that employees can wear anything they want.

The reasonability of an accommodation often depends on the circumstances of the particular case, including the type of business and the employee's job. Courts will most often uphold an employer's dress code and grooming rules if the rules are applied consistently among all employees. To be legal, the codes must involve legitimate employer concern for employee or guest safety.

FOOD AND SERVICE SAFETY

A clean uniform reflects an image of an operation that is well managed and sanitary. The uniform portion of a dress code should take into account the fact that proper dress in a restaurant or foodservice operation allows for the safe service of food.

Dirty clothing may harbor pathogens, which are microorganisms that can cause illnesses. To minimize the chances of spreading an illness caused by pathogens, foodhandlers, including servers who handle food, should follow food safety rules:

- Wear a clean hat or other approved hair restraint to keep hair out of food and to keep wearers from excessively touching their hair. Depending on the operation's policy, servers who do not handle food may not be required to wear a hair restraint.

- Wear clean uniforms daily; changing into uniforms, if at all possible, after arriving at work rather than changing into uniforms before going to work. Dirty clothing that is stored in the operation must be kept away from food and prep areas.

- Wear clean aprons that are changed when they get dirty. Aprons should be removed before taking out garbage or using the restroom.

- When directly handling food, remove decorative jewelry, because jewelry may contain harmful microorganisms. Wearing some types of jewelry may also pose a hazard when working around food or pieces of restaurant or foodservice equipment. Servers who do not directly handle food may be allowed to wear jewelry if allowed by company policy.

- Wear clean, polished, and appropriate solid-toed and slip-resistant footwear.

KEEPING IT SAFE

One of the most important parts of an operation's dress code relates to allowable footwear. Because most restaurant and foodservice workers do their jobs while standing on their feet, comfortable shoes are essential. But shoes must be safe as well as comfortable. For that reason most managers require their employees to wear slip-resistant, rubber-soled, and low-heeled shoes.

Most managers also prohibit the wearing of open-toed shoes in kitchens and in dining rooms to avoid injury that could result from spillage of hot liquids. Appropriate footwear is so important it needs to be specifically addressed in every operation's dress code.

Personal Hygiene

In addition to dressing properly, servers must take care to ensure that they practice proper personal hygiene. Good personal hygiene is one key to the prevention of foodborne illness: a disease transmitted to people by food. For all restaurant and foodservice professionals, including servers, good personal hygiene requires a variety of safe practices:

- Following hygienic hand care and hand-washing practices
- Maintaining personal cleanliness
- Wearing clean clothing
- Avoiding unsafe habits and practices
- Maintaining good health
- Reporting illnesses

Clean hands are essential to proper sanitation and high-quality customer service. Servers should wash their hands before they start work, after using the restroom, and after clearing tables or busing dirty dishes. There are other times when hand washing is required depending on whether or not servers will be directly handling food:

- Before and after handling raw meat, poultry, or seafood
- After touching hair, face, or body
- After sneezing, coughing, or using a tissue
- After handling chemicals that might affect the safety of food
- After eating, drinking, smoking, or chewing gum
- After taking out garbage
- After touching clothing or aprons
- After touching dirty equipment, work surfaces, or wiping towels
- After handling money

Servers must also maintain personal cleanliness:

- Take a bath or shower each day.
- Use perfumes and colognes only sparingly.
- Brush teeth and tongue daily.
- Keep nails short and clean; avoid fingernail polish and artificial nails unless allowed by company policy.
- Tie back hair or use an effective hair restraint as required and approved by local health codes, if directly handling food.
- Cover any cuts, infections, or sores appropriately.
- Use single-use, disposable foodhandling gloves if handling foods directly.

OPEN FOR BUSINESS

KEEPING IT SAFE

Proper hand washing is a key to safe foodhandling, and servers should be instructed to wash their hands frequently and as needed. Proper hand washing takes only about 20 seconds and the National Restaurant Association recommends a five-step process:

Step 1: Wet hands and arms with running water as hot as you can comfortably stand. It should be at least 100°F (38°C).

Step 2: Apply enough soap to build up a good lather.

Step 3: Scrub hands and arms vigorously for 10 to 15 seconds, cleaning under fingernails and between fingers.

Step 4: Rinse hands and arms thoroughly under warm running water.

Step 5: Dry hands and arms thoroughly with a single-use paper towel or hand dryer.

Exhibit 4.3

Managers play a critical role in the effectiveness of a personal hygiene program and perform essential tasks:

- Establish proper personal hygiene policies.
- Train servers on personal hygiene policies, and retrain them when necessary.
- Model proper behavior for servers at all times (see *Exhibit 4.3*).
- Supervise food safety practices continuously, and retrain servers as necessary.
- Revise policies when laws and regulations change and when changes are recognized in the science of food safety.

PERSONAL ATTRIBUTES

Chapter 2 described the challenge of providing excellent guest service related to inseparability. Recall that inseparability is the tendency of restaurant and foodservice customers to connect the quality of service provided with the personal characteristics of the individual staff member who delivered it. Experienced managers and servers know that a guest's view of service quality and his or her view of the individual employee providing the service are inseparable.

As noted, guests assess servers based on the server's appearance and their personal hygiene habits. Guests also assess servers based on the personal attributes the server possesses and displays. Desirable personal characteristics of servers may vary somewhat based on the industry segment in which they work. However, all servers should possess and exhibit key **attributes**: courtesy, friendliness, and tact and diplomacy.

Courtesy

All guests expect courteous service. In life, courtesy means being polite, gracious, and considerate toward others. For professional servers, courtesy means putting the needs of guests before their own. Courtesy should be automatic and be given to every guest. Courtesy is displayed though words and actions.

In most cases, even difficult guests who are treated courteously will return the gesture. The few who will not are rare. Servers must do their best to remain professional and not take personally the actions or the words of those few guests who insist on being rude.

THINK ABOUT IT . . .

Have you ever been treated rudely by a business's customer service representative when making a purchase? How did you feel about the business? How did you feel about the product or service?

Friendliness

The best servers consistently provide friendly service. Customers often appreciate a smile and short, pleasant conversations upon their arrival, during their visit, and at the time of their departure. Servers should always keep their conversations with guests positive and should never discuss personal issues. Rather, small talk should be kept pleasant and informative. There are a variety of topics that friendly servers can talk about with guests:

- Daily specials or favorite menu items
- Historical facts about the operation
- Special events and attractions in the area
- Weather

While servers should be encouraged to chat with guests, managers should not tolerate a server making negative comments about the operation, its products, or other servers. Neither should servers be allowed to share with others information of a confidential or personal nature.

Tact and Diplomacy

Tact and diplomacy mean saying and doing the right thing, using the right words, at the right time. It is also an intuitive sense of what to do or say, or not do or say, to avoid offending another. Tact and diplomacy are attributes servers must possess when challenging service-related situations arise. The number and nature of such situations will vary based on the specific type of business. However, some situations requiring tact and diplomacy are common to many operations:

- When a credit card given by a guest for bill payment is rejected
- When small children dining with parents are unruly
- When a dining party is excessively loud
- When a guest appears to be intoxicated
- When a guest must be refused the additional service of alcohol
- When guests become angry and direct offensive language toward servers
- When guests make sexually suggestive comments or try to engage in physical contact with servers

Servers should exercise tact and diplomacy in all challenging situations. However, they must also be taught that, if the situation escalates beyond their control, they should summon a manager immediately.

THINK ABOUT IT . . .

Can friendliness be taught? Is it easier to hire naturally friendly people or to teach those who are not naturally outgoing how they can become friendlier?

Manager's Memo

Some in business are fond of saying that "The customer is always right." In fact, the customer is not always right.

Sometimes customers are offensive, rude, and unruly, or may behave in ways managers simply cannot allow. This is especially true regarding the sexual or other harassment of employees by guests. Managers are responsible for ensuring their employees can do their jobs in a harassment-free environment. That means protecting employees from harassment by managers, coworkers, and also from guests.

All servers should be taught to use tact and diplomacy when dealing with customers whose remarks or actions are offensive. Servers should also be taught, however, to immediately inform their managers if the offensive behavior continues despite the employee's tactfully applied efforts to stop it. In such cases, it is the manager's job to make the harassment stop immediately or to insist that the customer leave immediately or be escorted off the premises.

WHAT'S THE FOOTPRINT?

Farm-to-fork is an increasingly popular term used to describe the handling of food through the stages of growing, harvesting, processing, packaging, preparing, and serving. Also referred to as farm-to-table, managers are finding that, in ever greater numbers, customers are asking about how the foods they order were obtained and handled prior to their choosing them from the menu.

More and more guests are expressing concern about the quality of the environment. These customers also prefer to patronize operations that share those concerns. As a result, servers must be increasingly knowledgeable about the menu items offered in their operations and their organizations' commitment to serving quality foods in ways that minimize their negative impact on the environment. Managers should ensure servers know about their operation's commitment to serving quality foods in earth-friendly ways. Servers should also know about farm-to-fork initiatives so that they can freely share that information with guests.

PRODUCT KNOWLEDGE

Customers of all types want good value when they select menu items. Recall that guests often ask themselves, "Will the item I am ordering provide value for the price I will be paying?" These guests carefully consider the item's selling price as they decide.

Establishments that consistently provide value for customers attract large numbers of guests. Establishments that consistently exceed guests' value expectations, giving guests more than they expect for their dining dollars, are even more highly successful.

Guests are highly satisfied when they receive the menu items that match what they believed they ordered. To be effective salespersons, servers must know much about the products they sell. Servers must be able to inform guests about the important characteristics of those products. These include the taste, size, and price of menu items. To be truly effective, however, servers must also possess knowledge in two additional menu item–related areas: preparation methods and ingredients.

Preparation Methods

Customers certainly do not expect servers to be chef-experts in food-production methods. However, they do expect their servers to know the basics of how menu items are prepared so questions they may have can be readily addressed. Of course, the specific preparation methods used in each restaurant or foodservice operation will vary. Therefore, it is the responsibility of managers to ensure that their servers are well trained in the production methods used in their own operations.

There are some culinary terms used to describe menu items, with which most servers should be familiar. For example, the following are culinary terms used in meat and seafood preparation:

- **Grilled:** Grilling is cooking over a high heat source, generally in excess of 650°F (343°C). This leads to searing of the surface of the meat, which creates a flavorful crust.

- **Broiled:** Broiling is similar to grilling, except that grilling is usually performed with the heat source under the item to be cooked, and broiling is usually performed with the heat source above the item.

- **Roasted:** Roasting is a method of cooking that uses hot air to cook all the way around the item at the same time.

- **Pan fried or deep fried:** Pan and deep frying means cooking in oil. Pan-fried items are cooked with oil that does not cover the item, while deep-fried items are cooked by fully immersing the item to be cooked in oil.

- **Stewed:** Stewing involves immersing the entire item to be cooked in a liquid other than oil.
- **Braised:** Braising involves cooking items, which have first been seared, in a covered pan containing small amounts of flavored liquids, such as stock or wine.

In addition to how menu items are cooked, servers must very familiar with the toppings, sauces, side dishes, and other accompaniments that are typically served with the items on their menus.

Ingredients

In a large number of cases, guests can ask servers a variety of ingredient-related questions about their menu choices such as, "Does this dish contain monosodium glutamate (MSG)?" or "Does this item come with a sauce?"

As addressed in chapter 1, in some cases guests may be allergic to an ingredient and want to ensure they avoid eating it. In other cases, the guest may simply want to know more about an item than they can learn from the item's description on a written menu or from the server's verbal description.

In these cases, servers should know as much as is reasonably possible about the ingredients used to make the dishes they sell. If a server does not know, the server should inform the guest that he or she will check with the kitchen to find the answer. To avoid the loss of time involved in frequently checking with kitchen production staff, managers should train servers in the information needed to answer the most commonly asked questions about the ingredients used to make the operation's menu items.

Suggestive Selling

When servers know about the products sold in an operation, how the items are prepared, and the ingredients they contain, the servers are in a position to excel at suggestive selling and upselling.

Properly implemented, suggestive selling is the process of making recommendations or suggestions to guests about menu items guests may be interested in buying. A common example of suggestive selling occurs when servers inform guests about the daily menu specials offered in an operation. Suggestive selling also takes the form of recommending a particular type of wine when guests inquire about wines that would complement their menu selections.

Upselling is a selling strategy where the server provides guests with opportunities to purchase related or higher-priced products that the guest might want, often for the purpose of making a larger sale. A common example of upselling happens when a QSR (quick-service restaurant) employee asks a guest who has just purchased a hamburger, "Would you like fries with that?"

Both suggestive selling and upselling can make a significant impact on an operation's average sale per guest. The average sale per guest in an operation is calculated as the sales achieved for a specific time period divided by the number of guests served in that time period:

$$\text{Sales} \div \text{Guests served} = \text{Average sale per guest}$$

For example, if an operation achieved sales of $75,000 in one month, and served 5,000 guests, the average sale per guest would be:

$75,000	$\div$	5,000	=	$15
Sales		Guests served		Average sale per guest

Exhibit 4.4

The average sale per guest in a restaurant or foodservice operation is also often referred to as the check average—the average amount of the bill each guest must pay for his or her menu selections.

Suggestive selling and upselling can be powerful personal selling strategies that significantly increase an operation's total sales. In a restaurant or foodservice operation, suggestive selling can optimize guest satisfaction and increase the average sale per guest, resulting in increased profitability (see *Exhibit 4.4*).

Suggestive selling programs that target food items or alcoholic beverage products work. As a result, every manager should implement an ongoing and effective suggestive selling program. To do it well, managers undertake essential activities:

1. Develop program standards for measuring suggestive selling effectiveness.
2. Communicate to all service employees management's program expectations.
3. Train employees in the skills needed for effective suggestive selling.
4. Observe employees as they apply approved suggestive selling techniques.
5. Evaluate suggestive selling program results.
6. Alter the suggestive selling program, as required, to improve results.

When establishing standards for their suggestive selling programs, managers consider important items:

• What results should the program seek to achieve?

• Which employees should be included in the program?

• What, if any, employee incentives will be offered for good performance?

• What will be the budget for employee incentives?

• How will employee input about the program be solicited?

• How will the program's success be measured?

The success of suggestive selling depends on having the right people, with product knowledge, effective communication skills, and appropriate sales training. Some employees are reluctant to suggestive sell because they are shy, or they think that suggestive selling makes them too pushy, or they are uncomfortable with selling. All these reasons for hesitating to suggestively sell can be handled with proper training. Even so, it is a good practice to hire waitstaff and bartenders who are comfortable with effective suggestive selling and upselling techniques.

Managers who train servers to suggestive sell commonly point out that it will increase the guest's check size. As a result, the server's tip will likely increase. The increased tip happens because most guests base the amount of the server's tip on the total amount of their bill. However, suggestive selling involves a lot more than just selling additional menu items. The best servers use suggestive selling and upselling, for example, to suggest an appetizer, side dish, or dessert that they feel will truly enhance the guest's dining experience and maximize guest satisfaction. Emphasizing this fact is most often extremely effective in training restaurant and foodservice employees to suggestive sell.

A good suggestive selling training program addresses many important goals:

• Enhancing servers' communication skills so they can be effective with customers

• Developing servers' product knowledge so they can vividly and accurately describe items to customers, as well as mention ingredients that may cause allergic reactions

• Learning the menu items that complement each other so they can be suggested to customers

• Anticipating guests' needs so servers can be ready with suggestions

MANAGER'S MATH

A manager's operation achieved the following sales, and served the following number of guests last week. Complete the chart by calculating the average sale per guest. Then answer the questions that follow.

Weekday	Sales	Guests Served	Average Sale per Guest
Monday	$ 1,525	125	$
Tuesday	1,385	110	$
Wednesday	1,415	117	$
Thursday	1,783	135	$
Friday	2,955	182	$
Saturday	3,552	198	$
Sunday	1,985	141	$
Total	$14,600	1,008	$

1. What was the average sale per guest on Monday? _____

2. What was the average sale per guest on Tuesday? _____

3. What was the average sale per guest on Wednesday? _____

4. What was the average sale per guest on Thursday? _____

5. What was the average sale per guest on Friday? _____

6. What was the average sale per guest on Saturday? _____

7. What was the average sale per guest on Sunday? _____

8. What was the average sale per guest for the week? _____

(Answers: 1. $12.20; 2. $12.59; 3. $12.09; 4. $13.20; 5. $16.23; 6. $17.93; 7. $14.07; 8. $14.48)

Exhibit 4.5

Manager's Memo

In addition to taking a customer service approach to encourage suggestive selling, managers can develop employee incentives and reward programs. There are many examples of how managers can use incentive programs:

1. Reward all servers who attain a specified guest check average.
2. Give sellers a commission for selling nonentrée items, such as appetizers and desserts.
3. Hold sales programs that reward all servers who sell more than a specified number of bottles of wine.

These programs work well, but managers should recognize that there can be challenges when using them. Managers must be cautious when implementing incentive programs. It can be difficult to design incentives and contests that are fair to all servers on all shifts. Also, managers must be careful to avoid creating a culture where servers practice suggestive selling or upselling only when there is an incentive or other reward given for doing so.

In addition, good suggestive selling and upselling training provides employees with specific sales opportunities:

- Suggesting specific items; for example, "Would you like lemonade on this hot day?" rather than asking, "Would you like something to drink?"
- Suggesting items that servers themselves enjoy
- Suggesting products that sell well
- Suggesting the establishment's best and most popular items to increase the probability that the customer will be happy with them
- Using props such as dessert trays to sell visually as well as verbally

Managers should prioritize ongoing personal selling training for service staff. A manager or trainer can conduct the training formally. As well, the manager can also discuss the topic at staff meetings (*Exhibit 4.5*). In these meetings, managers can discuss suggestive selling best practices and challenges and allow employees to sample new menu items. Finally, informal training can occur continually through observation, coaching, and formal feedback.

FOOD SALES

Servers can implement suggestive selling and upselling strategies when they know an operation's preparation methods and the major ingredients used in its menu items. Clearly guests want their dining experiences to be as pleasant as possible. As a result, guests appreciate when servers recommend food items that enhance a meal.

Of course, servers should never persist in trying to sell customers items they do not want. Rather, servers should provide information guests can use to make their own menu selections:

- Our Béarnaise sauce makes an excellent addition to that steak!
- For only $0.99 more you can make that sandwich a combo and get a large drink with free refills.
- Would you like to add an Irish Cream liqueur to your after-dinner coffee?
- You can upsize that appetizer for only $3.00.
- Would you like to order the large pizza? We have take-home boxes in case you can't finish it all here.
- We have full pies available for take-home. Would you like me to box one up for you?

Managers know customers do not like to be surprised with charges for food or beverages they did not know about. For that reason, servers should ensure that guests know about any charges they will incur when following a server's menu suggestions.

ALCOHOLIC BEVERAGE SALES

When developing suggestive selling programs related to alcoholic beverages, managers must ensure these products are always sold responsibly. It is perfectly responsible for managers, for example, to encourage servers to suggest a beer, wine, or cocktail that would make a good accompaniment to a guest's entrée choice. It would not be responsible, however, for managers or servers to encourage overconsumption of alcohol by guests.

Responsible suggestive selling related to alcoholic beverages can be creative. It could, for example, take the form of recommending specialty New Orleans–style Hurricane drinks during an operation's specially promoted Mardi Gras celebration. This can be a fun way to encourage beverage sales during the event. The *number* of such drinks sold to a single customer during such a promotion, however, should not be different than at any other time.

In all cases, alcoholic beverages targeted for promotion in a suggestive selling program should be served to guests just as carefully and as responsibly as any other drink that is not being specially promoted. Alcoholic beverage promotions such as "buy one, get one free" or "pay one price" to receive unlimited alcoholic beverages are used less frequently than they used to be and may even be illegal in some areas. These and similar approaches to upselling alcohol are often viewed as encouraging irresponsible drinking.

Experienced managers understand that suggestive or high pressure selling in a manner that encourages irresponsible drinking is unwise. But they also know that most drinkers are responsible and often like to try new, different, and sometimes higher-priced beverages. As a result, the effective in-house promotion of *responsible* alcohol consumption can lead to significantly increased drink check averages and operational profits.

The best managers know that the effectiveness of their suggestive food and beverage selling programs must be continually monitored. Managers can do so by asking specific questions on a regular basis:

- Have per-guest sales increased?
- Are all order takers and servers performing as trained?
- Are incentive programs working?
- Are employees comfortable participating in the program?
- Is guest feedback about the program positive?
- Is additional employee training needed?

Manager's Memo

There are times when servers must be aware of the reasons for a guest's hesitancy to respond positively to suggestive selling and upselling techniques.

When guests are price-conscious they may be unwilling to spend any additional money. Similarly, if guests are in a hurry, they simply may not have the time to order suggested appetizers or after-dinner desserts or beverages. Other guests may not be interested in additional menu items because they are not hungry or are on special diets.

It is not always easy to determine if guests will be interested in making additional purchases, but managers can train servers to be perceptive and seek to match their selling techniques to the special circumstances of their customers.

When managers continually evaluate their suggestive selling programs they can make improvements that increase their programs' effectiveness.

TEAMWORK

A team is a group of people who work together to complete a task or reach a common goal. Working in teams is important. Even though one person can and should make a difference to an operation's success, no one person has enough knowledge, creativity, and experience to ensure guests consistently receive outstanding customer service. Team members share common goals. The act of cooperating and working together to complete tasks and reach common goals is called teamwork, and teamwork is absolutely essential to an operation's delivery of high-quality customer service.

Servers are part of the front-of-the-house team primarily responsible for ensuring high levels of guest service. Servers are also part of the operation's overall team that includes those back-of-the-house staff primarily responsible for ensuring high levels of product quality.

Exhibit 4.6

Importance of Teamwork

Managers must ensure their staff works together as a team. When managers facilitate teamwork, effective teams offer many benefits to restaurant and foodservice operations. These benefits typically include greater productivity and better assurance that products and services will consistently meet required standards (see *Exhibit 4.6*). Other benefits include more effective use of limited resources including time and money.

Team members who work closely together generally have increased creativity as they make decisions, solve problems, and help plan how to deliver products and services. Professional managers know that the quality of teamwork relates directly to the quality of the customer experience that is provided. Teamwork offers additional benefits:

- **Positive work environment:** Team members feel a closer connection to their coworkers, managers, and the operation and its goals. This closeness promotes a sense of common purpose and focuses the team's efforts more effectively. Teamwork also reinforces the contributions each member makes to the operation.

- **Open communication channels:** Teams help break down barriers that can exist between departments or groups. For example, consider an operation that has customer complaints about slow service. The cooks may blame this on servers who make mistakes when taking and submitting orders. The servers may blame the cooks for producing requested items too slowly. In contrast, members of a team that includes cooks and servers can make suggestions that range across departmental lines. Their emphasis will be on fixing the problem, not on blaming others.

- **Employee support systems:** Teams can help their members feel less stress when something goes wrong. Team support can also make it easier for an inexperienced member to tackle an assignment without fear. He or she will have the confidence of knowing others in the organization will provide needed support. This support creates greater opportunities for more employees to be successful. Also, more employees can receive recognition for their contributions to team goals.

- **Workplace diversity:** The ability to blend a diverse workforce together to complete tasks and solve problems can help everyone value the talents and differences that each member brings to the job.

Pre-Shift Service Team Meetings

One good way managers can help ensure teamwork among servers and back-of-the-house staff is by holding a pre-shift team meeting. Pre-shift team meetings are brief team gatherings held prior to the beginning of a work shift. These meetings provide an opportunity for managers to gather team members before their work begins. In a pre-shift meeting, managers share new information, address issues of concern, and review team goals. Effective managers holding pre-shift team meetings are most often concerned with three distinct types of team goals:

1. **Team-building goals:**

   - Introducing new team members. Formal introductions of new team members help the new member feel part of the team.

   - Getting to know each team member. Teams are most effective when the members discover each other's backgrounds, skills, and work styles.

   - Learning to work together. Teams need to identify the strengths of each member and set processes in place to work efficiently together.

   - Setting ground rules. Members need a common understanding of how the team will conduct itself and what is acceptable and unacceptable behavior. Some of the topics for discussion are meeting attendance, promptness, courtesy, assignments, and breaks.

   - Discussing decision-making procedures. One problem with ineffective teams is that decisions just seem to happen. Teams need to discuss how decisions will be made and who will make them to avoid conflicts.

Manager's Memo

Despite having common goals, conflict among team members can occur. One method managers can use for addressing team member conflict uses a three-step approach:

Step 1: Address the problem on a person-by-person basis. The manager can informally talk to the employees involved in the conflict and see if a solution to the conflict can be identified.

Step 2: As a one-on-one mediator, the manager can gather information, talk with team members, and consider the problem in the context of meeting the needs of the customers, the team, and the operation.

Step 3: If the first two steps do not work, a team meeting can be held. Its purpose should be to identify the facts and relate the problem to the needs of customers, the team, and the business. Then the manager should try to identify a team decision to which all members will agree.

Manager's Memo

All teams need a coach or team leader. In a restaurant or foodservice operation, the manager most often serves this role. Managers must encourage each team member to be service-minded. Managers can do this by performing well in three key areas.

First, managers can serve as role models by exhibiting the attitudes, words, and actions that emphasize high-quality customer service. Team members most often see their managers as team leaders and will imitate the actions of the manager.

Second, team members must be continually reminded that their leaders will provide them with required customer service training whenever it is needed. Team members should never feel as if they are "all alone."

Third, managers should reward team members who excel at customer service by positive reinforcement on the job and by favorable performance appraisals that include reference to the workers' contributions to the achievement of team goals.

2. **Information goals:**

   - Identifying new menu items, daily specials, or changes to the menu.
   - Identifying menu price changes.
   - Getting updates from team members on progress.
   - Communicating with other employees and teams, including production staff who explain new menus items.
   - Tasting new menu items or daily specials.

3. **Work-related goals:**

   - Understanding the tasks and each team member's responsibilities. Team members should be able to ask questions about their tasks and the expectations of those who make their work assignments.
   - Identifying the business needs supported by the goals. Managers must be able to explain how the team's goals relate to business needs. If they cannot or do not, team members will have difficulty trying to reach these goals because they will not see the reason for their assignments.
   - Understanding service standards. Team members need to understand the standards in place and the specific tasks that are their responsibility.
   - Identifying the resources that are needed. Team members should discuss resources that might be needed sooner rather than later in the decision-making process. This discussion ensures that necessary resources will be available when needed.
   - Developing plans and procedures to reach goals. Without a roadmap, teams can flounder. The manager or team leader should discuss work procedures with team members. Breaking the process into smaller steps and assigning duties will help the team members cooperate. Teams should continue to review and revise these plans as they move toward reaching their service goals.

SUMMARY

1. **List and describe the two factors that most affect a server's ability to deliver high-quality service.**

   Professional servers must possess specific characteristics if they are to deliver high-quality service to guests. In all restaurant and foodservice operations, two factors most impact a server's ability to deliver high-quality customer service: skills and empowerment. Servers must possess the specific skill sets required to do their jobs properly and to do them promptly. In addition, servers must be empowered. An empowered service staff member is one who is encouraged to use his or her own good judgment in meeting the needs of guests. Because guests often have special needs, the ability of servers to make guided, but independent, decisions in meeting guest needs is essential.

2. **Explain the importance of server appearance to service quality.**

   A guest's visual first impressions of servers are based on servers' uniforms and their personal hygiene. Uniforms are those garments worn to identify the wearer as an employee. All employees should wear well-fitting and clean uniforms each day to make a good appearance and to ensure the safe service of all food and beverage products. Dirty clothing may harbor pathogens that can cause illnesses. Good personal hygiene is also key to the prevention of food-borne illnesses. For restaurant and foodservice professionals, good personal hygiene requires following proper hand care and hand-washing practices, maintaining personal cleanliness, wearing clean clothing, avoiding unsafe habits and practices, and maintaining good health.

3. **List and describe the personal attributes all professional servers must possess.**

   While needed personal characteristics of servers vary somewhat, all servers should possess and exhibit the key attributes of courtesy, friendliness, and tact and diplomacy. Courtesy means being polite, gracious, and considerate toward others. For professional servers it means putting guest needs and feelings first, and their own second. The best servers also consistently provide friendly service. They do so by smiling and engaging in short, pleasant conversations with guests upon arrival, during their visits, and at the time of their departure. Tact and diplomacy comprise the art of saying and doing the right thing, and using the right words at the right time. It includes actions and words designed to avoid offending others. Tact and diplomacy are attributes all servers must possess, and especially when addressing challenging service-related situations.

4. **Describe the relationship between servers' product knowledge and effective suggestive selling programs.**

   Guests will be most satisfied with the menu items they receive when they match exactly the items they thought they ordered. To be effective, servers must know a good deal about the products they sell. Servers must be able to inform guests about the important characteristics of those products. In some cases guests may be allergic to an ingredient and want to ensure they avoid eating it. In other cases, the guest may simply want to know more about an item than they can learn from the item's description on a written menu. To be effective salespersons, professional servers must possess knowledge of food-preparation methods and the ingredients used to make the menu items they sell. When they do, servers can better use effective suggestive selling and upselling techniques.

5. **Explain how an employee suggestive selling program is implemented.**

   Managers implementing a suggestive selling program start by developing objectives and standards for the program. When establishing the standards, they consider important issues such as the specific results the program seeks to achieve and how the program's success will be measured. Next they must communicate the program's expectations, train employees appropriately, and then observe the results of the training.

   After the suggestive selling program has been implemented, managers evaluate the program's success and make changes if needed. When assessing suggestive selling programs, managers measure changes in per-guest sales, consider the level of employee participation in the program, and weigh the suitability of current employee incentive programs. Managers also consider guest feedback about the program. Managers who make careful assessments in these and other areas are in a good position to use the information they gain to make positive improvements to their suggestive selling programs.

6. **Explain the importance of teamwork to the effective delivery of high-quality customer service.**

A team is a group of staff members who work together to reach a common goal. Effective teamwork can increase productivity and better ensure that service levels will meet an operation's service-related standards. Team members who work closely together have increased creativity as they make decisions, solve problems, and help plan how to deliver high-quality customer service. Experienced managers know that the quality of teamwork relates directly to the quality of the customer experience that is provided. They also know that the manager is an important service team member. Managers can encourage teamwork by holding pre-shift team meetings. Held regularly, these meetings can be brief but still allow time to address a variety of important areas including team-building, providing new information, and achieving the organization's goals.

APPLICATION EXERCISE

Answer the following questions related to how you would define customer service:

1. Think of a restaurant or foodservice experience where you received very poor customer service. Describe in detail what the server did or said that made it so poor.

2. Think of the restaurant or foodservice experience in which you received the best customer service. Describe in detail what the server did or said that made it the best service.

3. Based on all your restaurant and foodservice experiences, describe what servers must do to make customer service excellent for you.

4. Reverse the viewpoint and describe what *providing* excellent customer service might mean to a restaurant or foodservice server. Pinpoint any differences in viewpoints you can identify and describe what you think managers could do to address the differences you found.

REVIEW YOUR LEARNING

Select the best answer for each question.

1. **Why are some managers afraid to empower their workers?**
   A. They think their labor costs will increase.
   B. They fear guest service levels will decline.
   C. They fear their employees will make poor decisions.
   D. They think the quality of the products they serve will be reduced.

2. **When should employees put on their work uniforms?**
   A. After they arrive at work
   B. When they first get dressed for the day
   C. Just before they leave their homes to go to work
   D. Immediately after they shower or bathe in the morning

3. Which type of jewelry is permitted in the dress codes of most restaurant and foodservice operations?

   A. Chains

   B. Bracelets

   C. Lapel pins

   D. Wedding rings

4. What must servers do after eating, drinking, smoking, or chewing gum?

   A. Change uniforms

   B. Wash their hands

   C. Put on a fresh apron

   D. Replace their hair restraints

5. What characteristics do servers find most useful when dealing with challenging customers?

   A. Friendliness and dedication

   B. Loyalty and efficiency

   C. Enthusiasm and zeal

   D. Tact and diplomacy

6. What must managers do if a guest persists in harassing a server after the guest has been politely asked to stop doing it?

   A. Refuse to serve the guest any more menu items.

   B. Immediately assign a different server to that guest.

   C. Make sure the guest leaves the operation immediately.

   D. Inform the guest that he or she will not be welcomed back in the future.

7. What is the culinary term used to indicate the cooking of an item when the heat source used is located above the item to be cooked?

   A. Braising

   B. Broiling

   C. Grilling

   D. Roasting

8. What would be objective evidence that a manager had implemented an effective suggestive selling program?

   A. Increase in per-guest sales

   B. Increase in number of guests served

   C. Increase in number of menu items offered

   D. Increase in the use of standardized recipes

9. What is the impact of a successful upselling program?

   A. Average sale per guest decreases and total sales decrease.

   B. Average sale per guest decreases and total sales increase.

   C. Average sale per guest increases and total sales decrease.

   D. Average sale per guest increases and total sales increase.

10. What is a team-building goal that could be addressed in a pre-shift team meeting?

    A. Explaining business objectives

    B. Introducing a new menu item

    C. Setting ground rules

    D. Identifying needed resources

5

Greeting and Seating Customers

INSIDE THIS CHAPTER

- The Importance of First Impressions
- Guest Arrival
- Guest Greeting
- Casual and Fine-Dining Table Management
- Menu Delivery and Server Assignments

CHAPTER LEARNING OBJECTIVES

After completing this chapter, you should be able to:

- Explain how proper facility maintenance impacts arriving guests' impressions of service quality.

- List the steps managers use to address guests' on-arrival hospitality experiences.

- Identify the information included in a properly made guest reservation.

- Discuss the importance of professional wait list management to guest satisfaction.

- Describe the impact of effectively managing the table assignment and seating process.

KEY TERMS

deuce, p. 114

flag, p. 111

four-top, p. 114

foyer, p. 105

greeter, p. 109

grounds, p. 105

maître d'hôtel, p. 115

menu board, p. 108

no-show, p. 111

server station, p. 114

table assignment,
p. 113

table management
system, p. 113

three-top, p. 114

two-top, p. 114

wait list, p. 107

walk-in, p. 112

CASE STUDY

"So tell them to leave," said Ms. Richards to Leo, the host on duty at the Mayfield Lodge. "They have my table."

The problem, as Leo had tried to tell Ms. Richards, was that the establishment only had one table that would hold 10 people. And Ms. Richards had a reservation for 9 people.

Her reservation was for 8:00 p.m., and it was now nearly 8:30. And the later it got, the more upset she became.

Leo reviewed the events that led up to this issue. The party of 10 currently occupying the establishment's one large table also had a reservation. They had been scheduled to arrive at 6:00 p.m. Since it took the average dinner party just under two hours to eat at the Mayfield, it should have been easy to seat Ms. Richards and her party when they arrived at 8:00.

But the 6:00 p.m. party did not all arrive until well after 6:30. And now, because it was a birthday celebration for the 80-year-old grandmother of the guest who reserved the table, they were still opening gifts and lingering over their after-dinner coffee.

"Did you hear me? Either you tell them to leave right now or we're leaving," said Ms. Richards to Leo.

1. What would you do now if you were Leo?

2. What would you advise the manager of the Mayfield to do to avoid problems of this type in the future?

Exhibit 5.1

THE IMPORTANCE OF FIRST IMPRESSIONS

Guests' first impressions take place long before they are seated at a table and handed menus (*Exhibit 5.1*). Today, guests might form a first impression when viewing the operation's Web site or calling for a reservation. Or they may form an impression when they pull up to a quick-service restaurant's drive-through menu board. In all cases, however, it would be hard to overstate the importance of creating a positive first impression on guests.

First impressions are most often lasting impressions. If guests do not form an initial good impression, they will likely be suspicious of an operation's overall service levels. They may also question its food quality. It is much easier to take the steps needed to impact arriving guests positively than it is to change a bad first impression.

Managers and servers cannot typically change key operational issues in a business such as its location, building, and décor. However, they can address several specific areas to ensure guests form a positive initial impression:

- Guest arrival
- Guest greeting
- Table management
- Menu delivery and server assignment

REAL MANAGER

THE LITTLE OPERATION SOMETIMES HAS TO WORK HARDER TO GET CUSTOMERS THAN THE BIG OPERATION.

When I started out working at the Burger Shack, we had a long conveyor belt of customers that mechanically rotated in front of the cash registers. But when I was out on my own running a hot dog cart with no signage or structure to attract customers, I had to yell and wave my arms and joke with passersby to attract customers.

GUEST ARRIVAL

When guests arrive at a restaurant or foodservice operation, they form immediate impressions. Chapter 3 explained that an operation's physical facilities affect guests' perceptions of service quality. The parking areas, grounds, building, equipment, and furnishings of an operation all make up the business's physical environment. Guests will assess that environment upon their arrival. Therefore, managers must take great care to ensure that guests form positive first impressions. Guests assess both the external and internal areas of an operation when they arrive.

External Areas

A guest's initial reaction to an operation may be first shaped when he or she calls ahead to make a reservation. But many guests form first impressions when they arrive at the establishment. They observe the parking lot, signage, and the operation's exterior. For that reason, managers must consider how best to manage two key external areas: the parking lot and the grounds.

PARKING LOTS

Easy-to-enter, tidy, and well-lighted parking and walk-up areas are a critical part of forming positive guest perceptions. They also speak volumes about a manager's attention to detail. When, for example, guests see multiple cigarette butts or litter in a parking area, they assume that the operation's staff see them as well but do not care enough to clean them up. For that reason, the exterior parking and walk-up areas of an establishment must be kept completely free of litter and debris (*Exhibit 5.2*).

GROUNDS

Grounds in a restaurant or foodservice operation include the plants, flowers, trees, and décor placed around the building that houses the operation. If there is landscaping around the property, it must be kept well trimmed, mowed, and weed-free. If trash and cigarette receptacles are placed on the grounds they should be situated in an area permitted by local smoking laws, if applicable. They should also be kept clean, checked daily, and emptied frequently.

If the operation's trash areas are visible to guests these should be kept neat. All trash should be placed in leak-proof, waterproof, and pest-proof containers. This is important both from an aesthetic point of view and to avoid the attraction and breeding of insects, vermin, and other pests.

Managers should inspect an operation's outside areas daily to ensure they are well maintained. Managers must also create and implement cleaning programs to keep these areas looking their best. Taking the steps already listed ensures that customers will not have cause to doubt the quality of service they will receive based on their upon-arrival impressions of the operation's external areas.

Internal Areas

Guests immediately notice an operation's entrance areas. While the specific areas contained in different operations vary, most include three key locations accessible to guests: foyers, restrooms, and waiting areas.

FOYERS

Foyers are the doorways, hallways, and lobbies that make up an operation's entrance. These areas must be kept clean and free of clutter. If stickers are placed on entrance doors or windows, the stickers should be appropriate for the facility and be kept to a minimum. Floors should be kept swept and mopped or vacuumed. Flooring in foyer areas should be kept meticulously clean and safe to walk on. If there is signage related to the business operation at the entrance to the operation, it must be accurate and kept in good repair.

Exhibit 5.2

THINK ABOUT IT . . .

Have you ever arrived at an establishment but, because of its external appearance, decided not to go in and eat there? What caused you to change your mind?

KEEPING IT SAFE

Wet floors in an entrance can be difficult to detect, and their slippery surfaces can cause unexpected slips and falls. These falls can result in serious injuries and liability expenses for a restaurant or foodservice operation. Extra attention to proper floor care during rainy or snowy weather is essential.

Managers can help prevent accidents by ensuring that service staff monitor entrance areas and dry any wet spots on floors immediately. Wet floors should always be well lit to help expose potential dangers to those walking on them.

If floors will likely remain wet due to heavy use, the wet areas should be clearly marked with standard "Caution: Wet floor" signs. In cases of continued introduction of water, snow, or ice on floors during inclement weather, managers can also install mats or rugs as needed to help ensure floor safety.

In some cases, foyers will include a coat check area. The coat check room should be staffed with professionally dressed service personnel who greet guests and may assist them with removing their outer coats. If seating is provided in a foyer area, it should be inspected regularly to ensure it is in good repair, is sturdy, and is kept clean. Artwork on walls should be hung properly and their surfaces kept clean.

RESTROOMS

Restrooms are an extremely critical part of a business's public area. A dirty or unpleasant-smelling restroom can cause guests to question the sanitation practices of the entire operation. Restrooms should be inspected and cleaned by employees on a schedule developed by management. If local health codes dictate specific supplies such as hand soap and hand drying materials be in place, managers must ensure they comply with these codes.

Managers can personally help ensure the continued good condition of restrooms by regularly inspecting them using a formal inspection checklist similar to that shown in *Exhibit 5.3*.

Exhibit 5.3

12-POINT MANAGER'S RESTROOM INSPECTION CHECKLIST

Manager's Restroom Inspection Checklist

1. Lighting	Bright ____	Dim ____ Bulbs need replacing ____	
2. Graffiti	None ____	Light ____ In need of removal ____	
3. Floors	Clean ____	Littered ____ In need of mopping ____	
4. Sinks	Clean ____	In need of cleaning ____	
5. Countertop	Clean ____	In need of cleaning ____	
6. Mirrors	Clean ____	In need of cleaning ____	
7. Diaper changing area	Clean ____	In need of cleaning ____	
8. Toilets	Clean ____	In need of cleaning ____	
9. Toilet paper	Adequate ____	Needs replenishing ____	
10. Liquid soap	Adequate ____	Needs replenishing ____	
11. Paper hand towels/drier	Adequate ____	Needs replenishing ____	
12. Waste basket(s)	Clean ____	In need of emptying ____	

Inspection date _____   Inspected by _____

WAITING AREAS

Waiting areas can range from small spaces in front of ordering or dining areas to extensive seating areas or lounges. The areas should be comfortable for guests and should be kept meticulously clean. Many operations provide music in their waiting areas, but if they do, volume levels must be kept low enough to ensure waiting guests can hear their names being called for seating.

GUEST GREETING

Whether guests arrive at a drive-up window or enter the most upscale of dining rooms, their formal greeting is a key moment of truth for all restaurant and foodservice operations. In some cases guests can be greeted and seated, or served, immediately. In other cases, the guests' names and the size of the dining party will be placed on a wait list: a record of the names of guests who have arrived at an establishment but who have not yet been escorted to their tables. The ways in which managers ensure guests are properly welcomed to an operation will vary somewhat. However, all managers follow specific steps as they manage employees that affect the experiences of arriving guests (see *Exhibit 5.4*).

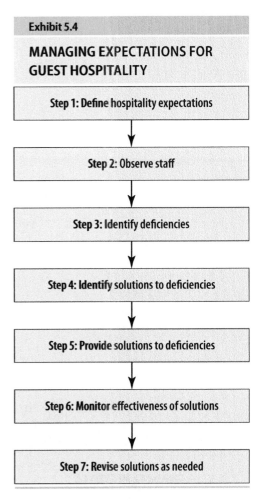

Exhibit 5.4

MANAGING EXPECTATIONS FOR GUEST HOSPITALITY

Step 1: Define hospitality expectations

Step 2: Observe staff

Step 3: Identify deficiencies

Step 4: Identify solutions to deficiencies

Step 5: Provide solutions to deficiencies

Step 6: Monitor effectiveness of solutions

Step 7: Revise solutions as needed

Step 1: Define hospitality expectations for arriving guests.

In this step, managers determine the exact experience they want arriving guests to receive. This addresses directly what guests will see and hear as the staff greets them. Managers must, of course, inform staff of their operations' preferences for how guests are treated upon arrival. This includes identifying what is to be said to arriving guests. For example, a manager may want the staff who will be seating guests to mention the special of the day to them. Staff meetings or individual employee training are among the methods managers can use to educate staff on expectations that have been set for arriving guests.

Step 2: Observe staff performance in meeting expectations.

In this step, managers monitor staff performance so they are continually aware of the experiences guests actually receive.

Step 3: Identify staff deficiencies in meeting expectations.

In some cases, managers may observe that guests are not receiving the intended experience. If this is observed, managers note exactly how guest experiences are not meeting the operation's standards.

Step 4: Identify solutions to staff deficiencies.

Once deficiencies have been identified, managers consider alternative actions needed for correction. For example, if guests are not immediately greeted upon arrival, managers may need to assess whether the problem relates to staffing levels or if it relates to insufficient training of existing staff.

Step 5: Provide solutions to staff deficiencies.

In this step managers determine, from their identified alternatives, the best corrective course of action. Managers then communicate to employees any changes made to the establishment's operating procedures during staff meetings or by individual employee training.

Step 6: Monitor effectiveness of solutions.

When a solution to the identified deficiency has been implemented, managers then monitor the solution's effectiveness to ensure that it has addressed and corrected the service-related problem.

Step 7: Revise solutions as needed.

Monitoring an operation's ability to achieve hospitality expectations is an ongoing process. As a result, managers revise their implemented solutions when it becomes necessary.

While all managers must address the entire guest arrival and greeting process, these processes vary most based on the industry segments in which their operations are located:

- Quick-service restaurant (QSR) and fast casual
- Casual and fine dining

QSR and Fast Casual

Guests at QSRs either dine inside the establishment or order via the drive-through. For drive-through customers, a guest's initial greeting may take the form of that person looking at the operation's menu board. The menu board is the large visual listing of menu item descriptions or pictures that show what is offered for sale. Properly functioning menu boards should be designed and installed to maximize the information provided to guests and to minimize the time required for guests to place their orders.

Increasingly, owners of QSRs provide one menu board in drive-through lanes for use by customers waiting in line and another where orders are actually placed (see *Exhibit 5.5*). Ample lighting in external menu board areas is essential to ensure that customers can easily read the board, and feel safe at night.

OPEN FOR BUSINESS

RESTAURANT TECHNOLOGY

Technology plays an increasingly important role in the guest experience received by drive-through customers. In some QSR organizations, the guest's initial greeting is given by an employee who may be hundreds or even thousands of miles away from the guest's physical location.

These remotely located employees are notified electronically when a guest arrives in a QSR's drive-through area. They then greet the guest, take his or her order, and announce the amount owed. In addition, because they specialize in order taking, those workers are most often trained well in the suggestive selling and upselling techniques described in chapter 4.

Exhibit 5.5

There are several issues related to the external menu board and drive-through that managers should address:

- The menu board, consisting of a quality speaker and microphone or a window for customers to place orders, must be welcoming.

- Inside the operation, employees greeting guests and taking their orders must have a quality speaker and microphone or wireless headset system.

- The window or windows where employees take orders, deliver menu items, and receive guest payments must be clean, well-lit, and easy for customers to access.

Some QSR operations include electronic display areas on menu boards. These displays show guests the items they have ordered and the amounts they are to pay. Other restaurants display the same information at the pickup window.

Drive-through orders may comprise 50 percent or more of some QSR's business. However, most QSRs and nearly all fast-casual operations also serve guests who physically enter the establishment. Managers must also address expectations of these arriving guests:

- Clean entrance and ordering areas
- Professionally groomed and friendly service personnel
- Easy to read and understand menu display boards
- Clean order placement and order pickup counters
- Correct filling of all orders
- Accurate and efficient payment processing
- Clean dining areas

Casual and Fine Dining

In casual and fine-dining operations, the first individual that guests come into contact with has an important impact on the guests' experience. Every member of the service staff, including owners, managers, hosts, and waitstaff, should know how to properly welcome a guest to the operation.

How to best verbally greet arriving customers will depend, to some degree, on the type of operation. In an informal casual establishment, a suitable greeting by a server, greeter, or host may be, "Hi, I'm Sara, welcome to Bennett's!" In an extremely formal setting, a better greeting might be, "Good evening, welcome to Bennett's."

In formal operations, a designated host may offer the greeting. In a more casual operation, a server may be the one greeting guests. In all cases, greeters are the employees who initially welcome guests and they should offer guests a smile, a pleasant attitude, direct eye contact, and a brief but sincerely offered welcoming phrase.

RESTAURANT TECHNOLOGY

OPEN FOR BUSINESS

Digital menu boards used in many QSR and fast-casual operations are new, easy to use, and versatile. Digital menu boards allow managers to change the wording and graphics displayed on menu boards by using computer software to modify the board's content. For example, a single menu board can be programmed to display breakfast menu items in the morning, then change to lunch and dinner menus later in the day.

Digital menu boards provide managers many advantages:

- Can be centrally controlled for multiunit operations
- Allows display of menu board content by time of day
- Can update displayed prices and items from anywhere
- Permits easy addition of new menu items or daily specials
- Eliminates unnecessary photo and print costs related to menu board updates

CASUAL AND FINE-DINING TABLE MANAGEMENT

In most casual and fine-dining operations, the initial greeting of guests is just the first in a series of guest services and processes that are interrelated:

- Reservations
- Managing wait lists
- Managing table assignments
- Guest seating

Reservations

One of the more frustrating things a customer experiences is a lost or incorrect reservation or special seating request. Many guests make reservations because they must carefully schedule their own time. If a customer's visit starts with a significant reservations-related error, it can be difficult to turn the visit into a positive experience. That is why it is extremely important to have an accurate system that records reservations and special requests.

First, managers must have an effective procedure, including a place for recording reservations and special requests. The type, speed, and complexity of the operation determines how sophisticated the procedure is and what technology is used. For example, a fine-dining restaurant with table service may record reservations and special orders in a book or computer at the greeter's station.

When taken, a guest's reservation record should include key information:

- Proper spelling of the guest's name
- Date the reservation is requested
- Time the reservation is requested
- Number in dining party
- Special seating or other requests
- Preferred method to contact guest, such as telephone or email
- Name of employee taking the reservation

There should only be one place for saving reservation records. There should also be a standard for the information recorded, including how and by whom it should be recorded. Then, managers must consistently enforce the operation's approved reservation procedure. The reservation procedure used should allow the operation's host to complete several important tasks:

- Record needed reservation information including the customer's name, requested seating time, and the number in the dining party, and special seating or other requests.

- Identify the guest's party upon arrival.
- Confirm the reservation or special order with the guests before they arrive.
- Resolve any problems with the reservation or special request.

Confirming all reservations and special orders is good customer service, makes the guest feel important, and protects the establishment against no-shows. A no-show is the industry term for a guest who makes a reservation but does not arrive to claim it. Managers can design systems that allow them to confirm by telephone, fax, email, cell phone app, or any other style that works well for the operation. This same information can be used for marketing purposes such as notifying guests of upcoming special events or the introduction of new menu items.

After the reservation or special order is recorded, there must be a system to communicate this information to staff. First, managers must link the reservations and special requests to the proper day and time. Managers can have separate reservation book pages or computer files for each day, meal, and time slot, or some other form of organization.

The reservation or special-order recording procedure must include checking for conflicts with prior reservations and checking for food availability. Then, table setup requirements must be given to the dining-room staff, and food or drink requirements must be given to the kitchen staff.

The service staff must also be given this information with enough time to complete the requests. In many operations, the point-of-sale (POS) system is programmed to perform this function. The POS system is the computerized system used to record guest purchases, payments, and other important operational information.

If needed, managers should preassign special requests to specific cooks, servers, or staff in dining-room sections that are capable of handling a variety of common special requests. For example, a guest who communicates in sign language must be assigned to a server who can also do this. Or, a guest who is limited to a wheelchair must be assigned to a table or room that can best accommodate a wheelchair.

With special requests, it is important to have a way to flag, or call special attention to, the action needed to fulfill the request. In this way the request can be forwarded to the direct attention of cooks, service staff, or others who will address them. Taking reservations and completing special requests seem like simple tasks, but they actually take a lot of planning and organization. With proper planning, managers can avoid staff making mistakes in these situations and thus avoid disappointing guests.

RESTAURANT TECHNOLOGY

Most customers appreciate the convenience of booking restaurant or foodservice reservations ahead. However, if a guest gets a busy signal, is placed on hold, misses a reservationist's return call, or visits an operation's Web site and finds no way to book a reservation online, the convenience—and the reservation—can be lost.

Today, many managers choose to provide their guests with the ability to book reservations online. The best of these online booking systems are electronically interfaced with the operation's POS system. When they are, managers make it easy for guests to make reservations and the manager can also easily access complete reservation histories by guest or by date.

Exhibit 5.6

OPEN FOR BUSINESS

RESTAURANT TECHNOLOGY

Increasingly, managers rely on automated wait list management programs that are fully integrated with their POS and reservation systems. Automated wait list management programs allow managers to more accurately project wait times. That allows an operation to better manage the seat assignment process and reduce guest waiting times.

A well-designed wait list management program assesses the number of guests already seated and estimates when they will complete their meals. It also assesses the number of reservations and their respective party sizes, and the speed of service typically achieved at the time of day for which the reservation was made. In addition, it calculates how long each waiting party has been waiting. All of these data are then analyzed to arrive at the most accurate guest seating time estimates possible.

When properly used, automated wait list management programs allow managers to improve customer relations, seat more guests, and increase sales.

Managing Wait Lists

Not all guests make advanced dining reservations. Walk-ins are guests who arrive at an operation without having made a reservation in advance. In the ideal case, guests arriving with a reservation, as well as walk-ins, would be able to be seated immediately (see *Exhibit 5.6*). When an operation is very busy, however, those arriving guests who do not have reservations may not be able to be seated immediately. Also, there may be times when even those diners who have reservations cannot be immediately seated. When that is true, it is in the best interest of guests and the operation to create and manage wait lists in a way that minimizes wait times for guests and maximizes the number of guests who can be seated.

It is critical that managers understand and teach employees that there are specific goals to be obtained in the management of wait lists:

1. Provide waiting guests with realistic estimates of how long it will be until they are seated.

2. Manage the wait list in a manner guests perceive to be fair to all.

Regardless of how well a wait list is managed, guests rarely like being asked to wait before they are seated and served. Managers and service staff, however, can take steps to make guests' waits as pleasant as possible:

- Provide a clean and pleasant waiting area.

- Ensure that guests with reservations are given first priority in seating. Walk-in guests should be seated on a strict first come, first served basis.

- Allow guests easy access to continually updated information regarding the estimated length of their wait times.

- Provide guests the option of alternative seating arrangements where practical. For example, offer immediate bar area seating if no dining area seating is immediately available.

- Provide music or television programming to make wait times pass more pleasantly and quickly.

- If appropriate for the setting, provide waiting guests with menus so they can review the operation's product offerings in advance of their seating.

- Inform all busing and service staff that there are waiting guests. Then employees are aware of the urgency of doing their work, so guests can be seated as quickly as is reasonable.

- Use an effective system to let waiting guests know immediately when their tables are ready.

In the case of guests who have reserved tables in advance, arrive on time, but cannot be immediately seated, managers must take special steps:

- Apologize for the delay.
- Explain the reason for the delay.
- Seat the guests at the earliest possible time.

The proper management of wait lists is important to quality guest service. Therefore, managers must take care to ensure the process is fully integrated into the establishment's table management system, or the methods used to control the flow of guests to tables in the dining area. In many modern POS systems, reservations, wait list management, and table assignments are integrated.

Managing Table Assignments

Table assignment is the placement of guests at specific tables and seats in an operation. The effective management of table assignments and seating capacity in an establishment is one of a manager's most important tasks. The reason for this can be readily understood when the restaurant business is viewed through a different lens.

Historically, those in the restaurant and foodservice industry are said to be in the business of selling food. Thus, for example, a restaurateur operating a steak house is said to sell steaks. That is one way to view the manager's business. Another way to view this manager, however, is as one who rents seats to customers who buy steaks.

In most cases, establishments have a fixed number of seats. Each seat has the potential to generate varying amounts of income to the operation based on how many customers occupy the seats, how long each customer is seated, and the amount each customer buys. As more seats are occupied, more sales are produced.

It is important to recognize that each hour a seat is unoccupied represents a loss of income that cannot be regained. From that perspective, a manager's inventory of available seats is different, for example, from its inventory of available steaks. If a steak goes unsold one night, it may be sold the next night. If, however, a seat goes unrented one night, revenue from that time period can never again be recouped.

When viewed from the perspective of managing table assignments to maximize seat rentals, several issues become important:

- What is the total number of rentable seats?
- What proportion of seats is rented at peak dining times?
- How long is each seat rented?

RESTAURANT TECHNOLOGY

In many cases, operations provide waiting guests with buzzers or lighted devices designed to inform these guests about when their tables are ready.

Increasingly, managers incorporate cellular phones into their wait list management systems. If customer cell phone numbers have been obtained at the time of reservation or upon arrival at the establishment, the host can send a text or other message to waiting guests to update them on their likely seating time. In other cases, managers secure email addresses from waiting guests and can send an email to be retrieved and viewed on their cell phones for guests.

Waiting guests want to know when they will be seated or how long their wait will be. Tech-savvy managers should continually monitor advancements in electronic communications to ensure they are using all the tools available to them to meet this desire on the part of their guests.

WHAT IS THE TOTAL NUMBER OF RENTABLE SEATS?

An effective table assignment system begins with knowing the total number of seats and tables available in an operation. In many cases, this number will not vary because dining-room sizes and table arrangements do not vary. However, in some operations dining-room sections may be closed and opened based on customer demand. In other operations, the number of service staff scheduled to work may dictate the number of available seats in dining areas that can be reasonably occupied while still ensuring high-quality guest service. In all cases, those managing reservations, wait lists, and guest walk-ins must know the precise number of tables and seats that can be filled at any given point in time that the operation is open.

WHAT PROPORTION OF SEATS IS RENTED AT PEAK DINING TIMES?

To manage table assignments well, managers seek to achieve as close to 100 percent seat occupancy as possible. That means seating guests to fill the maximum number of seats. It is important because in many cases, the number of tables and available seats in an operation will not match perfectly with the number of guests to be seated.

To illustrate the service-related issue that can arise in proper guest seating, consider an establishment whose dining area contains many "two-top" tables. Two-tops are tables that seat two guests (*Exhibit 5.7*). Two-top tables are also commonly referred to as deuces. Assume this operation also contains several

Exhibit 5.7

three-top tables that hold three guests and several four-top tables that seat four guests. On a busy night all two-top tables are filled. Six couples, who are not dining together, are on the wait list. If each of the six dining couples waiting to be seated were seated at currently open three- and four-top tables, these guests' waits will be reduced, but the operation will not be seating guests in a way that helps it achieve the highest possible proportion of seats filled. Effective table assignment means doing a good job of balancing the desire of waiting guests to be seated as quickly as possible with the need of the operation to fill the largest proportion of seats possible during busy time periods. In those operations where tables can be rearranged easily to create smaller or larger seating arrangements, the table assignment process is less complex.

HOW LONG IS EACH SEAT RENTED?

The length of time a seat is in use directly affects the total number of guests that can be seated during a specific meal period. Guests should never be rushed, but tables should be cleaned and reset as quickly as possible during busy meal periods (see chapter 5). Also, server stations, the specific number and location of tables and seats assigned to each waitstaff member, must be balanced so no server is overloaded with guests and so all customers can be served as quickly and efficiently as possible.

In some cases, waiting guests can become agitated if they see empty tables in a dining room while they are waiting to be seated. This can occur when a customer without a reservation sees empty tables reserved for guests who have not yet arrived to claim their reservations. When that happens, a polite explanation of the situation to waiting guests is desirable.

Seating Guests

Whether guests have been assigned a specific table by service staff or if guests are allowed to choose their own table, the actual seating of guests is an important moment of truth. Managers establishing standards for the guest seating address three key areas:

- Who should seat guests
- Where to seat guests
- How to seat guests

WHO SHOULD SEAT GUESTS

In some more formal operations guests may be seated by a maître d'hôtel, a staff member specially designated and trained to greet guests, make table assignments, and manage the operation's entire service staff. In other operations, a manager, host, or member of the waitstaff may seat guests. In all cases, however, the person seating guests controls the flow of traffic into the dining area and to specific server stations. It is important that this person be cordial and confident in his or her tasks. The person should, of course, also be instructed never to seat a guest at a dirty table.

WHERE TO SEAT GUESTS

Where guests are seated in a dining room often matters to guests as well as to the operation. In some cases, guests can be seated anywhere in a dining room that they prefer. When that is the case, special requests from guests seeking to be seated, for example, in a booth, by the window, near the fireplace, or away from the television should be granted.

In other cases, the decision of precisely where in a dining room guests should be seated takes on great importance to the establishment. Where an operation has established multiple server stations, the employee seating guests must make sure customers are dispersed evenly among the stations to avoid overloading any one server.

In many cases, the employee seating guests will be called on to use good judgment:

- In those jurisdictions where smoking in restaurants, bars, or casinos is permitted, guests should always be asked if they prefer smoking or nonsmoking areas.

Manager's Memo

The assignment of server stations is necessary so each waitstaff member knows which tables and guests he or she is responsible for serving. This helps maximize efficiency but can also give rise to a "that's not my station" response from servers when guests to whom they have not been assigned make a request of them.

Managers should emphasize the importance of teamwork when guests are served. A server who receives a request from a guest who is not seated in his or her station should accommodate the guest if at all possible. He or she should promptly relay the guest's request to the appropriate server or a manager if he or she is not able to immediately assist.

• Groups celebrating events that could potentially be louder than other diners may best be seated in areas of the dining room that would minimize their disturbance of the other guests.

• Large groups should be seated together whenever possible.

• Guests with mobility issues should be seated in areas that minimize the distances they must walk.

• When an operation offers a good interior or exterior view it makes sense to seat guests in areas that allow them to take advantage of the view.

• If guests request a specific seating area or table and the requests are reasonable, they should be granted whenever possible.

HOW TO SEAT GUESTS

Guests require seating as a result of having a reservation or being called next on a wait list. In other cases, however, walk-in guests may be greeted and seated immediately. In these cases guests should be given the appropriate initial greeting and then asked, "How many are in your party?" If a guest appears to be alone, some managers instruct greeters to ask "How many in your party?" Greeters should never ask, "Are you eating alone?" or inquire, "Just one?" because the guest may view comments such as these negatively.

The staff member who is seating guests should walk slightly ahead of the guests and slowly enough to ensure that the guests can follow easily. If the dining area is not crowded, guests may be asked to indicate their own seating preferences because this is a no-cost way to enhance the guest's dining experience.

Some managers may instruct those seating guests to pull out chairs for women or, in more formal operations, for both women and men. When guests are seated at booths or at tables along walls, the staff member seating guests may pull the table top away from the booth or wall to provide easy entrance.

Special attention may be required when seating guests who are disabled (see chapter 2). Many disabilities relate to mobility and as a result some guests using wheelchairs, crutches, canes, or walkers will require extra assistance in seating and storing mobility aids. The service staff must ensure guests are seated and aids are stored in ways that are safe for all guests.

Special attention may also be required when seating families with small children. It is important to ensure an adequate number of clean and safe high chairs and booster seats are available. However, those seating guests should be trained to allow parents to take the responsibility of actually placing their children in the high chairs or booster seats.

> **THINK ABOUT IT . . .**
>
> Booth or table? Which do you prefer when dining out? Why? Do you think most guests feel the same? What are the advantages and disadvantages of each?

Upon arriving at the guest's table, the staff member should, of course, check to ensure that the table is clean and that there are a complete set of condiments on the table as well as complete place settings for each guest seated. In most operations that pre-set their tables, the seating of guests is concluded by removing any extra place settings or glassware that the seated guests will not be using (*Exhibit 5.8*).

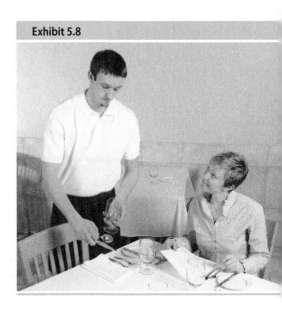

Exhibit 5.8

MENU DELIVERY AND SERVER ASSIGNMENTS

The final step in a casual or fine-dining guest's arrival, greeting, and seating process occurs when guests receive their menus and are given information about their servers. This step includes three distinct activities:

- Presenting the food menu

- Presenting the drink menu or wine list

- Communicating the server assignment

Presenting the Food Menu

In some operations, menus remain on the table between guest seatings. In other operations, food and wine menus are presented to guests after they are seated. A menu should be distributed to each diner old enough to read it. In many operations, the employee distributing the menu will open it for guests before handing it to them. This should be done in the most convenient manner possible based on table style and seating arrangements. In most cases, this means presenting the menu on the guest's right with the presenter's right hand or on the guest's left with the presenter's left hand.

At the time of menu presentation, the waitstaff should inform guests of any daily specials offered in addition to those items listed on the menu. Employees describing specials should explain them clearly and indicate their prices. Diners should also be told of any items listed on the menu that are not available for guest ordering.

Presenting the Wine List

In some operations, managers instruct waitstaff to present a wine list to every dining table. In other operations, waitstaff are instructed to ask "Will you be having wine this evening?" or "Would you care to see our wine list?" In those cases, servers can respond appropriately to the guests' replies.

The wine list is presented to the host of the dining party if that person is readily known. If not, wine lists are given to guests who request them from the guest's right side, if possible. At that point, the server should leave the table and allow the guest time to review the operation's wine selections. Upon returning to the table after an appropriate amount of time, the server may then ask if the guest has any questions about the wine list.

Communicating the Server Assignment

The final act of guest seating occurs when the host seating guests informs the diners about the name of the staff member who will be serving them, using statements such as the ones that follow:

- "Brisia will be serving you tonight."
- "Your server today will be Todd, and he will be right with you."
- "I'll send Dimitri over right away because he will be your server today."

After menus have been delivered, and the service staff member assigned to the table has been identified, the employee responsible for seating guests should ask if there is anything else the guest needs. If the answer is yes, the guest's request should be addressed. If the answer is no, the employee should leave that table with a smile and a final pleasant comment such as "Please enjoy your meal."

SUMMARY

1. **Explain how proper facility maintenance impacts arriving guests' impressions of service quality.**

   If guests do not form initial positive impressions of an operation they may be suspicious of its service levels and even its food quality. It is essential that managers take the steps needed to ensure positive first impressions.

   Many guests will form first impressions when they arrive at a facility and observe the parking area or entranceway. These areas, as well as the grounds surrounding the business, must be kept tidy and well maintained.

   When entering an operation, guests will immediately take notice of its interior entrance areas. These areas vary by the type of operation but for most all of them the condition of foyers, restrooms, and waiting areas play a critical part in forming guests' first impressions. The areas must be inspected regularly and kept well lighted, clean, and attractive.

2. **List the steps managers use to address guests' on-arrival hospitality experiences.**

   Managers use a multistep process when they seek to manage and control hospitality expectations. In the first step, managers define the expectations they have for arriving guests. Next, these expectations are communicated to service staff, and staff are observed in their execution of the standards. In the third step, managers identify any deficiencies in meeting expectations. The fourth step involves the identification of alternative solutions to the problem. In step five, managers choose the best identified solutions and implement them. In step six, managers assess the effectiveness of their solutions. In the final step, they make ongoing service quality assessments for the purpose of identifying and modifying future solutions as the need for them is identified.

3. **Identify the information included in a properly made guest reservation.**

   The accurate recording of reservation information is critical to ensuring guest satisfaction with the reservation and seating process. When designing a proper reservation records system, managers must ensure the following information is recorded for every reservation made: the full and proper spelling of the guest's first and last name; the date for which the reservation is being made; the time of day for which the reservation is requested; the number of persons for which the reservation is being made; special seating or other requests that should be made known in advance; and a way for the operation to reach the guest in the event a change must be made in the reservation and to maintain up-to-date customer records.

4. **Discuss the importance of professional wait list management to guest satisfaction.**

   When an operation is very busy, not all arriving guests may be able to be seated immediately. In that situation it is in the best interest of guests and the operation to create and manage wait lists in a way that minimizes wait times for guests and maximizes the number of guests who can be seated. There are two goals to be achieved in the effective management of wait lists. The first is to consistently provide waiting guests with realistic estimates of how long it will be until they are seated. The second is to manage wait lists in a manner guests perceive to be fair. Managers use a variety of techniques to ensure these two goals are met so the experiences of waiting guests does not detract from the guests' view of the operation's commitment to high-quality service.

5. **Describe the impact of effectively managing the table assignment and seating process.**

   Managers must ensure proper table assignment and seating of guests for several important reasons. When table assignments are made properly, the number of occupied seats in an operation can be optimized, service levels are improved because no server station is overloaded, and guest satisfaction is maintained at high levels.

   When seating guests, managers address who should seat guests, where they are to be seated, and how they are seated. Managers should ensure that any guest requests for specific table or seating assignments are granted whenever it is reasonable to do so. Finally, special care must be given to seating guests with disabilities and those guests arriving with small children to help ensure the safety of these guests as well as that of all other guests in the operation.

APPLICATION EXERCISE

The greeting offered by staff when guests arrive in an operation is important. Team up with another student in your class. Draft the specific initial guest greeting you would want your staff to use in the following operations:

Note: *Use your own name as the name of each operation.*

1. A quick-service restaurant featuring burgers and fries

2. A fast-casual restaurant featuring made-to-order burritos, tacos, and nachos

3. A casual restaurant featuring Northern Italian cuisine and Italian wines

4. A fine-dining restaurant featuring USDA Prime steaks as well as a wide selection of fine wines, beers, and spirits

When you have finished drafting your welcome, role-play your suggested greetings with your teammate for his or her reaction and critique.

Then allow your teammate to role-play his or her suggested greetings with you for your reaction and critique.

Discuss with your teammate the reasons that managers would likely script different guest greetings in different restaurant or foodservice operations.

REVIEW YOUR LEARNING

Select the best answer for each question.

1. **Why must trash held on the exterior grounds of a restaurant or foodservice operation be kept in an appropriate container?**
   A. To reduce the cost of trash removal
   B. To speed the removal of trash from the operation
   C. To avoid attracting insects, vermin, and other pests
   D. To ensure the maximum amount of trash can be held for pickup

2. **What is true of informational stickers affixed to exterior entrance doors in a restaurant or foodservice operation?**
   A. They should be kept to a minimum.
   B. They should be replaced on a monthly basis.
   C. They should be placed on the door well below eye level.
   D. They should be big enough to be the first thing guests see when entering the door.

3. **Parking areas in a restaurant or foodservice operation must be**
   A. well lighted and litter free.
   B. placed in the front of the operation.
   C. placed in the back of the operation.
   D. sufficient to park one car for each seat in the operation.

4. **What hospitality expectation do managers establish for guests?**
   A. The number of seats available in dining rooms
   B. What guests will see and hear upon their arrival
   C. The average number of walk-in guests on wait lists
   D. The style of menu used to make it easy for guests to place orders

5. **The best way for servers to present menus is**
   A. behind the guest with the presenter's left hand.
   B. behind the guest with the presenter's right hand.
   C. on the guest's right with the presenter's left hand.
   D. on the guest's right with the presenter's right hand.

6. **What information is NOT typically required from guests at the time they seek to make a reservation?**
   A. Number in the guest's party
   B. The guest's mailing address
   C. Date of the guest's requested reservation
   D. Time of the guest's requested reservation

7. **In what order should walk-in guests be seated?**
   A. Women first
   B. Largest parties first
   C. Smallest parties first
   D. First come, first served

8. **What should managers do *first* if guests with a reservation cannot be seated at the time of their reservation?**

   A. Apologize to the guest

   B. Cancel the reservation

   C. Place the guest on the wait list

   D. Explain the reason for the delay

9. **How many guests can be seated in a dining room containing 20 deuces, 10 three-tops, and 5 four-tops?**

   A. 70

   B. 80

   C. 90

   D. 100

10. **Where should hosts walk as they escort guests to their assigned tables?**

    A. Slightly behind the guests

    B. To the left side of the guests

    C. Slightly ahead of the guests

    D. To the right side of the guests

FIELD PROJECT

Visit one of the largest restaurant or noncommercial foodservice operations in your area. When you arrive, sketch the dining-room layout, taking special care to identify the location and number of all seats available to guests. Carefully study your drawing and then address the following questions:

1. What is the total number of seats available to guests?

2. What is the total number of two-top tables?

3. What is the total number of four-top tables?

4. What is the total number of six-top tables?

5. What is the total number and capacities of tables or booths of other sizes?

6. How would you assign your servers in this operation on a day when only two servers were needed?

7. How would you assign your servers in this operation on a day when four servers were needed?

8. How would you assign your servers in this operation on a day when six servers were needed?

9. Are there seats in the operation that you believe some guests would prefer more than others? Why?

10. Are there seats in the operation that you would instruct hosts to fill last during less than 100 percent capacity meal periods? Why?

6

Dining-Room Service

CHAPTER LEARNING OBJECTIVES

After completing this chapter, you should be able to:

- List the key areas to be addressed in dining-room table *mise en place*.

- State the key factors to address when taking guest orders in QSR and fast-casual, as well as in casual and fine-dining operations.

- Explain the importance of properly delivering guests' ordered menu items.

- Explain the importance of responsible alcoholic beverage service, and the major steps managers take to ensure responsible service of alcohol.

- Identify the two factors most affecting the proper delivery of take-away food orders.

- Describe the process required for resetting dining-room tables.

CASE STUDY

"My last table tipped me only $1," said Cindy, a server at the York's Old Mill restaurant. Cindy is on a 15-minute break with Amber, her coworker, who is also on the restaurant's waitstaff.

"Why? What happened?" asked Amber.

"Well, it was a couple," said Cindy. "The woman ordered a diet cola and the man ordered a regular cola. When I delivered the drinks I got mixed up."

"You gave the diet cola to the guy and the regular to the woman?" asked Amber.

"Right," said Cindy. "You know they look the same. The colas I mean. And I got mixed up. He was really upset when he took a big drink of the diet soda," said Cindy.

"And you think that's why your tip was so small?" asked Amber.

"Well that's probably part of it," said Cindy. "I don't think it helped when I forgot to tell the kitchen that the guest wanted dressing for his chef's salad served on the side."

"So you served his salad to him with the dressing already on it?" asked Amber.

"Right," said Cindy. "I guess today just wasn't my day."

"Doesn't sound like it was a very good day for your customers either," said Amber.

1. How important is accurate order taking and menu item delivery to ensuring guest satisfaction in restaurant and foodservice establishments?

2. Who at the Old Mill restaurant is responsible for teaching Cindy how to accurately take and deliver guest orders? What will likely happen if that is not done?

DINING-ROOM *MISE EN PLACE*

If guests are to enjoy a positive experience, dining areas must be kept clean and inviting. In addition, the dining tables in an operation must be properly prepared for the arrival of guests.

Mise en place is a French term that means "everything in its proper place." The term is traditionally thought of as a back-of-the-house culinary term, in which it means having all ingredients prepared and ready to combine and cook. However, *mise en place* is also applicable to the operation of a professional dining room. Chapter 5 indicated that preparing tables requires the proper placement of condiments and the availability of menus. In most operations those employees responsible for *mise en place* related to dining tables address additional key areas:

- Linens and napkins
- Flatware
- Dishware
- Glassware

Linens and Napkins

In the restaurant and foodservice industry, **linen** is the term used to refer to tablecloths. Today's tablecloths may be made from the flax plant that was the original source of "linens." However, they are more likely to be made of cotton or of synthetic fabrics such as polyester. In many cases, the tablecloths and napkins will be a blend of natural and synthetic fibers. This blend allows for ease of cleaning. The laundering of cloth linens and napkins is not typically done on premise in most operations. Yet clean and soiled items must be carefully handled to minimize cleaning costs. Operations also seek to avoid any laundry vendor charges made as a result of damage to rented linens and napkins.

Napkins can be made of cloth or paper. Cloth napkins are usually set on the table folded in half, in quarters, or in a manager-approved shape or fold. Paper napkins may be placed on tabletops or in dispensers. Both cloth and paper napkins may also be used for decorative purposes or for holding eating utensils (see *Exhibit 6.1*).

When preparing dining areas for guests, linens are carefully and evenly placed on tables. A silence cloth or second tablecloth is often used to help reduce noise and clatter from plates and glasses being placed on guest tables. When setting tables, great care must be taken to ensure all linens and napkins are clean and wrinkle-free. If they are not, they will not aid in making the most positive impression possible.

Exhibit 6.1

Tablecloths should be changed when they become soiled, but during service periods in fine-dining restaurants bare tabletops should never be visible to guests. Some operations use a second tablecloth or paper underliner on tables to ensure bare tabletops are not shown when tablecloths are changed.

When preparing a dining room for service, managers must ensure that tablecloths and napkins are properly used:

- All linen and cloth napkins are clean and wrinkle-free.
- Tablecloths are not ripped, frayed, or snagged.
- Tablecloths are centered or placed properly on tables.
- Chairs are pulled slightly away from tables so tablecloths drape naturally.
- At least one napkin is in place for each guest to be seated.

Flatware

Tableware is the industry term used to collectively describe three categories of tabletop items: flatware, dishware, and glassware. Flatware consists of the eating utensils used by guests and is sometimes referred to as cutlery or silverware. While silver-plated flatware is used in some very upscale operations, the flatware used in most operations is made of stainless steel and is sold in three quality-related levels:

Medium weight: This is the lightest flatware typically sold for use in commercial restaurant or foodservice operations. It is also called economy flatware because of its low cost. This type of flatware is somewhat fragile because, while it will not readily break, it can be easily bent by the user.

Heavy weight: This flatware is very durable, not easily bent, and makes for a nice presentation. It is used in a large number of casual and fine-dining establishments.

Extra heavy weight: Extra heavy weight flatware is used in finer establishments that seek to offer guests the highest levels of flatware quality. This type is very durable and sturdy and is difficult to bend.

The actual weight of a dozen knives, forks, or spoons will vary based on the shape and size of the individual flatware pieces purchased. A variety of flatware pieces are available to fit the needs of operations. Some of the most common are shown in *Exhibit 6.2*.

The specific pieces of flatware used in an operation will vary based on the menu items served and the manager's service standards. When pre-setting tables, or bringing flatware to guests, all servers must ensure they hold it only by the handle. Servers should not touch the flatware's food contact surfaces (*Exhibit 6.3*). Food contact surfaces are those areas of an item that will come into direct contact with food.

Exhibit 6.2

COMMON FLATWARE

Spoons	Bullion
	Demitasse
	Dessert
	Iced tea
	Soup
	Tablespoon
	Teaspoon
Forks	Cocktail
	Dinner
	Fish
	Oyster
	Salad
Knives	Butter spreader
	Dinner knife
	Steak knife

Exhibit 6.3

125

All flatware should be clean and spot-free when used. If a table is pre-set with tableware, servers may wrap or roll the flatware used in each place setting in a napkin. A **place setting** refers to all of the flatware, dishware, and glassware pre-set for use by one guest. If extra place settings are on a table when guests are escorted to it, the extra settings are typically removed when guests are seated. If extra wrapped or unwrapped place settings are left on tables after guests have been seated, all of these pieces must be removed and washed properly after guests have left the table.

Dishware

Dishware in a restaurant or foodservice operation refers to the reusable plates, cups, and bowls used to serve menu items. Some managers use the term *china* when referring to dishware and some very upscale operations do in fact purchase this high-quality form of porcelain for their dishware. In most operations, however, dishware will be made from less expensive materials. Dishware used in the restaurant and foodservice industry is commonly made from a variety of materials:

- Plastic
- Metal
- Ceramic:
  - Bone china
  - Clay
  - Porcelain
  - Stoneware
- Glass

In some operations, coffee cups and saucers or other dishware items are pre-set on tables prior to guest arrival. If dishware is pre-set on tables, care must be taken that servers do not touch their food contact surfaces. Any pre-set, but unused, dishware items should be removed and washed properly after guests have left the table.

Glassware

Glassware is the restaurant and foodservice term for individual beverage containers. In many cases, glassware in an operation may be made from nonglass materials including paper, Styrofoam, plastic, and metal. Glass is such a popular material for making drinking vessels, yet the term *glass* is often used to refer to most of the drink containers in an operation. However, the term *glassware* is best applied only to reusable glasses.

Glass is made by fusing, or heating, sand (silica) in combination with soda and lime. Additions of metals such as lead can change the properties of glass. **Crystal** is glass that contains high levels of lead and has been hand or machine cut with facets to create a "sparkle" in the glass. Crystal is of high quality, fragile, and expensive. Some restaurant and foodservice managers refer to the glassware used in their operations as "crystal," but most managers find that lower-cost, more durable types of glassware are best for their operations.

Distinctive glassware can enhance the image of any restaurant or foodservice operation. Regardless of the materials from which they are made, or the styles and shapes used in an operation, glassware must be handled carefully because it is breakable. If glassware is delivered to guests or pre-set on tables, the glasses should be free from chips and cracks. They must also be clean and spot-free.

GUEST ORDERS

After guests have been properly greeted in quick-service restaurant (QSR) or fast-casual operations, or greeted and seated in casual or fine-dining operations, service staff take their menu orders. Taking orders properly requires servers to use excellent communication skills. In a restaurant or foodservice operation, communication mistakes can lead to errors in customer service, from misunderstanding a request to delivering the wrong menu item to the wrong guest.

Communication is an extremely complex process. The sender–receiver model (see *Exhibit 6.4*) shows the communication process.

Exhibit 6.4

THE COMMUNICATION PROCESS

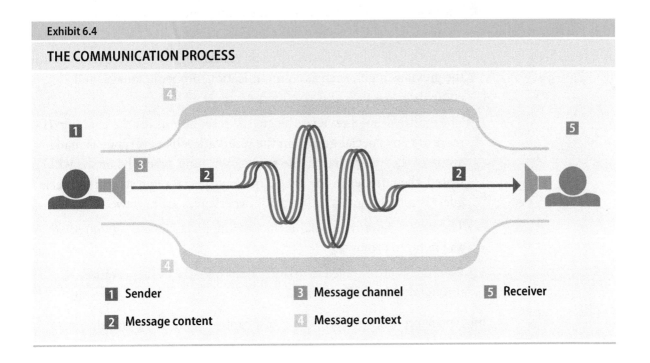

1	Sender	3	Message channel	5	Receiver
2	Message content	4	Message context		

KEEPING IT SAFE

Managers must ensure that all menu items are served safely. Managers training and supervising staff should instruct them in safe foodhandling procedures used in the dining room:

- Wash hands after smoking, eating, drinking, and using the restroom.

- Do not wipe dirty hands on aprons or clothes.

- Never touch food, such as butter, bread, or ice, with bare hands.

- Avoid touching food contact surfaces on flatware, dishware, and glassware.

- Do not use tableware of any type that has fallen on the floor until it has been properly cleaned.

- Do not serve food or beverages in chipped, cracked, or soiled dishware or glassware.

- Do not use soiled service cloths or towels to clean food contact surfaces.

The sender is the person who has a message to communicate, whereas the receiver is the person who gets the sender's message. The sender needs to send the message and get feedback that it was received accurately. Here are some examples of miscommunication in a restaurant or foodservice operation:

- A guest asks a server who is unfamiliar with American slang, "What's hot on your menu tonight?" The server responds by listing the menu items that are served at a hot temperature, while the guest wanted to know what items were popular.

- A server recognizes a guest from past visits and assumes that the guest knows the menu items. Therefore, the server does not highlight items that the establishment wants to promote. As a result, the customer does not consider these items when ordering.

- A server states, "What will *we* be having tonight?" and thus offends a guest who finds the server's comment offensive because of its too casual familiarity.

Clear communication is the solution for these situations. Managers should familiarize employees with common guest questions. In addition, servers should be trained to avoid making any assumptions about a guest, even if the guest is a frequent visitor.

In chapter 4, pre-shift meetings were cited as an example of a method managers use to improve internal communication. The following example shows how one fine-dining restaurant uses pre-shift staff meetings as a way to address and communicate important information:

- The maître d'hôtel and the chef require every scheduled staff person to attend a meeting before opening the dining room. The meeting agenda is fairly consistent each day.

- The maître d'hôtel reviews any positive and negative service issues from the previous night, such as communication, proper language, and etiquette.

- The maître d'hôtel reviews the guests' reservations for the evening. If there are any special guests on the reservation list, everyone is made aware of the guest's name, the reservation time, where he or she will be seated, the number in the party, and any special requests. If the special guest is returning, his or her prior experiences are reviewed.

- The chef reviews and explains the evening menu, including ingredients and items to promote.

- Everyone is encouraged to ask questions and discuss expectations throughout the staff meeting.

This type of pre-shift meeting can significantly help identify and eliminate many internal communication problems.

Communicating clearly means listening carefully. The best servers have good listening skills because sending a message is only half of the communication model. Listening, or receiving, is the other half. Good listening skills are critical to good service.

To listen effectively, a person must be interested in what is communicated and pay attention to the sender. The receiver should not interrupt and should let the sender complete the message. In general, servers follow the principles for effective listening shown in *Exhibit 6.5*.

Taking the Guest Order

The professional and accurate taking of guest orders is essential to high-quality service in every restaurant and foodservice segment and in every food and beverage operation. All guests expect their orders to be taken by qualified servers.

They also expect those taking their orders will be knowledgeable:

- Servers should know what is on the menu, including basic item ingredients and preparation methods.
- Servers should know descriptive words used to explain the menu items offered.
- Servers should know the time required to prepare menu items.
- Servers should know what accompaniments are served with each menu item.
- Servers should know which menu items complement each other. For example, lighter wines with milder food and more robust wines with more intensely flavored food.
- Servers should know the prices charged for each menu item offered.

While all customers expect order takers to be well-trained, knowledgeable, and professional, the most critical factors related to taking guest orders varies by industry segment. The requirements for QSR and fast-casual tend to be different than those for the casual and fine-dining segments.

QSR AND FAST CASUAL

Like those in all segments of the industry, staff taking guest orders in the QSR and fast-casual segments of the industry must be good communicators. In addition, they must emphasize the two traits most important to high-quality order taking in their specific segments: friendliness and accuracy.

FRIENDLINESS Some managers believe high-quality customer service is dependent only on timing, efficiency, and the specific steps needed to record and accurately deliver guests' menu item selections. These are important factors. However, a vending machine can deliver a sandwich efficiently, but only friendly people can provide hospitality.

Exhibit 6.5

PRINCIPLES OF EFFECTIVE LISTENING

- Prepare to listen.
- Stop talking.
- Pay attention.
- Do not interrupt.
- Practice listening.

Understanding the importance of hospitality to high-quality service delivery requires managers to focus on people as well as procedures. Unfriendly order takers may be able to perform their order-taking tasks efficiently. These servers cannot, however, make a positive impact on a guest's feelings about an operation. Connecting with others can take many forms. In the hospitality industry it begins with servers who are genuinely caring and friendly.

ACCURACY   Because of their very nature, the processing of guests in the QSR and fast-casual segments of the industry moves quickly. In many cases, it is speed of service that draws guests to these operations. As a result, guest orders are most often taken and filled quite rapidly. Accuracy and attention to detail are of critical importance when order taking.

To illustrate why accuracy is especially important in the QSR and fast-casual segments, consider the server in a casual dining table-service operation who forgets if one of his guests ordered extra onions for her chef salad, or if she did not want any onions on the salad. In this case, the server can quickly return to the guest's table to clarify the order. On the other hand, if a guest placed a takeout pizza order by telephone, the staff member actually making the pizza will be completely dependent on the ability of the order taker to have accurately recorded whether the guest preferred extra onion, or no onion, on the ordered pizza. Rapid guest processing and the difficulty of clarifying orders with drive-through and some customer types illustrate the need for accuracy of order taking in QSR and fast-casual operations.

CASUAL AND FINE DINING

In casual and fine-dining operations, professional order taking also addresses two key issues:

- Exhibiting an appropriate demeanor
- Optimizing the dining experience

EXHIBITING AN APPROPRIATE DEMEANOR   Chapter 3 defined ambience as special atmosphere or mood created by a particular environment. Server demeanor is the way a server behaves when doing his or her work. In casual and fine-dining operations the demeanor of servers must be consistent with the ambience created in the operation's dining area. The demeanor of servers consists of several behavioral characteristics:

- Appearance
- Attitude
- Mannerisms
- Image

In casual-dining operations, server demeanor should reflect the casual service approach likely offered in that operation. In fine-dining operations, server demeanor must reflect and reinforce the ambience offered in those unique operations. Guests do not like pretentious service or snobbish servers. It is essential that servers behave in ways that guests feel are consistent with the overall physical environment they have chosen for their dining experience.

OPTIMIZING THE DINING EXPERIENCE   Friendliness and accuracy are key factors in providing excellent guest service in QSR and fast-casual restaurants. Servers in casual and fine-dining operations seek to provide their guests with a truly memorable dining experience, and in many cases that includes friendly service and accuracy in order taking and food delivery. But in most cases it requires even more.

A memorable meal includes good food, but it is also most often the result of servers striving to optimize their guests' dining experiences. The best servers do this using a variety of techniques:

- Presenting a professional appearance
- Knowing their menu offerings well
- Responding properly to guest questions about menu items and menu item preparation
- Using appropriate suggestive selling techniques
- Taking and delivering menu orders efficiently and accurately
- Anticipating guests' needs and providing attentive, but not intrusive, service
- Presenting a demeanor in keeping with the operation's overall ambience

When servers use these techniques and exhibit these characteristics they have an excellent likelihood of optimizing each guest's dining experience. Doing so helps the operation reach its customer service goals, increases guest satisfaction, and assists the operation in achieving its profit goals.

Recording and Placing the Guest Order

The manner in which service staff members takes guest orders varies by industry segment. For example, in QSRs large numbers of guests order at drive-through windows while others place their orders with counter personnel. In fast-casual operations, guests give their orders to designated service staff or production staff members who may take orders and prepare requested menu items.

In casual and fine-dining operations, guests make their selections in dining areas. Trained waitstaff take the orders and give them to production staff. In all of these cases, and in all segments, it is essential that servers complete two critical tasks well: recording the order and placing the order.

REAL MANAGER

PEOPLE WILL PAY MORE FOR AN EXPERIENCE THAN THEY WILL FOR JUST FOOD.

Because I was making my hot dog cart more about my personality than the hot dogs, people felt compelled to leave me a little something extra. I never put out a tip jar, but there was usually a bit of spare change sitting on the cart when customers walked away. As far as I knew, I was the only person in the park earning tips, and I was going home each night with enough change stuffed in my pockets to equal my hourly wages for the day. I had *doubled* my income!

THINK ABOUT IT . . .

Have you ever had a meal delivered to your table that you did not order? How do you think that happened? How did you feel about the level of service you received in that operation?

Recording guest orders means accurately communicating with guests to precisely determine their menu selections. The types of questions commonly asked by servers when properly recording orders vary based on the menu items offered. There are many examples of order details that servers must record properly:

- **Doneness:** for steaks and burgers
- **Cooking method:** for eggs
- **Size:** for items such as beverages and pizzas
- **Condiments:** for sandwiches
- **Dressings:** for salads
- **Toppings:** for ice-cream dishes
- **Side dishes/accompaniments:** to identify guest choices of menu item alternatives included in an entrée or meal's selling price

After determining what guests want to order, service staff must properly place, or enter, the orders into the operation's production system so item preparation can begin. The methods used to record and place guest orders vary somewhat, but managers typically use one of four methods:

- Checklist
- Guest check
- Notepad–POS system
- Interfaced POS system

CHECKLIST

When using the checklist method, the server checks or circles ordered items from a preprinted list of menu options. The checklist is submitted to production personnel for order preparation. In this system the completed checklist serves as both the record of guest orders and the manner in which orders are placed into the operation's production system.

The checklist is filled out by the guest or a server and is manually delivered to production staff for order preparation. This method is best used when the number of menu options offered to guests is limited and, as a result, the ordering process is uncomplicated.

GUEST CHECK

When using the guest check method the server writes down guest orders on a guest check. The guest check is then manually delivered to the operation's production personnel. In this system the guest check serves as the record of guest orders and the document used to place the order into production.

When managers use guest checks with multiple copies, one copy of the guest check may be given to production staff and another copy retained by the server for eventual use in preparing the guest's final bill. This system is commonly used in smaller operations where servers and production staff are in close proximity and can communicate easily.

NOTEPAD–POS SYSTEM

When using the notepad–point-of-sale (POS) system method, the server writes down guest orders on a notepad. This typically occurs in the dining area, after guests have been seated and reviewed the menu. The server then uses an order entry terminal in the dining area or kitchen to place the guest's order into the operation's POS system. In this method, the facility's production staff members will monitor their operation's POS display terminals or order printers located in the production areas to receive incoming orders. These orders tell the production staff what menu items must be produced (see *Exhibit 6.6*).

In most cases the display terminals or order printers used by production staff also display the name of the server placing the order. This information is especially helpful if production staff members have questions about the order or how the order should be prepared. The notepad–POS system method is the one most commonly used in casual and fine-dining operations where guest orders are taken, or recorded, at the guest's table.

INTERFACED POS SYSTEM

The newest order recording and placement approach is the interfaced POS system method. To **interface** means to electronically connect two systems. In this case the two interconnected systems are guest order *recording* and guest order *placement*.

To illustrate the method, assume that in a QSR a customer orders a beverage. The counter staff person records the order by entering it directly in the POS system. Display terminals or printers in production areas immediately display the guest's order and preparation of the beverage can begin.

The interfaced POS system method was originally used only in QSR and fast-casual operations, where guests place orders with counter or window personnel. Today, wireless handheld order entry devices allow servers at guests' tables to take orders and automatically enter them in an operation's POS system. As a result, the notepad–POS system method traditionally used in casual and fine-dining operations is, in many operations, giving way to this more technologically advanced method of guest order recording and placement. Some handheld order systems can even recognize a server's handwriting, read it, and then place the server's orders directly into the operation's POS system.

Exhibit 6.6

OPEN FOR BUSINESS

RESTAURANT TECHNOLOGY

The taking of guest orders is an important moment of truth. In most cases, guest orders are taken after guests arrive in an operation. Increasingly, however, guests can use technology to place their orders *prior* to arriving at an operation.

Guests can place orders via computer if the operation has designed their Web site or email accounts to accept them in this manner. Other operations allow guests to use smartphones to text message orders. Some even allow users to use social media programs to place orders.

In all of these cases, an electronic record of guest orders is obtained, but in most cases these orders must still be manually placed into the operation's POS or manually delivered to production staff to ensure the orders are recorded and then prepared properly. When they are, this moment of truth can be handled well even before guests arrive.

DELIVERING THE GUEST'S FOOD ORDER

Accurately recording and submitting guest orders to production personnel are the first steps toward ensuring guests actually received what they have ordered. Delivering those items to the correct guest is the second step. This is especially important when the items are delivered to individual guests at their tables. Servers who take guest orders must be extremely careful to record which guest ordered which item. Doing so avoids the very poor service received by guests when a server arrives at a table, holds a plate in the air, and loudly pronounces, "Who's the chicken sandwich?"

Types of Meal Service

In the restaurant and foodservice industry, there are several different styles of table service that date back for generations (see *Exhibit 6.7*). These different meal service styles typically are found only in casual and fine-dining establishments. Each style demands different preparation and presentation procedures. The more labor intensive the style of service, the more costly it is for the establishment owner to provide.

Exhibit 6.7

STYLES OF TABLE SERVICE

American-style service: The food is placed onto a plate for each diner and then brought out to the customer. The plates are distributed to the proper diners. This is the most common form of table service in the United States.

English-style service: Also known as familystyle dining, this type of service is the simplest and least expensive. The food is brought to the tables on platters and serving bowls. The host of the table then serves the meal on the plates for the other diners, or the dishes are passed around the table so diners can serve themselves.

French-style service: While this is the most elegant of the styles of service, it is also the most expensive. The food is placed into serving dishes and then brought out on a cart. It is then served onto the diners' plates at the table. The food is kept hot by a warming unit in each cart. This type of service is expensive to implement because of the expensive carts and the additional skills required of the servers.

Russian-style service: Each diner's hot food is placed onto hot plates and cold food onto cold plates. All the diners' plates are brought to the table on a cart where they are distributed to the diners. A small investment is required by the restaurant owner for the expense of the carts.

The types and extent of products and services provided affect the delivery of guest orders. Several factors must be taken into account when managers make critical decisions about the table-service method they use:

- Target market chosen and how well an operation can meet its demands
- Size, décor, and cost of the facility, its equipment, and its furnishings
- Number and types of employees, the skills they must have, and the amount of compensation they require
- Types and costs of the food and nonfood supplies
- Extent and nature of the operation's marketing, advertising, and promotion efforts

Basically, the more service provided, the more investment required and the more ongoing expenses incurred. As a result, more must be charged for the meals because in nearly all operations, meals are the primary source of revenue. The primary goal of every table-service method used is the same: to deliver and properly place the correctly ordered menu items in front of the appropriate guests.

Special Cases of Meal Service

Exhibit 6.7 shows traditional methods used to serve guests, but two additional methods of meal service are also common: self-service and tableside preparation.

SELF-SERVICE

When guests are allowed to select some, or all, of their menu items in self-service food and beverage operations, the role of the server must be somewhat modified. In many cafeterias and in buffet settings (*Exhibit 6.8*), guests may be allowed to select and carry to their own tables a variety of products such as beverages, appetizers, salads, entrées, side dishes, and desserts.

Exhibit 6.8

In some operations, such as all-you-care-to-eat buffets, guest may be allowed to return to all self-serve areas, or food bars, multiple times. In cafeteria settings, guests may be charged for the items they select each time they go through the serving line. In still other settings, guests may be allowed refills on some items such as beverages while other items such as entrées are not unlimited. In all cases, however, when guests serve themselves, the role of the food

KEEPING IT SAFE

Here are some additional rules for keeping food bars safe:

- Maintain proper food temperatures.
- Keep raw meat, seafood, and poultry areas separate from ready-to-eat food in self-service areas.
- Protect food with approved sneeze guards or food shields.
- Identify all food items.
- Do not let customers refill soiled plates or use soiled utensils at the food bar.
- Never use the ice provided to keep food or beverages cold as an ingredient.

KEEPING IT SAFE

Managers contemplating the addition of flambéed items to their menus must consider many things. The single most important factor to consider, however, is the safety of guests and employees. Employees assigned to tableside cooking work with highly flammable alcohol-based ingredients. If they are not well trained and extremely careful, servers creating the fires needed to cook food and create the show associated with flambéed items can easily injure themselves or guests.

Regardless of the dishes to be offered, or how they are to be prepared, the addition of tableside cookery to an operation's product offerings should be undertaken only after meticulous attention has been paid to the ability of the operation's staff to prepare the dishes safely—every time.

server is expanded to include promptly removing soiled dishware from the guests' table. This is important for several reasons:

- To minimize crowding on the guest's table
- To keep the guests' tables clean and attractive looking
- To minimize the risk of contamination that would result from guests returning to food display areas to refill previously used plates and glassware

In self-serve operations, managers may assign staff to replenish food bar items and dishware and even to hand out fresh plates for return visits. Managers can also post polite tips about food bar etiquette. These actions can go a long way toward keeping self-service areas more sanitary.

TABLESIDE PREPARATION

The tableside preparation of menu items is a special style of table service that is used in many fine-dining operations. When using this unique and showy preparation method, selected food or beverage items are prepared in the dining room and at the guest's table.

Menu ingredients are arranged on trays or dishes and placed on a special wheeled cart called a *gueridon*. The cart will also be loaded with the tools required to prepare and serve the dish as well as with a *rechaud*—a portable heating unit used for tableside cooking. The cart is then wheeled to the guest's tableside for item preparation.

Some tableside items, such as Caesar salads, are made without flambéing, or flaming, the item at the table. Many other dishes are flambéed tableside. The showmanship exhibited in professionally executed tableside cookery can make truly remarkable and memorable dining experiences for guests ordering flambéed items and for other diners observing these menu items' tableside preparation.

Popular tableside cookery items include entrées such as steak Diane and veal scallopini Marsala. Popular desserts include items such as cherries jubilee, crepes Suzette, and bananas Foster. Popular flambé beverages include Irish coffee and café diablo.

When considering the addition of tableside prepared items to their menus, managers must consider the ability to move carts easily through dining areas, the time required for at-the-table item production, product costs, required staff training, safety, and the challenges of ensuring product consistency.

ENSURING ACCURATE AND RESPONSIBLE BEVERAGE SERVICE

Few activities are more enjoyable and relaxing than enjoying beverages with, or without, meals. Nearly 100 percent of guests who purchase food in a restaurant or foodservice operation will drink a beverage as an accompaniment to the food. In some operations, such as coffee shops and bars, guests may be more likely to visit an operation for its beverages than for its food. Professional managers know that the vast majority of beverages served in the restaurant and foodservice industry *do not* contain alcohol:

• Coffee

• Tea

• Milk

• Juice

• Soft drinks

• Bottled water—still or carbonated

• Tap water

Servers taking and delivering guest's non-alcoholic beverage orders know it is important that these tasks be done properly. Those who serve alcoholic beverages know that these popular beverages require special management attention:

• Alcoholic beverages

• Wine service

• Guest intervention

• Responsible alcohol service

Alcoholic Beverages

There is no doubt that many diners enjoy alcoholic beverages with their meals. In other cases, guests enjoy alcoholic beverages without meals. In both cases, the service of alcoholic beverages requires special information and care. The alcoholic beverages served in a restaurant or foodservice operation are of three basic types:

Beer: An alcoholic beverage fermented from cereals and malts, and made with yeast and hops, which is a flower added to flavor the beverage

Wine: An alcoholic beverage produced from grapes or other fruit

Spirit: An alcoholic beverage produced by distilling, or removing water from, a liquid that contains alcohol

Exhibit 6.9

In moderation, alcohol has a tranquilizing effect. It relaxes and stimulates the appetite. In large quantities, it can become an addictive and even a deadly toxin. Because of alcohol's physiological effects, the service of alcoholic beverages is tightly regulated. The responsible sale of such beverages is critically important to managers. As a result, managers must ensure that all alcoholic beverages are sold in keeping with all local and state laws related to their sale.

Wine Service

For many guests, elegant wine service heightens a dining experience. Those operations with high-volume wine sales may employ a wine steward or a sommelier. These staff members advise customers about wine selection, take wine orders, and present and serve the wines that are selected. Most operations, however, do not have this specialized assistance available. In establishments without wine stewards or sommeliers, a trained food or beverage server is responsible for offering guests information about the wines available on the wine list. Often, they are also responsible for serving wines (*Exhibit 6.9*).

An important first step in selling wine is to make product knowledge about the wines available. Servers should also know how to properly pronounce the name of each wine offered. In some establishments, tables are set with wineglasses, perhaps a glass appropriate for white wine and a separate glass appropriate for red wine. In this instance, if a wine is not ordered, both glasses should be removed from the table. If one type of wine is requested, the glass that is not needed is removed. In other establishments, wineglasses are not set on the table before the customers arrive and, instead, they are brought to the table only if wine is ordered.

In all cases, wines should be served professionally. *Exhibit 6.10* outlines 10 key steps in professional bottled wine service.

Manager's Memo

Wines are sold in many establishments by the glass, carafe, or bottle. Wine bottles come in various sizes that are regulated by the government and are based on the metric system of liquid measurement.

Bottle Size	Name	Description
0.100 liter	Miniature (mini)	A single-serving bottle
0.187 liter	Split	1/4 of a standard bottle
0.375 liter	Half-bottle	1/2 of a standard bottle
0.750 liter	Bottle	Standard wine bottle
1.5 liters	Magnum	Two bottles in one
3.0 liters	Double magnum	Four bottles in one

Note: *1 liter = 33.8 ounces.*

Step 1: Present the Wine List

Wine lists, like food menus, represent the operation's brand. They should be clean and neat because they are significant selling tools. They should be brought to the table for presentation to the customer with a comment such as, "I am proud to present our wine list." This can be followed with the suggestion, "If you have any questions about our wines, I will be happy to answer them. Otherwise, please take a few moments to look over the list." In some establishments, wine lists are placed on the table when it is set for service. In this case the server should point out the wine list on the table.

Step 2: Assist Customers with Wine Selection

Some customers are likely to be very knowledgeable about wine and will not desire or appreciate assistance. Others may have questions about the type of wine to select relative to the food being ordered or the quantity to order. It is important to note that there are approximately five servings (5 ounces each) per bottle; a full bottle holds 25.6 ounces. A full bottle will likely be sufficient for two to three people depending on portion size.

Step 3: Take the Wine Order

The wine order should be taken and repeated to ensure there is no communication problem.

Exhibit 6.10

10 KEY STEPS IN BOTTLED WINE SERVICE

Step 1: Present the wine list.

Step 2: Assist customers with wine selection.

Step 3: Take the wine order.

Step 4: Collect the wineglasses and obtain the necessary wine.

Step 5: Bring the glasses and wine to the table.

Step 6: Present the wine to the guest.

Step 7: Open the wine after guest approval.

Step 8: Allow the guest to taste.

Step 9: Pour the wine after guest approval.

Step 10: Refill the wineglasses.

Step 4: Collect the Wineglasses and Obtain the Necessary Wine

Some establishments use the same wineglass regardless of the wine type selected; others use specific glasses for specific types. Establishments use various systems for servers to obtain the wine ordered. White wines are typically served chilled. Many wine experts agree that wines are best served at **cellar temperature**, generally considered to be between 65°F and 70°F (18°C and 21°C). The best temperatures for long-term storage of five or more years for red wines is lower, usually between 55°F and 60°F (13°C and 16°C). Depending on the operation and its storage facilities, different wines may be stored in different locations within an operation until they are issued to service staff.

Step 5: Bring the Glasses and Wine to the Table

If wineglasses are not pre-set, they should be brought to the table on a small serving tray and handled by their stems, not by their bowls or rims. They should be placed to the customer's right. Red wines can be brought to the table on a tray or in a wine basket. Chilled white and sparkling wines should be brought to the table on a small serving tray or in a wine cooler or wine bucket. In some establishments, wine coolers are placed on the table; in others, a cooler stand is placed on the floor to the guest's right to provide more table room.

Step 6: Present the Wine to the Guest

In most cases, the individual who ordered the wine should be presented with the wine bottle; however, the decision of who at the table will taste the wine is the guest's, not the servers. The host should be allowed to read the wine bottle's label while the server pronounces the wine's name. The guest should agree that this is the correct wine that was ordered.

Step 7: Open the Wine after Guest Approval

The server should use the knife blade attachment on a corkscrew to remove the foil, which is then placed in the server's pocket or apron. The corkscrew is inserted into the center of the cork and is screwed in as far as it will go. The lever is placed on the bottle's lip, and the cork is levered up until it can be removed. Once removed or unscrewed from the corkscrew, the cork can be presented to the guest, who may wish to examine it.

Step 8: Allow the Guest to Taste

A small sample of the wine is poured into the guest's glass for sampling. When the wine is poured, the wine bottle's label should be facing the customer, and when pouring is complete, the bottle should be twisted at the same time it is tipped up to reduce drips. Glasses are not removed from the table as wine is poured unless, for example, the customer is seated against a wall or in a booth, or there is another reason that pouring with the glass in place is impractical.

If the host does not approve the wine, the server should retrieve a second bottle. Improper processing, transporting, or storing conditions sometimes yield an unsatisfactory bottle of wine. Sometimes, however, the customer may just be unsatisfied with the wine's taste. Care should be taken that this is not caused by an improper description on the wine list or by the server. Alternatively, the server may suggest a different wine or request that the manager or other staff member with more extensive wine knowledge assist the customer. When a new bottle of wine is brought to the table, steps 6 through 8 should be repeated.

Step 9: Pour the Wine after Guest Approval

Begin with the woman nearest the host's right; serve all other women, then male guests, and finally the host. The manager should establish the portion size to be poured in wineglasses, and this decision will be based in part on the shape and size of wineglass. As a general rule, wineglasses should never be filled more than halfway full.

Step 10: Refill the Wineglasses

Servers should know when to refill glasses. When a guest's wineglass is almost empty, the server can inquire, "Would you care for more wine?"

There is a great deal of tradition and showmanship in professional wine service. Proper use of these procedures is appreciated by many customers and is an important part of their enjoyment of wine and of the meal it accompanies.

Professional Guest Intervention Procedures

Managers know that they must please their guests. They also know that they and their employees must follow the law. In most cases it is easy to do both, but not always. This can be the case, for example, when a guest who appears to be intoxicated wishes to purchase additional alcohol. It is illegal to serve alcohol to intoxicated guests. If the guest is refused service, it is very likely he or she will not be happy. While that is unfortunate, experienced managers know that in such situations guest safety and following the law is more important than short-term guest happiness.

In cases where intoxicated individuals cause damage or injury to themselves or others, society has deemed it appropriate to place a portion of the responsibility on those who sold or served the alcohol. The laws that address liability for serving alcohol illegally are complex. Managers must understand that there are at least three parties involved when an accident results from the illegal sale of alcohol:

- **First party:** the individual consuming the alcohol
- **Second party:** the operation serving the alcohol
- **Third party:** the injured person(s) not involved in this instance of selling or consuming the alcohol

To illustrate the third-party perspective of improper alcohol service, assume that Randy, a guest (the first party), is served an excessive amount of alcohol by Monica, the bartender at an establishment (the second party). As a result, Randy drives a car and causes an accident that severely injures Bob (the third party).

In such a situation, this establishment and, in some states, even Monica the bartender, may be held liable for Bob's injuries. This legal concept, known as third-party liability, forms the basis for what is referred to as dram shop legislation. This legislation has the intent to penalize those who serve alcohol improperly and to compensate innocent victims.

To avoid potential liability, it is essential that both managers and employees know and perform their respective roles in serving alcohol safely. Doing so ensures that all guests will be provided a safe environment and the operation will fulfill its duty of using reasonable care in the service of alcohol.

INTERVENTION BY BARTENDERS AND SERVERS

It is illegal in all states to serve alcohol to an intoxicated guest. Intoxication is the physiological state that occurs when a person has a high level of alcohol in his or her blood. As a result, all bartenders and servers should be trained to identify the signs that indicate a guest has had too much to drink. Effective intervention by bartenders and servers begins the moment a guest enters the operation. Keeping guests from becoming intoxicated is just as critical as stopping service to them after they have become intoxicated.

Exhibit 6.11

Bartenders and servers should evaluate customers when they order their first drinks (*Exhibit 6.11*). This is done simply by greeting the guest, initiating a brief conversation with them, and noting key guest characteristics:

- Does the guest appear tired, stressed, or depressed?
- Does the guest speak clearly, not slurring his or her words?
- Is the guest already intoxicated?
- Does the guest make comments, either seriously or in jest, indicating his or her desire to "get drunk"?
- Will the guest be ordering food?

If the bartender or server has any indication that the guest has already consumed some alcohol or is consuming alcohol at a rate likely to elevate the guest's blood alcohol content (BAC) dramatically, they may encourage the guest to eat; to switch to non-alcoholic drinks, such as coffee or water, or lower-alcohol drinks; or to "slow down" their consumption.

Blood alcohol content (BAC) is the amount of alcohol that has been absorbed into the bloodstream of a drinker. A BAC of 0.10 means there is about 1 drop of alcohol for every 1,000 drops of blood in the bloodstream.

While the effect of alcohol varies widely by individual, the impact of different BAC levels has been well studied and generalizations about their effect can be stated:

0.02–0.03 BAC: No loss of coordination, slight euphoria and loss of shyness. Depressant effects are not apparent.

0.04–0.06 BAC: Feeling of well-being, relaxation, lower inhibitions, sensation of warmth. Some minor impairment of reasoning and memory will occur.

0.07–0.09 BAC: Slight impairment of balance, speech, vision, reaction time, and hearing. Judgment and self-control are reduced, and caution, reason, and memory are impaired. A BAC of 0.08 means the drinker is legally impaired; it is illegal in all states to operate a motor vehicle at this level.

0.10–0.125 BAC: Significant impairment of motor coordination and loss of good judgment. Speech may be slurred; balance, vision, reaction time, and hearing will be impaired.

0.13–0.19 BAC: Gross motor impairment and lack of physical control. Blurred vision. Judgment and perception are severely impaired.

0.20–0.25 BAC: Feeling dazed, confused, or otherwise disoriented. May need help to stand or walk. Blackouts are likely, so drinkers may not remember what has happened. All mental, physical, and sensory functions are severely impaired.

0.30 BAC and above: Drinkers may pass out suddenly and be difficult to awaken. Coma and even death is possible due to respiratory failure.

In some operations, beverage servers who are concerned about a guest's BAC will slow service to the guest, but the manager must approve this approach. In many operations, it is a policy that managers be alerted any time a server is concerned about a guest's BAC. Doing so ensures that the manager is aware of the possibility of their future involvement in addressing such a guest's continued alcohol consumption.

Bartenders and servers must be trained to look for indications that they must stop serving guests additional alcohol:

- If the guest shows physical or behavioral signs of intoxication
- If the bartender or server is concerned about the impact of the number of drinks the guest has consumed on the guest's BAC

Some operations allow bartenders and servers to stop service in such situations but require them to notify the manager. Other operations require managers to stop the service. In all cases, bartenders and servers should be fully trained in responsible alcohol service and follow their own operation's guest intervention policies.

INTERVENTION BY MANAGERS

In many operations, it will be the manager's job to intervene when a guest is refused service of additional alcohol. In such cases, it is essential that the operation's preestablished policies be followed and that the incident is documented in an incident report. In addition to stopping service to a guest, managers may face other intervention challenges, including guests who arrive intoxicated and intoxicated guests who seek to drive away from the operation.

Sometimes guests who are already intoxicated arrive at an operation that serves alcohol. In this situation, managers have a legal obligation *not* to serve such a guest. Many managers feel they also have a professional obligation to help the guest depart safely. Managers can take specific steps if guests arrive intoxicated:

- Try to refuse entry.
- Ensure guests are not served alcohol if they insist on entering.
- Call local law enforcement personnel to have the guest removed if he or she causes a disturbance.

Sometimes guests who arrive intoxicated or who appear to become intoxicated while in the operation may decide to drive away when they are refused service. In such a case, managers should take specific actions:

- Determine if the guest is the only available driver or if a safe driver is available to drive him or her.
- If the guest is the only driver, ask for his or her keys.
- If the guest agrees not to drive, arrange for alternative transportation.
- If the guest refuses to surrender his or her keys and insists on driving, notify local law enforcement.

KEEPING IT SAFE

In some cases, guests who are refused alcohol service may become threatening or even violent. In such cases employee safety, as well as the safety of other guests in the operation, must always take first priority. Employees serving alcohol must avoid any physical confrontations with guests and summon their managers for assistance if needed.

Employees should also be carefully taught about the circumstances in which local law enforcement officials should be summoned to deal with unruly guests. But in no case should employees ever be instructed to place their own personal safety at risk when dealing with unruly guests.

Managers are responsible for following the law related to the service of alcoholic beverages, but these laws may change. As a result, it is essential that managers stay abreast of legal changes regarding beverage alcohol service.

Responsible Alcohol Service

Managers whose operations serve alcohol must ensure they have the right policies and procedures in place to protect themselves, their guests, and their operations. Managers must take a number of important steps to help ensure the safe service of alcohol in their operations and to demonstrate to others, if the need arises, that they have done so:

1. Developing an incident report form
2. Providing training and certification
3. Monitoring licensing and certificates
4. Monitoring alcoholic beverage service
5. Resolving beverage service problems and concerns
6. Reviewing resolutions of service-related problems and concerns and taking corrective action if alcohol service–related problem patterns emerge

DEVELOPING AN INCIDENT REPORT FORM

Managers must be prepared if a critical incident related to alcoholic beverage service occurs. If it does, a record must be made about the event. An **incident report** is the form used to document what happened and what was done in response. There are a variety of situations in which managers may decide to mandate the completion of an incident report:

- If alcohol service has been stopped to a guest
- If alternative transportation has been arranged for an intoxicated guest
- If an illegal activity has been observed
- If a fight or altercation occurs
- If a guest becomes ill and requires medical treatment

If a significant event such as those listed occurs, it can be stressful and emotions can run high. A manager must take control of the situation immediately for two reasons:

- To ensure the safety of the guests
- To protect the operation legally

Managers can accomplish these goals if employees are trained to respond properly in an emergency situation. Part of that training involves promptly completing and filing an incident report. Employees such as bartenders or servers who witness or who are involved in an incident should be taught to notify the appropriate person, communicate the problem, and take the steps needed to keep themselves and guests safe. When they do, managers or other responsible persons should record the event. Doing so will allow owners or insurers to know about the event in the future. *Exhibit 6.12* shows an incident report form that can be used to record critical information about beverage service–related issues.

Exhibit 6.12

INCIDENT REPORT FORM

(Facility Name and Location)

Date Prepared _____

Completed By *(print)* _____ Title _____

Date of Incident _____ Reported By _____

Time of Incident _____ (a.m.) (p.m.) Location_____

Summary of Incident:

_____

_____

_____

Type of Incident: ☐ Guest Refused Service   ☐ Injury/Fight   ☐ Other

If Injury:

Was 911 called?	☐ Yes	☐ No
Was injured party capable of requesting medical attention?	☐ Yes	☐ No
Did injured party request medical attention?	☐ Yes	☐ No
Was medical attention provided? *(If yes, provide information below.)*	☐ Yes	☐ No

Nature of Medical Attention: _____

_____

If Fight/ Disturbance:

Were police summoned?	☐ Yes	☐ No
Was a report taken?	☐ Yes	☐ No
Was an arrest made?	☐ Yes	☐ No

Attending Officer's name *(print)* _____ Badge Number _____

If Other:

Description of Action Taken: _____

_____

Witness to the Event: _____

Name _____ Position _____

Contact Information _____

_____

Telephone _____

Report Submitted to _____ Title _____

Date of Submission _____

If an incident related to beverage service should occur, managers must ensure the appropriate staff members are familiar with the incident report and know how to fill it out properly. Keeping a record of beverage service issues as they occur helps managers prevent future issues, modify training if needed, and be prepared for potential legal action against the operation. In addition, how managers respond to and document an incident may affect their operation's insurance coverage.

PROVIDING TRAINING AND CERTIFICATION

Managers whose operations serve alcohol must ensure that they or their staff members do not serve intoxicated persons and others not permitted to drink. One way to ensure that relevant employees are qualified is by requiring or encouraging certification.

Certification refers to the confirmation that a person possesses certain skills, knowledge, or characteristics. In most cases, some form of external review, education, or assessment supplies this confirmation. One of the most common types of certification is professional certification. In most cases, the certified person has demonstrated an ability to competently complete a job or task. Typically he or she does so by passing a formal examination.

Increasingly states require that managers and, in most cases, bartenders and other beverage servers complete an alcohol service training course. They must complete such a course to become officially certified in the safe service of alcohol and as a condition of keeping an operation's liquor license. In many cases, those companies that provide insurance to beverage-serving operations make the same requirement.

Managers can receive help in this task because training and certification in the safe service of alcohol is provided by several organizations, including the National Restaurant Association. ServSafe Alcohol is the name of the responsible alcohol server program developed by the National Restaurant Association.

Whether managers are required to be certified by their employer, by the state issuing their liquor license, by their insurance companies, or simply because they wish to improve their professional skills, training in the safe service of alcohol is important for them, their entire beverage service staff, and their customers.

MONITORING LICENSING AND CERTIFICATES

Every state requires sellers of alcoholic beverages to be licensed. Applying for and maintaining a liquor license is a complex process. To maintain a liquor license, most states require managers to comply with, and document their compliance with, a variety of policies or laws. Managers must be very familiar with these licensing and certifying requirements. They must also ensure that they stay abreast of any changes in laws related to alcohol service so that they and their operations are in compliance at all times.

MONITORING ALCOHOLIC BEVERAGE SERVICE

Personally monitoring alcoholic beverage service is one of a manager's most important steps (*Exhibit 6.13*). Managers should observe servers and bartenders as they follow policies and procedures designed to ensure they serve alcohol safely.

RESOLVING BEVERAGE SERVICE PROBLEMS AND CONCERNS

Another of a manager's most important tasks is to help resolve beverage service problems and concerns as they develop. Despite excellent staff training, certain incidents will likely occur and will require the manager's intervention:

Exhibit 6.13

- Refusing entrance to guests who appear intoxicated
- Refusing all alcoholic beverage service to underage drinkers
- Stopping alcohol service to drinkers who appear intoxicated

REVIEWING RESOLUTIONS OF SERVICE-RELATED PROBLEMS AND CONCERNS AND TAKING ACTION IF PROBLEM PATTERNS EMERGE

Sometimes managers will find that the same beverage service–related issues occur frequently. When this happens, managers can use a formal problem-solving process to address and correct the recurring issue:

- Defining the problem
- Determining the cause of the problem
- Assessing alternative solutions
- Selecting the best course of action
- Documenting the action

DEFINING THE PROBLEM   The best way to define a problem is to think about who or what is affected, and a questioning process can be used for this purpose. Depending on the problem, different groups including employees, managers, owners, or even customers could be asked to help explain why the problem exists.

DETERMINING THE CAUSE OF THE PROBLEM   Problems affecting policies and procedures are often blamed directly on affected employees. However, problems often can have other causes. Most beverage operations are made up of a series of complex systems including those for admitting guests, taking orders, serving guests, and collecting payment. Problems can occur when one or more of these systems breaks down or was not carefully developed in the first place. Managers must carefully review their systems to determine where their problems regularly reappear.

ASSESSING ALTERNATIVE SOLUTIONS   An alternative is simply a possible solution to a recurring problem. A beverage service–related problem likely has a number of possible solutions. After potential alternatives have been generated, they should be analyzed to determine which would best correct the problem. Key questions can be asked:

- What will happen if we use this alternative?
- Who will be affected and how will they be affected?
- Is the alternative better than any other alternative?
- Is it cost-effective? Will the solution cost more than the problem?
- Is it reasonable? Does the alternative have a good chance to succeed?

SELECTING THE BEST COURSE OF ACTION   Wise managers choose solutions carefully. An incorrect solution will likely create the need to repeat the problem-solving process, and the negative impact of the problem will also continue. After a manager chooses the best solution, he or she develops an action plan. An action plan is a series of steps that can be taken to resolve the problem. Communicating the action plan is essential. Managers should also communicate the action plan's expected outcomes to everyone involved so they know what must be done and how they will be impacted.

DOCUMENTING THE ACTION   The purpose of documentation is to record information for future use. Changes in job procedures and activities used to implement the solution should be recorded so staff training can be modified as needed. The continual review and modification, if necessary, of all alcohol service activities, policies, and procedures are an essential part of every beverage manager's job.

TAKE-AWAY ORDERS

Increasingly, fast-casual, casual, and even some fine-dining operations receive "take-away" or "to-go" orders from guests. Guests placing these orders may be in a setting that prevents them from eating in the establishment, such as work. Or, they may simply prefer to eat the food in their own homes.

Historically, some food types such as Chinese, Thai, and other Asian cuisines have been popular takeout choices. Others popular takeout choices include deli sandwiches and pizzas. In fact, two of the three largest pizza franchise companies generate the majority of their revenue selling carryout or home delivery pizzas.

Whether they sell carryout items to guests who pick up their own orders, or they deliver the items to guests, managers responsible for ensuring high-quality service related to items sold for away from operation consumption focus on two key areas: order accuracy and proper packaging.

Order Accuracy

Order accuracy is even more critical with take-away orders than with food eaten in an operation's dining room. In many cases, guests will not detect any errors until they have left the operation. Such errors cannot be readily corrected. For example, an office worker volunteers to pick up lunch for a group of co-workers from a local establishment. That guest is not likely to inspect each of the orders closely when he or she picks them up.

Rather, it is the responsibility of the operation to carefully ensure each take-away order has been properly filled. When errors in order accuracy do occur, it leads to inconvenience on the part of the guest and significant reductions in customer perceptions of the operation's service quality.

Proper Packaging

Take-away food orders must be filled accurately. In many cases, it is equally important that the orders be packaged properly if they are to be well received by customers. In all segments of the restaurant and foodservice industry a variety of high-quality, affordable disposable packaging supplies is essential:

- Napkins
- Eating utensils
- Food containers or dishware
- Trays, boxes, or bags
- Wraps
- Condiments

Managers choosing take-away packaging seek to ensure food safety, maintain proper product temperatures, and present their menu items in the most attractive manner possible.

CLEARING AND RESETTING TABLES

Every operation will have policies and procedures for clearing and resetting dining area tables. Responsibilities of servers, busers, and others must be made clear to all. Tables with dirty dishes are unsightly to guests entering or already in the dining room.

Managers must address who will clean and reset the tables, when it is to be done, and how it is to be done. In all cases, however, the basic procedure for clearing and resetting dining-room tables includes steps that must be followed in order:

- Clearing
- Cleaning
- Rinsing
- Sanitizing
- Resetting

Clearing

The proper service of guests includes, of course, the removal of used items such as appetizer plates and wineglasses as guests are finished with them. Fully clearing tables involves the removal of dirty dishware, food containers, napkins, and if needed, tablecloths immediately upon guest departure. Areas around the tables, including floors, chairs, and booth seating, should also be cleaned. Servers should be sure to remove all crumbs, other food droppings, and spilled beverages.

The clearing of tabletop items can be done with bus tubs or trays. In addition, waitstaff can clear tables with only one or two items by hand, such as removing an empty cocktail glass. If bus tubs and trays are used to return items to back-of-the-house areas, they should not be overloaded.

Bus tubs and trays must be used carefully to avoid dishware or glassware breakage. Managers must also ensure employee safety when carrying soiled items. The most important factor in clearing dirty tables is that the process be performed quickly and quietly so as not to disturb other guests in the dining room.

Cleaning, Rinsing, and Sanitizing

Cleaning means removing food and other types of soil from a surface such as a tabletop or counter. Cleaning always follows clearing in the table resetting process. To clean a dining table, all used items including garnishes, breads, and other edible items that could have been touched by guests must first be cleared from the table. Tablecloths should be removed. The table is then ready to be cleaned, rinsed, and sanitized. Seating areas should also be cleaned.

After table areas have been cleared, cleaned, and rinsed, the surface of the table should be sanitized. Sanitizing means reducing the number of harmful microorganisms on a clean surface to safe levels. While cleaning removes soil that can be seen, sanitizing removes harmful microorganisms that cannot be seen.

The sanitizing of a surface always takes place after the surface has been cleaned and rinsed. Eating areas such as tabletops and countertops, including those eating areas on high chairs, should be sanitized between uses. Generally, seating areas need to be cleaned only between uses.

There are key steps employees should take when cleaning, rinsing, and sanitizing dining-room areas:

Step 1: Set up separate washing, rinsing, and sanitizing buckets for the dining room, and place a wiping cloth in each. Fill the washing bucket halfway with hot water and add the recommended amount of washing solution. The rinsing bucket should be filled with clean water. Finally, fill the sanitizing bucket with water and add the recommended amount of sanitizing solution. Use a test strip to test the sanitizer solution to confirm that the sanitizer is the correct strength.

Step 2: Remove large, visible food particles from the eating area. Then use the washing solution and a cloth or scrub pad to clean the surfaces of the table, booths, and chairs seats, taking special care to thoroughly wash high chairs and booster seat surfaces. Clean tabletops and edges of the table toward the underside, as guests' soiled hands frequently make contact with these areas.

Step 3: Finish cleaning all table and chair surfaces and rinse them by wiping them down using the separate cloth from the rinse bucket.

Step 4: Using a fiber-free cloth from the sanitizing solution, wipe the table, high chairs, and booster seat surfaces, including all edges, with the sanitizer-soaked cloth. Allow the areas to air dry without wiping off the sanitizer. Note: *Steps 1 through 4 should be performed after every use of eating areas.*

Step 5: Do a thorough cleaning of tables and seating areas at the end of each operating day, cleaning the tabletop as well as the table underside of any food debris or gum that may be present. Wash table legs, chair legs, and any other seating areas such as booths or stools, but do not upend chairs onto the sanitized tables unless the chair seats have also been sanitized.

Exhibit 6.14

Resetting

Items that should remain on tables, such as menus and condiments, and those items such as flatware and glassware that must be replaced when resetting tables will vary by operation. What is most important is that each service employee knows what these tabletop items are, and that each item is placed on the table in the proper number and in the proper location. When tables have been properly reset, they are ready for the seating of new guests (see *Exhibit 6.14*).

SUMMARY

1. **List the key areas to be addressed in dining-room table *mise en place*.**

   The four key areas related to dining-room table *mise en place* are linens and napkins, flatware, dishware, and glassware. Table linens refer to the tablecloths used to cover tables. These should be clean, wrinkle-free, and attractively placed on tabletops. Napkins may be cloth or paper, and each dining place setting should include at least one clean napkin. Flatware are the eating utensils used by guests. Whether they are pre-set on tables or delivered with the guest's meal, they should be clean and free from water spots. Dishware refers to the cups, bowls, and plates on which food is served. They may be made of a variety of materials.

   If dishware is pre-set on tables, care must be taken that servers do not touch their food contact surfaces. Glassware means drinking vessels. Glassware is fragile and care must be taken in handling these items. The size and types of glassware used will vary by operation, but all should be clean and spot-free when presented to guests.

2. **State the key factors to address when taking guest orders in QSR and fast-casual, as well as in casual and fine-dining operations.**

   The professional and accurate taking of guest orders is essential to high-quality service in every restaurant or foodservice segment because all guests expect their orders to be taken by qualified and knowledgeable servers. For servers in the QSR and fast-casual segments, professionalism dictates order taker friendliness and accuracy. Friendliness is essential because guest orders are processed quickly in these segments. An unfriendly server loses the opportunity to interact with guests on a personal level. Accuracy of order taking is especially important because speed of service is critical. Guests in these segments may not be on-premise for easy reclarification of orders.

   For servers in the casual and fine-dining segments, professionalism means exhibiting the proper demeanor. A casual approach is appropriate in casual establishments, while a more formal demeanor is appropriate in most fine-dining operations. In both of the segments an emphasis on ensuring that guests enjoy the best possible dining experience is a key factor when taking guests' orders.

3. **Explain the importance of properly delivering guests' ordered menu items.**

   The delivery of the correctly ordered item to the right guest is critical to ensure high levels of guest satisfaction. Establishments can choose from a variety of service methods. However, the primary goal of every table-service method used has the same goal: the delivery and proper placement of the right menu items to the right guest. The delivery of alcoholic beverages is a special case both in presentation, as in bottled wine service, and in the responsible service of these adult beverages. Managers must ensure that all service staff know how to serve alcoholic beverages as well as when they must not be served to guests.

4. **Explain the importance of responsible alcoholic beverage service, and the major steps managers take to ensure responsible service of alcohol.**

It is illegal in all states to serve alcohol to an intoxicated guest. As a result, managers and their service staff must be trained to identify the signs that indicate a guest has had too much to drink. Serving an intoxicated guest puts that guest's safety at risk. It also places risks on those whom that guest might harm because he or she is intoxicated. Finally, because of third-party (dram shop) liability laws, serving an intoxicated guest can put a business and even its employees who have served the alcohol at legal risk.

Managers responsible for the safe service of alcohol perform a number of critical tasks. These include developing an incident report form to document any problems their operations experience in the service of alcoholic beverages. They also provide comprehensive staff training at all employee levels. They monitor state licensing and certificate requirements as well as continually monitor alcoholic beverage service in their facilities. They stay up-to-date with any changes in laws regarding the service of alcohol. Finally, managers resolve beverage service problems and concerns as these occur and take appropriate correction action if alcohol service–related problem patterns emerge.

5. **Identify the two factors most affecting the proper delivery of take-away food orders.**

Those managers selling carryout items to guests or delivering products to guests must focus on order accuracy and proper packaging. Order accuracy is important because in many cases guests will not detect any errors in filling their orders until they have left the operation. As a result, the errors cannot be readily corrected. Packaging is also important. Managers packaging food products to be eaten away from their operations want to ensure the safety of the food products they sell. They also want to maintain proper product temperatures and present their menu items in the most attractive manner possible.

6. **Describe the process required for resetting dining-room tables.**

The most important factor in clearing dirty tables is that the process be performed quickly and quietly. First, set up separate pails and cloths for washing, rinsing, and sanitizing. The process used to reset dirty tables in dining areas begins with clearing: the removal of dirty dishware, food containers, napkins, and if required, tablecloths. The next step in the process involves cleaning: the removal of visible food and other types of soil from the tabletop or countertop and seating areas around the table. After table areas have been cleared and cleaned, rinse all of the cleaned surfaces. Tables may then be properly sanitized to reduce the number of harmful microorganisms on them to safe levels.

The sanitizing of a surface always takes place after the surface has been cleaned and rinsed. The sanitizer should be allowed to air dry. Finally, after the table has been cleaned, rinsed, and sanitized, front-of-the-house staff can set and replace tabletop items for new guests in the proper number and in the proper location on the table.

APPLICATION EXERCISE

Consider an establishment in the casual or fine-dining segments that you would like to own or manage and then prepare two training sessions for service staff.

1. The first session should address how tables are to be set. Include a diagram for setting a four-top table properly. In addition to other issues you feel may be important, be sure your session includes information on the following:
   * Who is responsible for table setting?
   * How should tablecloths be placed on tables?
   * Will flatware be pre-set on tables? If so, which pieces will be pre-set and where will they be placed?
   * Will dishware be pre-set on tables? If so, which pieces will be pre-set and where will they be placed?
   * Will glassware be pre-set on tables? If so, which pieces will be pre-set and where will they be placed?
   * Will napkins be pre-set on tables? If so, how will they be folded and placed?
   * What condiments will be pre-set on tables and where will they be placed?

   * What other items will be pre-set on tables and where will they be placed?

2. The second session should address how tables are to be cleared, cleaned, and sanitized. In addition to other issues you feel may are important, be sure your session includes information on the following:
   * Who is responsible for table resetting?
   * How should soiled tablecloths be replaced during meal service?
   * Where will soiled tablecloths and napkins be stored?
   * Where and how will dishware be scraped, stacked, and removed?
   * How should glassware be removed (i.e., tray, bus tub, or by hand)?
   * How should flatware be removed?
   * How should empty wine bottles or chillers be removed?
   * How should table areas be cleaned and sanitized?
   * How should special seating for children be cleaned and sanitized?

REVIEW YOUR LEARNING

Select the best answer for each question.

1. **What should servers avoid touching when placing flatware directly on cleaned and sanitized dining-room tables?**
   A. The tabletop
   B. The flatware's handles
   C. The underside of the table
   D. The flatware's food contact surfaces

2. **For which event would an operation normally complete an incident report?**
   A. Manager is given a promotion.
   B. Employee is continually late for work.
   C. Guest is refused additional alcohol service.
   D. Guest arrives late for a confirmed reservation.

3. Which is an example of a subjective slang statement that could confuse a guest?

    A. All our steaks are USDA Choice.

    B. All our house dressings are fat-free.

    C. Our chicken strips sell like gangbusters.

    D. Our dessert soufflé takes 30 minutes to prepare.

4. What is a sommelier's area of expertise?

    A. Soups

    B. Wines

    C. Sauces

    D. Pastries

5. What is the main advantage of using advanced technology, such as email or text messaging, for receiving guest orders?

    A. Menu items can be produced at a lower cost.

    B. Menu items can be more quickly entered in the POS.

    C. Guests can order menu items prior to their arrival at an operation.

    D. The operation can communicate menu changes more effectively.

6. What is the most important factor servers must consider when offering tableside preparation of menu items?

    A. Cost

    B. Taste

    C. Style

    D. Safety

7. At what blood alcohol content (BAC) will drinkers begin to experience minor impairment of reasoning and memory?

    A. 0.02–0.03

    B. 0.04–0.06

    C. 0.07–0.09

    D. 0.10–0.12

8. Lani is a bartender at an establishment owned by Dennis. One night Lani serves Steven five drinks. When driving away from the establishment Steven's car strikes Andrea's vehicle and Andrea is injured. If it is alleged a violation related to dram shop legislation occurred in this scenario, who is the third party?

    A. Andrea

    B. Dennis

    C. Lani

    D. Steven

9. What are the two most important factors affecting the preparation of take-away food orders for guest pickup or delivery?

    A. Speed and lowest cost

    B. Accuracy and lowest cost

    C. Speed and proper packaging

    D. Accuracy and proper packaging

10. In what order must waitstaff implement the steps used to reset dirty tables?

    A. Clear, rinse, reset, clean, and sanitize

    B. Clear, clean, rinse, sanitize, and reset

    C. Sanitize, rinse, clear, clean, and reset

    D. Rinse, clear, reset, clean, and sanitize

7

Guest Payment and Service Recovery

INSIDE THIS CHAPTER

- Importance of Professional Guest Payment Procedures
- Presentation of Guest Checks
- Accepting and Recording Guest Payment
- Payment for Take-Away, Delivery, and Drive-Through Orders
- Return Incentives
- Guest Departure and Service Quality Confirmation
- Service Recovery

CHAPTER LEARNING OBJECTIVES

After completing this chapter, you should be able to:

- Explain the importance of implementing a professional guest payment system.

- Identify the most commonly accepted forms of guest payment.

- List the steps to develop an effective guest feedback program.

- List the steps to manage an effective guest feedback program.

- Summarize the procedures managers use to address areas of recurring guest complaints.

- Describe the process that staff and managers should use when responding to on-premise guest complaints.

KEY TERMS

bounce back, p. 167

cash overage, p. 160

cash shortage, p. 160

comment card, p. 169

frequent diner program, p. 166

guest check, p. 159

guest check folder, p. 159

guest feedback program, p. 168

merchant copy, p. 162

mystery shopper, p. 170

quick-change artist, p. 159

reconciliation, p. 163

return incentive, p. 167

service recovery, p. 176

statistical analysis system (SAS), p. 173

void, p. 160

CASE STUDY

"But that's not fair. How were we supposed to know they were in such a hurry?" Tamarra asked.

Tamarra was an assistant manager in charge of the dining room at the Wallrich's Table restaurant. Wallrich's Table was a fine-dining operation known for its commitment to using locally grown and produced ingredients to create menu items of exceptionally high quality. Service levels provided to guests were also very high.

Tamarra and Gene, the operation's manager, were looking at a customer review that had been posted online in the "Out and About the Town" Web site. The site allowed users to post comments about, and rate, the quality of their dining experiences at local restaurants.

The posted review was from a diner who had given the restaurant only one "fork" on a scale of one to five forks. One fork indicates a poor rating, and five forks denotes an outstanding one.

"Well, this customer did say the food was exceptional. Every course." Gene said. "But they said they missed the opening of the play they had tickets to that night because it took so long for us to process their check."

"But we always let guests linger at their tables after they finish their meals. We don't want to rush them," Tamarra said.

"I hear what you're saying," Gene replied. "But these guests aren't happy. And the chef won't be happy either when he sees the low rating we got."

1. Do you think it's fair for guests to judge an operation favorably or unfavorably based on its service levels, as well as on its food? Do you think guests commonly do so?

2. What do you think Gene should do about the guest payment system in place at Wallrich's Table? What should be done about the posted review?

Exhibit 7.1

IMPORTANCE OF PROFESSIONAL GUEST PAYMENT PROCEDURES

Proper procedures for accepting payment are critical to the profitability of any restaurant or foodservice operation. Using proper procedures for all forms of payment is essential. Payment forms include cash, checks, money orders, credit or debit cards, gift certificates, gift cards, and coupons. The exact procedure will depend on the form of payment. But collecting payment alone (*Exhibit 7.1*) is not enough to ensure an operation's profitability. The payment must also be recorded and safeguarded until it is prepared for deposit in the operation's bank account.

Failure to properly process guest payments can result in a number of problems:

- The operation may not collect all of the money it has legitimately earned from the sale of its products.

- Servers may take advantage of deficiencies in an operation's payment collection procedures to defraud customers or the business.

- Customers may take advantage of deficiencies in an operation's payment collection procedures to defraud the business.

- Honest mistakes may be made that cause customers to question an operation's commitment to providing high levels of customer service or to view it unfavorably.

- The operation may not receive enough money to pay its bills and achieve its profit goals.

Managers must establish, train for, and enforce proper money collection procedures. If employees handle money, these staff members must be well trained. Training ensures that sales result in accurately collected and recorded revenue. Training for proper payment acceptance procedures is not just for cashiers. Servers must also record and charge for products and services rendered. In addition, servers total guests' bills, accept payment, and return change or receipts. If this training is not provided, employees might collect the wrong amount from guests.

Mistakes made while learning on the job are costly to the establishment. Managers should regularly spot check for consistent use of approved payment collection practices. This will help identify misunderstandings, shortcuts, and errors. It will also identify improper procedures and reduce the potential for fraud.

THINK ABOUT IT . . .

Have you ever been overcharged for a purchase you made at a business? How did that make you feel about the way that business was managed? What would you think if it happened again on your next visit?

PRESENTATION OF GUEST CHECKS

Servers should accurately total the diner's bill or guest check, the document that lists the amount owed by guests. In most QSRs and fast-casual operations, servers should do so when guests order or receive their food. In casual and fine-dining operations, this happens when diners have finished their meals. Servers then present the guest check to the diner in a professional manner.

In table-service establishments, servers present the guest check face down on the table, on an open tray, or in a guest check folder. A guest check folder is designed for use in check presentation, in payment collection, and to return change to the table's host on the host's left side. After a reasonable time, the server should return to the table to accept payment. The server then accepts the diner's money or other form of payment for processing.

ACCEPTING AND RECORDING GUEST PAYMENT

Customers often choose one or more methods when paying their bills. These methods include cash, payment cards, checks, or other payment forms.

Cash Payments

In today's business environment, cash payments are becoming less common. Even QSR operations now readily accept credit or debit cards. As a result, employees do not handle cash as frequently as in the past. Yet all applicable staff members still need cash-handling training. Cash-handling skills include counting change, dealing with large bills, correcting or canceling payments, and avoiding fraud. In addition, procedures should be developed and staff should be trained for special situations such as robbery, dealing with quick-change artists, and other risk management issues. Quick-change artists seek to confuse cashiers and steal from a business.

To process cash payments properly, managers must ensure that cashiers and servers are well trained. An employee accepting a cash payment should follow specific procedures:

1. Count the cash.
2. Make sure the cash amount covers the amount of the guest check.
3. If appropriate, ask the customer if he or she needs change.
4. Place the cash and guest check in a secure carrying device, such as the check folder, and carry them to the point-of-sale (POS) system or cash register.

Manager's Memo

Quick-change artists try to defraud operations by confusing cashiers. Here are some tips for cashiers seeking to avoid becoming a victim of a quick-change artist's scam:

1. Watch out for scam artists working in pairs. Sometimes one member of the pair will cause a distraction by asking questions of the cashier at the same time the other member pulls the scam.
2. Be wary of guests who pay for very small purchases with very large bills.
3. Focus carefully when returning change. The quick-change artist gets that name because the scam is intended to cause the cashier to give back more change than is due. Keep all bills visible and count change back slowly and carefully while announcing bill denominations out loud.
4. Call for a manager if you get confused.

In many communities, the local police will visit a manager's operation to provide specific training on quick-change artists.

5. Follow the operation's cash processing procedures. These will differ by the type of POS system and for each operation. It is important that both the guest check amount and the payment amount match in the system.

6. Put any change into the folder, carry it back to the table, and return it to the person paying the check.

7. Thank the customer for his or her business, and complete the remaining goodbye protocol of the operation.

8. Walk away from the table so the guest can leave a tip in private.

VOIDS

If a cashier makes a mistake such as ringing in a wrong amount or item, or a customer changes his or her mind about something after the electronic transaction has begun, the cashier needs to remove or void it from the computer system or register. A void is when a cash register entry has to be corrected by canceling the entry and entering the correct item.

In a line-item void, the payment has not been processed yet, but items have been rung up. Cashiers can either void these themselves or, more preferably, a manager must enter a code or use a key that allows an item to be removed or changed in the transaction. Voids should be monitored by dollar amount, shift, and cashier. These security measures help prevent cashiers from removing items from guest checks and still taking, and keeping for themselves, the money paid for the items.

Another type of void occurs when an entire transaction must be removed from the system after it has already been completely processed, including the payment. A manager must do this, since the threat of theft is even greater. If the entire transaction is voided because of a mistake or change of mind, a new transaction must be entered with the correct payment information.

CASH OVERAGES AND SHORTAGES

Tracking cash overages and shortages helps identify problems with employees' cash-handling skills. A cash overage occurs when an operation has more cash in the drawer than the POS system or register says it should have. Too many cash overages may indicate that cashiers are poorly trained and customers are negatively affected, because a cash overage normally results when a guest has been shortchanged. A cash overage may also be the result of improper voids, such as when a cashier voids one amount, then removes and keeps for himself or herself an amount of cash smaller than the voided amount. In that case, a cash overage will occur. If managers do not investigate all cash overages, over time the amount of money that could be removed by a cashier using this technique can be significant.

A cash shortage occurs when there is not enough cash in the register to equal the amount reported in the register. A large or regular cash shortage would most likely happen from not knowing proper procedures, carelessness, or theft. Poor cash counting procedures may be the cause of a shortage, but in that case only the counting is wrong and there is no actual shortage (*Exhibit 7.2*).

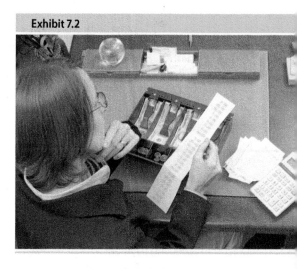

Exhibit 7.2

If a manager has eliminated the possibility of a counting error as the source of a cash shortage, he or she must determine whether the shortage was caused by lack of training, carelessness, or theft. If lack of training or carelessness is the cause, then employees must be retrained and assessed to ensure they know and follow proper cash payment procedures. However, if theft is suspected, it can be very difficult to prove unless someone is caught in the act, particularly if there is no established and enforced cash register operating process. The best prevention is having a consistent cash register operating process. If the process is enforced, this type of theft can be discouraged.

A one-time cash shortage may be the result of a quick-change artist, who tries to confuse the cashier while he or she is making change. Proper cash-handling procedures will prevent this fraud. That is why managers must train staff on their operation's approved cash-handling procedures, how to deal with suspicious transactions, and when law enforcement personnel should be informed of suspected illegal activity. In all cases, managers must recognize that frequent cash overages and cash shortages are an indicator that additional training or a change in cash-handling procedures may be necessary.

Payment Cards

Credit and debit cards are quickly becoming the preferred form of payment in all restaurant and foodservice operations. In general, there are three areas of credit or debit card payment that need to be addressed:

- Credit or debit card handling procedures at the point of purchase
- Handling procedures for "declined" or "denied" cards
- Credit or debit card reconciliation

PAYMENT CARD HANDLING PROCEDURES

To accept payment cards as authorized forms of payment, a manager's operation must have the software and equipment meant to be used for credit or debit card payment at the point-of-sale location. This is essential to implementing card payment policies and procedures. Usually, an operation's POS system determines the procedure to be used for accepting card payments. In these cases, managers can incorporate the POS system's documents and procedures into their payment processing training programs. Training should include the process for collecting and documenting card data and the data that management will need to reconcile the card transactions. While the individual payment processing procedures used in operations may

RESTAURANT TECHNOLOGY

Advancements in credit and debit card processing systems interfaced with POS systems make it easier than ever for managers to accept these popular forms of payment. Unfortunately, increased numbers of payment transactions also increase the number of security-related risks associated with the use of the cards. In addition to collecting payment processing information from credit or debit card transactions, managers must also consider key security issues. An operation must have a system for guest credit or debit card security that includes several key features:

1. Preventing card abuse, such as using an invalid card, using someone else's card, or using a falsified card

2. Maintaining the privacy of the guest's personal and financial card-related information

It is always the manager's job to ensure the security of cardholder information regardless of the technology system used in processing card payments.

vary somewhat, there are specific practices used by all properly designed systems:

1. Identify the form of payment as a credit or debit card so that it can be processed in accordance with the operation's credit or debit card procedures.

2. Swipe the guest's card.

3. Verify the card number with the numbers displayed onscreen.

4. Enter the charge amount into the POS system. At this point, most systems will automatically request card approval.

5. Once the amount is approved, two charge slips will print. One charge slip is called the **merchant copy**, which is the copy for the guest to sign and leave with the operation. The other slip is a receipt for the guest to keep.

6. After the guest has signed the merchant copy, reenter the POS system and verify the card number.

7. Enter the tip amount, if any.

8. Verify the correct payment amount.

9. Keep the signed merchant copy slip for use in the end-of-shift register close-out.

Regardless of the specific procedures used to charge the meal to the credit or debit card, there are important overall handling procedures that cashiers must use when accepting these cards for payment:

1. Cashiers take specific steps when the card is offered as a payment:
   • Verify that it is signed.
   • Keep in mind whose card was offered; it may not be the person to whom the guest check was given.
   • Ask for a picture ID and compare the picture to the customer if the establishment has had problems with customers using stolen credit or debit cards.

2. Take the card and guest check in a secure and private carrying device such as a guest check folder to the POS system or card swiper.

3. Servers take specific steps when processing card payments:
   • Keep the card and guest check near each other and in their possession.
   • Do not let others see the card number.
   • Swipe the card and avoid keying in the card number, if possible. Keying in the card number increases the card company's charges to the operation. If many cards do not properly swipe and must be keyed in, the swipe slot may need cleaning.

- Add the ZIP code to the card information. This is typically possible only through a POS system. The ZIP code adds extra verification information and reduces the card company's charges to the operation.

4. Put the card authorization form, receipt, and guest check into the folder and carry it back to the table. Servers should keep the card with them so they can verify the signature later.

5. Return the card to the actual card owner.

6. Leave the table so the guest can complete the tip and sign the card authorization form in private.

7. Watch the table so they know when the card authorization form has been signed. They should not let the guest sit for more than a minute or two after completion so that, if the guest is in a hurry, he or she is not needlessly delayed from leaving.

8. Return to the table when the guest has signed the card receipt.

9. Verify that the signature on the card receipt matches that on the back of the card.

10. Return the card to the customer.

11. Thank the customer for his or her business and the tip and complete the remaining goodbye protocol of the operation.

DECLINED PAYMENT CARD PROCEDURES

Sometimes a guest's credit or debit card will not be accepted for payment. "Not approved" or "Declined" credit or debit cards must be handled with dignity and respect for the guest. The guest should be politely and discreetly informed of the situation and asked for another method of payment. The manager should specify how this is done in the operation and include it in the staff training.

Staff should also be informed in their training that cards are declined for many reasons. For instance, electronic and operator errors are common in the approval process. Many times, a second running of the card will result in an authorization or approval. In the event that a server does not get an approval on a second attempt, servers should consider the guest's feelings and be empathetic when dealing with this type of situation.

PAYMENT CARD RECONCILIATION

An important part of ensuring an operation's profit is **reconciliation**. Reconciliation is the process of matching recorded sales against actual payments received. Guest check payments such as cash, checks, card transactions, or gift certificates are situations involving direct guest contact and, therefore, components of customer service. Credit or debit card

---

THINK ABOUT IT . . .

Have you ever had your credit or debit card information stolen? What did you have to do about it?

THINK ABOUT IT . . .

Has your credit or debit card ever been declined when you tried to use it? How did that make you feel? What did you do?

Exhibit 7.3

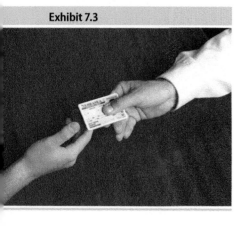

reconciliation requires money to be correctly accounted for, including properly accounting for servers' tips included on cards.

Also, mistakes can happen in all forms of payment processing, including credit or debit card processing. Therefore, it is important to reconcile daily card transactions with receipts kept by cashiers or servers to compare the dollar value and quantity reported per server or per register readings.

Reconciling credit or debit cards is easy if there are no mistakes or fraud. However, that is not always the case. Staff members who handle credit or debit card transactions should be trained on preventing card abuse. Managers must ensure that servers and cashiers follow specific procedures:

- Check personal identification when taking cards if that is the operation's policy.
- Check to see that the card is signed.
- Check to see that the signature on the card reasonably matches the signature on the personal identification.
- Check that the card's expiration date has not passed.

Checks

Staff members who receive payments should also be trained on handling payments by personal check. The fact that checks are being used less frequently makes this training even more important than in the past. Proper personal check handling practices require specific actions:

- Accept checks only for the amount of the purchase.
- Checks must have the guest's current address and phone number printed on them.
- Do not accept temporary, second-party, or payroll checks.
- Two forms of identification must be provided.
- Once accepted, all checks must be immediately stamped with the bank deposit stamp.
- Establish a policy for out-of-area checks.

Managers are responsible for policies and procedures for accepting personal checks. There are specific procedures that must be in place when a personal check is offered as payment:

1. Cashier takes specific steps when a check is offered as payment:
   - Verify that the amount covers the guest check amount.
   - Verify that the check is signed.
   - Ask for two picture IDs and compare the picture and signature with the customer's (*Exhibit 7.3*).

2. Take the personal and guest checks in a secure and private carrying device, such as the guest check folder, to the POS system or cash register.

3. When processing the personal check payment:

   • Keep the personal and guest checks near each other, and with the server.

   • Do not let others see the personal check account number.

4. Follow the personal check processing procedures for the operation's cash register or POS system. It is important that both the guest check amount and the payment amounts match in the system.

5. Return any receipts to the person paying the check.

6. Thank the customer for his or her business and complete the remaining goodbye protocol of your operation.

7. Leave the table so the guest can leave a tip in private.

There are important issues that commonly occur when dealing with personal checks:

   • Out-of-town checks

   • Second-party checks

   • Identification verification

Managers should ensure their operations' specific procedures for these issues are thoroughly covered in staff training. In addition to training staff on check payment policies and procedures, guests should also know an operation's check payment policies. Guests are typically notified via a sign near the cash register or a notice on the menu. In establishing the check payment policy, managers must be sensitive to their customers. In some settings, an outright policy of not accepting any checks may offend some guests. In other settings it may be best not to accept personal checks as an authorized form of payment.

Other Payment Forms

In addition to cash, payment cards, and checks, many operations accept additional forms of payment:

   • Gift certificates

   • Gift cards

   • Promotional coupons

   • Frequent diner program redemptions

Each of these payment forms may have special handling requirements:

Gift certificates: The amount of the gift certificate tendered by guests should be clearly indicated on the certificate. The expiration date should be checked to ensure that the certificate is still valid.

Manager's Memo

Traveler's checks are a special form of payment often used by international travelers. Managers establish specific procedures for acceptance of this payment form:

   • Advise the guest of the amount owed.

   • Tell the check holder the name he or she should make the check out to.

   • Ask the guest to provide his or her signature in the designated area of the traveler's check. The signature must be completed in the cashier's presence. If the customer has already signed the check, have him or her sign it again on the back.

   • Compare the second signature that was done in your presence to the original signature on the check. If the signatures do not match, do not accept the traveler's check.

   • Provide the customer with change (if any).

   • Treat the traveler's check like cash.

Manager's Memo

Every operation should establish a standard payment-handling process for cash, checks, and payment cards.

A proper cash-handling process includes the following:

- Establishing a cash drawer amount based on average check size, ease of replenishing the drawer, and proportion of guests who pay with cash, among other factors.
- Reducing the amount of cash in the register periodically to the established amount.
- Limiting cash register access.
- Instructing staff to immediately notify the manager of any suspicious activity.
- Exchanging and balancing the cash drawer at every shift change.
- Instructing staff to complete each transaction before beginning another. For example, if a guest requests change for a $20 bill while paying for a meal, the payment transaction should be completed before making change.
- Closing the cash drawer between transactions and when not in use.
- Taking periodic cash register readings to record and monitor actual cash sales amounts.

Gift cards: Gift cards are issued in various amounts. In some cases change will be returned to guests. In other operations the amount of change will remain on the card.

Promotional coupons: Promotional coupons may include "dollars off the purchase" as well as others that provide for "free" items, "two for ones," or other discounts. In all cases, these should be entered in the POS and retained in the cash register as if they were cash payments.

Frequent diner program redemptions: Frequent diner programs are used to increase customer loyalty and provide an incentive to customers who purchase a specified number of meals or items or visit a restaurant a required number of times (see chapter 8 for more details). In most cases redemptions of program awards are made by guests at a time of their own choosing. In these cases, the redemptions by guests of free menu items or even free meals must be properly recorded in the POS and in the records of the frequent diner program.

How these various forms of payment are recorded in an operation's POS and accounting system can vary. In some cases they are considered to be current revenue as of the date of sale. In other cases they may be considered as a debt owed to the guest until the payment form is redeemed. Either method has accounting implications. The procedures for redeeming these payment forms will depend on a manager's preferred system, which must be taught to all cashiers.

PAYMENT FOR TAKE-AWAY, DELIVERY, AND DRIVE-THROUGH ORDERS

Take-away, delivery, and drive-through orders are popular alternative dining methods. They bring an opportunity for additional revenue and profit. Also with them come more opportunities for cashier mistakes, abuse, and theft. To ensure customer satisfaction and profitability, the following order placement and production systems should be in place and consistently used:

- A POS system that can accommodate these types of sales
- Staff training on the POS system and procedures for these orders
- Procedures for confirming orders made via regular phone, smartphone application, fax, text message, tweet, and email
- A way to get the orders to the kitchen staff
- A way to get prepared orders and information about their pickup or delivery to the servers who will package them
- A system for storing and identifying these orders between packaging and delivery or pickup

To ensure proper guest payment collection and recording, the following procedures should be in place and consistently used:

- Policies, procedures, and systems for collecting payment for deliveries, including cash, checks, and credit or debit cards

- A procedure for getting money paid to delivery staff back to the operation and properly matched to the order in the POS system

- Procedures to confirm that deliveries were received and drive-through and take-away orders were picked up

Cell phones and other advanced technology systems are driving forces in the popularity of these alternative dining methods. POS systems address the technical aspects of take-away, delivery, and drive-through orders. However, a manager's staff should be properly trained to handle these alternative methods. They should be trained on the previously mentioned systems and their procedures. They should also have additional skills, such as speaking with customers on the telephone. For example, assigning a designated employee to be responsible for take-away orders can be an effective way to reduce confusion.

RETURN INCENTIVES

Return incentives are an often overlooked area of good customer service. They are also an excellent source of potential added revenue. A return incentive is a tool used to give guests a good reason to come back in the future. Return incentives are also known as bounce backs because they help encourage guests to come back soon. A manager might create a return incentive to encourage guests to buy a specific menu item or to attend a special event. Managers can use return incentives to do a variety of important things:

- Invite guests back to buy, at a reduced price, a menu item they may not have already tried.

- Announce the date a new item will be added to the menu and invite customers to return then to try it.

- Encourage guests to return with one or more friends for a "Buy One, Get One Free" item.

- Give guests a specific reason to return. For example, offer them free appetizers with each dinner order.

- Give guests a reason to return on a specific day. For example, offer them reduced price appetizers on Monday.

- Give guests a specific reason to return at a specific time. For example, offer them reduced price appetizers daily between 4 p.m. and 6 p.m.

Bounce backs can be used to encourage guests to try new items or increase check averages. They can also help increase the number of people in a customer's dining party or increase the number of times a guest visits an operation.

Return incentives usually take the form of a printed handout given to guests upon departure. They are a low-cost and convenient way for most operations to increase future revenue and future profits.

GUEST DEPARTURE AND SERVICE QUALITY CONFIRMATION

It might seem that once guests have received their orders, finished their food, and paid their bills, the delivery of customer service is complete. In fact, managers must take several additional steps to ensure the consistent delivery of high-quality guest service. One of the first steps that must be undertaken is the development of an effective guest feedback program.

Guest Feedback Programs

A **guest feedback program** is a formal system for receiving and analyzing customers' assessments of an operation's service and product quality. To develop a formal guest feedback program, managers undertake specific tasks:

- Determine the type of feedback wanted.
- Determine the method of collection.
- Determine the type of measurement to use.
- Design the feedback tool.
- Produce program materials.

DETERMINE THE TYPE OF FEEDBACK WANTED

The specific type of feedback managers seek will depend on their operation's service style and goals. There are some common areas of customer assessment, however, that are of interest to most managers:

- Facility cleanliness
- Menu layout
- Menu selection
- Product quality
- Service timing
- Service quality

DETERMINE THE METHOD OF COLLECTION

Managers can obtain information about a customer's satisfaction level either through face-to-face questioning or through objective methods. As much as possible, managers should use objective methods of gathering data. Objective methods involve gathering information without using a person whose interpretation or memory of what was said could change the feedback. For example, an establishment might have a customer feedback form on its Web site (see *Exhibit 7.4*) that customers can use anonymously after they have been directed to this feedback opportunity.

There are several objective methods available to the restaurant or foodservice operation to gather information about how well they are serving their customers' needs and expectations. **Comment cards** solicit feedback from the guests about their dining experiences.

Comment cards can take many forms. Cards could be incorporated into the table setting, presented with the guest check, printed on the guest receipt, or made available online through a Web site. There are principles to be considered when using comment cards as part of an operation's guest feedback program:

- Comment card content should be limited and focused.

- Guests should be able to complete their comments in a short time.

- Guest's personal information may be necessary to allow managers to respond.

- Managers should retain comment cards for future reference and use.

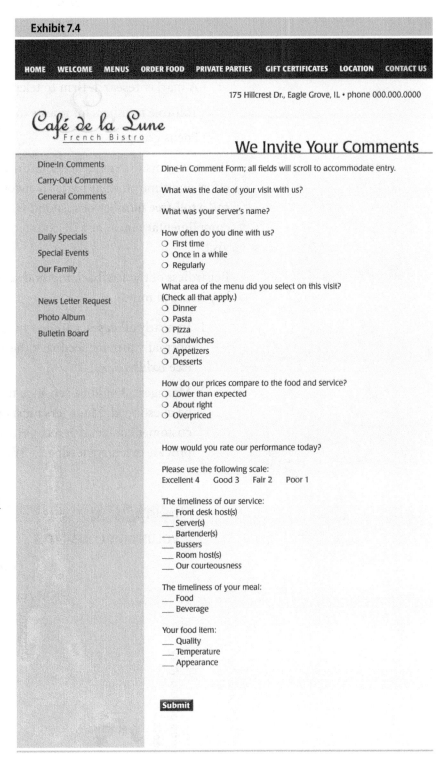

Exhibit 7.4

HOME   WELCOME   MENUS   ORDER FOOD   PRIVATE PARTIES   GIFT CERTIFICATES   LOCATION   CONTACT US

175 Hillcrest Dr., Eagle Grove, IL • phone 000.000.0000

Café de la Lune
French Bistro

We Invite Your Comments

Dine-In Comments
Carry-Out Comments
General Comments

Daily Specials
Special Events
Our Family

News Letter Request
Photo Album
Bulletin Board

Dine-in Comment Form; all fields will scroll to accommodate entry.

What was the date of your visit with us?

What was your server's name?

How often do you dine with us?
○ First time
○ Once in a while
○ Regularly

What area of the menu did you select on this visit?
(Check all that apply.)
○ Dinner
○ Pasta
○ Pizza
○ Sandwiches
○ Appetizers
○ Desserts

How do our prices compare to the food and service?
○ Lower than expected
○ About right
○ Overpriced

How would you rate our performance today?

Please use the following scale:
Excellent 4   Good 3   Fair 2   Poor 1

The timeliness of our service:
___ Front desk host(s)
___ Server(s)
___ Bartender(s)
___ Bussers
___ Room host(s)
___ Our courteousness

The timeliness of your meal:
___ Food
___ Beverage

Your food item:
___ Quality
___ Temperature
___ Appearance

Submit

Objective methods can be used along with less objective methods such as direct customer interaction, discussions with individual service staff, and discussions at staff meetings.

Larger operations, such as chain restaurants, may use more far-reaching methods:

- Mystery shoppers, also called secret shoppers or just shoppers, who are consultants or employees who visit an operation, act as normal guests, and secretly report to managers on the food, service, facility, and their overall experience
- A market research firm to telephone customers and get their feedback
- Toll-free numbers for guests to call and discuss their dining experiences
- Focus groups

For customers to provide feedback through the phone or a Web site takes effort and time on their part. To encourage customers who take the time to call a toll-free number or respond via a Web site, some operations offer a complimentary meal or a discounted entrée or other menu item on a return visit.

Regardless of the feedback method selected for use, managers must keep two key issues in mind:

1. In nearly all cases, a higher proportion of people with complaints will normally provide feedback than those with neutral or positive attitudes (see *Exhibit 7.5*).
2. Managers should be sensitive to how much external customers want to be questioned. Managers must ensure that all staff with external customer contact can recognize a guest's cues that they do not want to provide extensive feedback. Training can help provide skills in this area.

Exhibit 7.5

VOLUNTARY COMMENTS

		Customer Opinion of Product or Service						
		Outstanding	Excellent	Very Good	Average	Poor	Bad	Awful
Likelihood of Voluntary Comments	Often					✕	✕	✕
	Sometimes	✕						
	Rarely		✕	✕	✕			

Voluntary comments tend to be biased toward the negative.

DETERMINE THE TYPE OF MEASUREMENT TO USE

The type of measurement used in a guest feedback system can vary. There are several popular forms:

- **Grades:** Feedback based on customers grading an operation using grades of A to F
- **Categories or rankings:** Excellent, Average, or Below Average, for example (see *Exhibit 7.6*)
- **Numerical Scales:** Feedback based on a scale of 1 to 10, with 1 being low and 10 being high
- **Symbols:** The awarding by guests of one to five Stars, Diamonds, Forks, or other symbols

The type of measurement selected for use should be easy for customers to understand and use and provide data that are easy for managers to interpret.

Exhibit 7.6

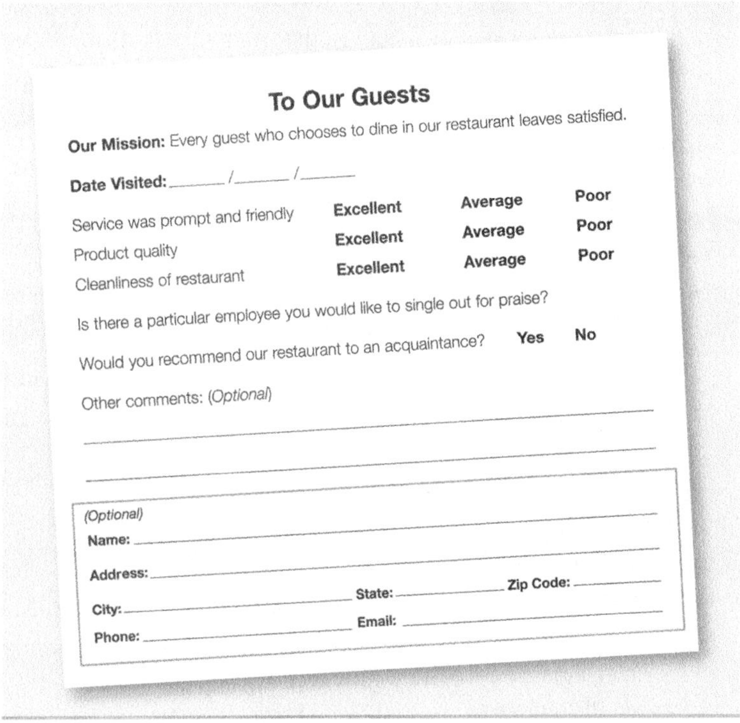

To Our Guests

Our Mission: Every guest who chooses to dine in our restaurant leaves satisfied.

Date Visited: _____ / _____ / _____

Service was prompt and friendly	Excellent	Average	Poor
Product quality	Excellent	Average	Poor
Cleanliness of restaurant	Excellent	Average	Poor

Is there a particular employee you would like to single out for praise?

Would you recommend our restaurant to an acquaintance?   Yes   No

Other comments: (*Optional*)

_____

_____

(*Optional*)

Name: _____

Address: _____

City: _____ State: _____ Zip Code: _____

Phone: _____ Email: _____

DESIGN THE FEEDBACK TOOL

Designing a feedback tool simply requires managers to incorporate all of the elements listed earlier. The feedback tool should include the identified areas of feedback interest, the collection method to be used, and the chosen measurement system when creating their operation's comment card format. In many cases managers will employ the services of a professional graphic designer or software specialist to create the actual feedback document. This may include creating attractive hardcopy surveys as well as feedback tools appropriate for delivery and return by email.

PRODUCE PROGRAM MATERIALS

Producing the actual materials needed for an effective guest feedback program requires managers to address several key areas:

- Printing of on-premise distributed comment cards in the desired size and number
- Printing of off-premise distributed comment cards or guest surveys in the desired size and number
- Design of Web site posted or other electronically delivered versions of feedback-related materials
- Design of versions suitable for email delivery and return

Manager's Memo

One of the easiest methods of soliciting external customer feedback is by simply asking for it. Servers should check with guests a few minutes after serving any beverage or food to see whether it is satisfactory. The guest should not be forced to wait very long to report a problem. Frequently, guests will request some small addition, such as butter or another eating utensil needed to make their meals more enjoyable. When addressed quickly, servers can easily turn these potential negative issues into positives.

Managers stop at tables to ask how everything is going. Doing so not only gives the guest an opportunity to comment on the menu items and service, but it also gives the guest an opportunity to meet the manager. The manager can discuss with guests ways to change or improve the operation, such as with the menu, décor, service levels, and other areas of importance.

Experienced managers know that face-to-face questioning is good for uncovering immediate problems or for getting a rough idea of the level of customer satisfaction. However, people do not usually like to report minor problems or dissatisfactions. Instead, customers will tend to say that everything is "OK" or "fine." This means managers should give only moderate weight to in-person feedback and should also use more objective methods of gaining feedback to get the most complete picture of their guests' views of service levels.

Analyzing Feedback Data

After managers have developed their guest feedback programs, they must manage those programs. To do so, they implement specific steps:

1. **Review the guest feedback program:** Managers review their programs to ensure that each of the steps required to develop them properly has been completed.

2. **Train employees:** Managers must train employees so each staff member understands his or her role in the guest feedback collection process.

3. **Distribute program materials:** Managers distribute the feedback collection materials needed to operate the program to employees, who will then give them to guests. Managers may also elect to distribute feedback materials directly to guests. Direct distribution to guests can take several forms:

   • Placement on dining tables

   • Presentation with guest checks or in guest check folders

   • Placement at exit points in the operation

   • Online posting for direct guest access

4. **Collect data from guests:** After feedback collection materials have been distributed to guests, managers must have a system in place to collect the completed feedback tools. This may include having a designated space in the manager's office to store returned hardcopy surveys until they can be properly analyzed. It may also mean designating specific guest feedback folders on the manager's computer. The contents of the folders are then readily available to be reviewed on a regularly scheduled basis.

5. **Analyze the data:** On a regular basis, managers must compile and analyze the feedback received from customers. This is one of the most critical parts of the management of guest feedback programs.

6. **Summarize the information and distribute it to key stakeholders:** Many staff members will likely be interested in the feedback received from guests. For example, chefs and kitchen managers will be

interested in feedback related to food quality. Dining area supervisors will be interested in feedback related to service levels (*Exhibit 7.7*).

Exhibit 7.7

7. **Revise the guest feedback program as needed:** Over time, managers may find that their feedback systems can be improved. The addition of new questions (e.g., "How was the quality of our WiFi service?") may be dictated by changes in customer wants and needs. Changes in how surveys are distributed, collected, and reviewed may also be undertaken as managers work to continually improve their guest feedback systems.

As stated, after managers have gathered guest feedback, they must analyze the data. Doing so will allow them to improve their operations' menus, food quality, or service processes. In most cases, failing to analyze and act on feedback can make bad situations worse. Most people, including guests, are unhappy to learn that nothing was done with their feedback. As a result, analysis and taking action should be a part of every manager's feedback plan.

One goal of analysis is to identify areas that need improvement. Another is to prioritize potential improvements in terms of costs and benefits. Analysis can also indicate areas that could be models to use in other aspects of customer service. Customer feedback is very valuable information. If used properly, it can mean the difference between good customer service and exceptional customer service.

In some cases, a market research firm or consultant will conduct market research. Statistical analysis systems (SASs) are used to tabulate and collate research data. The data are used to develop a research report. SAS procedures use descriptive analysis methods to analyze data. Descriptive analysis uses data to describe the average or typical respondent, and to what degree the person currently responding varies from the typical respondent.

The two most often used analysis methods are frequencies and means. The frequencies method tabulates and counts the frequency of responses to each question on a research instrument. Here is a typical question a manager might ask his or her guests:

How many times in an average month do you dine away from home?

- **Less than 4 times**
- **5–10 times**
- **11–15 times**
- **16–20 times**
- **More than 20 times**

The frequencies method counts how many times or how frequently each of the possible responses is selected. Frequencies can be provided as raw numbers, percentages, a combination of the two, or in a manager's preferred customized format.

The means method provides information about the mean, or average, number of responses to a variable. Standard deviation of a variable is another data analysis tool that can be determined using the means method. A standard deviation measures how far a response is from the mean.

Whatever analysis method is used, the first step is usually to count the data. Typically, the data are grouped into useful segments such as by menu item or meal period. This may also include time of day, day of week, month, or season. For example, a manager might have collected data about the following menu items:

- Hamburgers
- Pan fish
- Prime rib
- Roast pork

The manager may determine that the most useful time period to track these data is by the day of the week. The manager organizes the data into a table when counting the results, as shown in *Exhibit 7.8*.

Exhibit 7.8

TABULATED CUSTOMER SATISFACTION DATA

Menu Item	Sun		Mon		Tue		Wed		Thu		Fri		Sat	
	Good	Bad	Good	Bad	Good	Bad	Good	Bad	Good	Bad	Good	Bad	Good	Bad
Hamburger	16	7	22	9	18	3	26	1	14	3	28	5	26	8
Pan fish	11	1	18	1	25	2	19	1	22	2	19	6	12	9
Prime rib	47	1	4	24	12	4	19	2	34	2	41	3	44	2
Roast pork	33	3	30	19	18	4	27	2	29	2	36	3	35	1

Although the data are in a table, they can be difficult to understand and use. The easiest way to gain value from these data is to graph it. Graphs are great for tracking trends and cycles and making unusual data understandable. However, a manager may not want to graph all of the data in the table because that could be very confusing. Rather, the manager selects the parts he or she wants to better understand and then graphs only those data. In this example the manager wants to see how the prime rib does throughout the week at dinner, as illustrated in *Exhibit 7.9.*

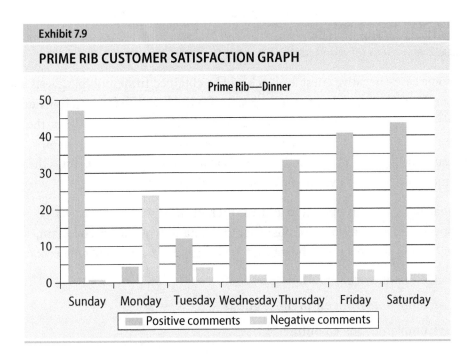

Exhibit 7.9

PRIME RIB CUSTOMER SATISFACTION GRAPH

The graph shows that prime rib grows in popularity from Monday through Sunday. Note also, however, that the bad comments far outweigh the good comments on Monday. This should alert the manager to some problems with this menu item on Monday. When the manager investigates, he or she may find that the operation was serving leftovers from Sunday, and they are not well received. Whatever the reason, the manager is now aware of a potential problem and can find out what it is so it can be corrected.

When analyzing data from comment cards, it is important to keep in mind that more people will complete a comment card if they have had a poor experience than if they have had a positive experience. If a negative comment describes a situation that happens only rarely, it may simply indicate a one-time error. However, the manager should still investigate the comment and respond to the guest. Consistent negative comments usually indicate a more serious problem. The same is true if negative comments follow a pattern. The managers should investigate the comment and respond to the guest. The manager also may have to take action to revise a process or procedure to eliminate the problem.

SERVICE RECOVERY

Despite their best efforts, managers or their staff will, on occasion, receive direct negative feedback from guests. This feedback must be addressed and the method of doing so will vary depending on the circumstances of a guest's complaint. Service recovery is the process of identifying the cause of negative guest feedback or complaints and ensuring the circumstances that caused the dissatisfaction are corrected.

In some cases, negative guest feedback will be obtained from multiple guests and about the same situation. In other cases, the feedback will be from an individual guest and about a problem encountered only by that guest. In these cases, the guest complaint may be received when the guest is still in the operation or, because the Internet has become such a popular way for guests to express their opinions about an operation, the complaint may be posted online.

Managers must be prepared to address each of these varied situations properly. To do so managers must first understand why guests complain. They then must determine how best to address specific areas of concern:

- Complaints from multiple guests
- Complaints from on-premise guests
- Complaints posted online

Understanding Guest Complaints

Most managers have heard the expression "the customer is always right." This is not always true, but most customers believe it to be. That is why customers complain when they are dissatisfied. As a result, managers must use good service recovery techniques to respond to guest complaints in ways that consistently return customers to a high level of satisfaction.

Managers often find that customer complaints are the result of poor communication. Based on the amount of information the customer has at the time, their problem or complaint is probably valid. Providing the customer with a thorough explanation of the menu, ensuring that new customers are familiar with how the establishment operates, and training all employees to consistently communicate accurate information to customers helps minimize communication errors and complaints and to speed service recovery.

Even with excellent communication, some customer complaints and problems can occur. Organizations with a reputation for excellent service recovery, however, have distinct characteristics:

- There are standards and guidelines for each specific type of situation.
- The entire staff is trained on how to handle customer complaints.
- The staff has a high level of product knowledge.

- The first staff member who is made aware of the complaint is considered its "owner."

- An environment exists where staff are empowered (see chapter 4) and trusted to do what is right for the customer and the organization.

Exhibit 7.10

Important management actions can help ensure guest complaints are resolved properly:

- Establish a clear policy of who is responsible for handling complaints on each shift. Some operations choose the on-duty manager or shift supervisor. Others set a policy that the person receiving the complaint (*Exhibit 7.10*) is its "owner" and is responsible for handling it.

- Support employees' decisions when they are empowered and authorized to resolve the complaints. Doing so develops the needed trust for empowered employees. If the employee's decisions could be improved, managers should respectfully make the employee aware of a more appropriate solution. They can do so either in group training or in private, depending on the sensitivity of the situation and the employee.

COMPLAINTS FROM MULTIPLE GUESTS

In some cases a guest feedback system will indicate that many guests are experiencing the same service- or product-related problem. For example, a manager may receive multiple and consistent complaints about the cleanliness of restrooms. In this case, feedback on the condition of the operation's restrooms may be obtained either from comment cards, from conversations with guests, or both. In all cases, when managers receive the same complaint from multiple guests, the managers must take specific action:

1. **Review guest feedback data:** The identification of a specific and recurring service issue is often the result of carefully reviewing guest feedback data received from customer comment cards or in-person conversations. When the same complaint reoccurs frequently, it must be immediately addressed by managers.

2. **Recognize employees for good work and compliments:** In some cases, managers will receive consistently positive feedback about a product or an employee. When an employee is the subject of repeated positive customer comments, that employee should be complimented for his or her efforts.

3. **Identify operational changes or enhancements that may address specific issues:** When a specific problem area has been identified, managers must analyze their operations to determine what changes must be made to correct the problem. In some cases, menu items will need to be reviewed, service systems may need to be examined for modification, or current employee actions may need to be reassessed.

Exhibit 7.11

4. **Develop a plan to address needed changes or improvements:** After managers have assessed the problem area, they develop an improvement plan. The plan addresses the specific changes and improvements that must be implemented to remedy the problem.

5. **Retrain employees as needed:** In many cases, an operational change designed to correct a recurring guest service or product-related problem may require the retraining of service or production staff (see *Exhibit 7.11*). For example, new cooking methods may need to be used, new service techniques may need to be implemented, or changes in employee cleaning or other work assignments may need to be communicated in targeted training sessions.

6. **Implement operational changes:** After employees have been properly trained, managers can implement the changes designed to correct the recurring service or production problem. Managers then carefully evaluate the results of their improvement efforts to ensure that the recurring problem is no longer an issue that generates multiple customer complaints.

COMPLAINTS FROM ON-PREMISE GUESTS

In some cases, guests will voice a complaint to their servers or to a manager. There are proven ways servers and managers can best handle in-person complaints from guests:

- Listen to the guest.

- Treat the guest with courtesy and respect.

- Be patient and empathize with the guest.

- Paraphrase what appears to be the problem to confirm it with the guest. Servers and managers do this by saying, in their words, what they think they heard the guest say, and by describing the main details of the situation.

- Take responsibility for the situation and ownership for resolving the complaint.

- Offer a solution, explain to the guest what can be done to resolve the problem, or ask the guest how he or she wants the complaint to be resolved.

- If appropriate, record a brief description of the issue and the corrective course of action taken for future reference.

Staff can also apply proven techniques when concluding service recovery actions:

- Thank the guest for his or her concern and for bringing the issue to the attention of the operation.

- Thank the guest for being patient and request his or her future business.

In addition to the previous recommendations, *Exhibit 7.12* shows additional proven techniques for addressing customer complaints.

Exhibit 7.12

HANDLING CUSTOMER COMPLAINTS

Do	Don't
• Develop a written communication procedure for addressing complaints that are reported online, through company mail or email, or by other means. • Document how different complaints are resolved so employees learn from these real experiences. • Identify standards and guidelines for specific complaint situations. • Develop standard apology letters. • Determine reimbursement guidelines for each situation.	• Argue with the customer. • Embarrass the customer. • Accept responsibility verbally, or in writing, for a customer's injury or damage to property until properly investigated, and if necessary, insurance companies are contacted.

A well-trained staff is among a manager's best resources for resolving guest complaints. To reinforce skills in service recovery, some organizations regularly test staff on the menu, on service issues, on how to deal with customer complaints, on operational issues, and on other aspects of the business.

All employees should practice their service recovery skills on a regular basis. Staff meetings are a good time to discuss and practice handling customer complaints. Managers can take a few actual complaints and conduct a brief role-play where one employee acts as the customer and the other as the employee. Afterward, the manager can ask the staff if the complaint was handled well, or how the complaint could have been handled differently.

When training employees in service recovery, managers should also address staff safety, security, and any liability concerns and policies. They can also help employees practice in key areas of service recovery:

- Listening
- Being polite and empathetic
- Being genuine
- Acknowledging customer concerns
- Fixing the situation in the best way possible within their power
- Recognizing when situations cannot be fixed and apologizing appropriately

If all of the proper policies and procedures are in place, and all employees are thoroughly trained, an operation can successfully address on-premise customer complaints and recover well from them.

Have you ever posted a negative review of a restaurant or foodservice establishment online? Did the manager respond online to your posting with a sincere apology and a possible solution? How would you have reacted if he or she had done so?

COMMENTS POSTED ONLINE

Due to online social networks and the growing popularity of online restaurant reviews, the Internet has become a vehicle for customers to share comments about their dining experiences. While many postings describe positive experiences, a large number describe guests' negative service- or product-related experiences. When a negative guest comment is posted online, managers should respond to it if the Web site in question permits them to do so.

When responding, managers should ensure their responses are well written and have been carefully proofed to be grammatically correct. In their response to negative online postings, managers should do specific things:

- Start by thanking the reviewer. In this way, the manager's response always begins on a positive note.

- Apologize to the guest. Simply stating "We're sorry" is always a good way to show the reviewer you truly care about the incident that caused their dissatisfaction.

- Explain what happened. This section need not be long, but can help readers better understand what caused the problem. This section should address the "why" behind the complaint that was posted.

- Identify the solution. This section tells readers what the manager has done to help ensure this same problem will not occur in the future.

- Invite the person who posted the negative review to come again. This shows readers of the manager's response that the operation wants the chance to show it has improved and assures readers they will not likely experience the same problem if they visit the business.

- Close by again thanking the person who posted the review. This ensures the manager's response ends, as it started, on a positive note.

Some online review sites allow managers to post positive comments from other customers who have given official permission to do so. When managers can do that, it is possible to turn social media sites into a powerful source of positive advertising, even if the site also contains some less than positive comments about their operations.

SUMMARY

1. **Explain the importance of implementing a professional guest payment system.**

   A professional guest payment system is essential because an operation must collect all of the money it has legitimately earned from the sale of its products. A professional payment system minimizes the chances for employees to take advantage of deficiencies in the operation's payment collection procedures to defraud customers or the business. It also helps prevent customers from defrauding the operation. In addition, a poorly implemented payment system may result in errors that can cause customers to question an operation's commitment to high levels of customer service. Finally, the absence of an effective payment collection system may result in an operation's inability to receive all the money needed to pay its bills and achieve its profit goals.

2. **Identify the most commonly accepted forms of guest payment.**

   Customers in the restaurant and foodservice industry use a variety of methods for bill payment. In many operations, cash is a primary payment method. Increasingly, however, guests use payment cards to pay their bills, even in the QSR and fast-casual segments of the industry. Today, fewer operations accept personal checks. However, personal checks and traveler's checks are still an important form of payment in some operations. Other payment forms for which managers must train cashiers include gift certificates of various denominations, and prepaid gift cards. These must be processed according to the operation's approved payment acceptance procedures. In some operations, promotional coupons and frequent diner program redemptions represent payment forms with which an operation's cashiers must be familiar.

3. **List the steps to develop an effective guest feedback program.**

   To develop an effective guest feedback program, managers must first determine the type of feedback wanted. This can include feedback related to issues such as cleanliness, food quality, and service quality. Next, managers determine the method(s) of information collection they will use. These can include printed comments cards and guest surveys as well as feedback collected via Internet-based collection tools. Managers then develop a measuring system such as a ranking, symbol, or descriptive term that is easy for customers to understand and use, and easy for managers to analyze. Finally, managers must design and produce the tools they will use to collect customer feedback.

4. **List the steps to manage an effective guest feedback program.**

   To manage their guest feedback programs well, managers first review the programs to help ensure each of the steps required in their development has been completed. They then train their staff so all employees understand their role in the guest feedback collection process. Next, program materials are distributed to the employees for presentation to guests, or the materials are given directly to guests. Direct distribution to guests may include placement on tables, presentation with guest checks, placement at exit points in the operation, or the online posting of materials. Managers then collect and analyze the guest-supplied feedback on a regularly scheduled basis.

5. **Summarize the procedures managers use to address areas of recurring guest complaints.**

   If managers receive the same complaint from multiple guests, they must take specific action. First, they review feedback to identify the problem causing the complaints. If the recurring comment is positive, managers share the comments with employees; however, when a recurring problem is identified, managers analyze their operations to identify needed changes. They then develop an improvement plan to correct the problem. In many cases, the implementation of an operational change may first require the retraining of service or production staff. After employees have been properly trained, managers implement the change designed to correct the recurring problem, and carefully monitor the result of their improvement efforts to ensure the problem has been resolved.

6. **Describe the process that staff and managers should use when responding to on-premise guest complaints.**

When resolving guest complaints in an operation, staff and managers must listen carefully. They must always remember to treat guests with courtesy and respect. Guests will likely be upset in these situations, but staff and managers should always be patient and empathize with the guest. They should summarize their understanding of the problem and then confirm that understanding with the guest. Just as important, they must take responsibility for the situation and take ownership of the guest's complaint. They can do so by offering a solution, by explaining to the guest what can be done to resolve the problem, or by asking the guest how he or she feels the problem can best be resolved.

APPLICATION EXERCISE

We Hear Your Feedback!

Obtain permission from a restaurant or foodservice operation to collect or make copies of some of its guest comment cards to analyze and discuss in class. Collect these cards over a period of one week or more. The objective is to collect cards that cover each day part, or meal period, and day of the week.

After reviewing the cards, separate them into any number of categories, such as day of the week, meal period, references to menu, staff, cleanliness, and so on. For each category, count the number of positive and negative comments. Keep in mind that guests tend to comment when they have not been satisfied, so the ratio of negative to positive comments is not as important as the repeated occurrence of a particular comment.

After categorizing the comment cards, analyze the data. What are the comments telling you about the business? Is there a particular day that seems significant for one reason or another? Is there a theme? What are the positive comments saying? What are the negative comments saying? In some cases, things will be obvious; in others, you may have to really think about it. Do not limit or predetermine what the cards are telling you about the business.

Based on the collected data, try to reach some conclusions. From these conclusions, develop a list of those conclusions that need improvement, and of those that should be modeled. Prepare a report documenting what you did, what you found out, and your interpretations.

Based on all you have learned, make a list of actions you would take if you were the manager.

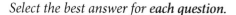

REVIEW YOUR LEARNING

Select the best answer for each question.

1. **What would be the most likely result of a failure to properly process guest payments in a restaurant or foodservice operation?**
   A. Revenue will be overcollected.
   B. Revenue will be undercollected.
   C. Operating costs will be overstated.
   D. Operating costs will be understated.

2. **How can quick-change artists succeed in defrauding an operation?**
   A. By skipping their bills
   B. By confusing cashiers
   C. By paying the amounts they owe with very large bills
   D. By paying the amounts they owe with very small bills

3. What will be the result if an employee voids a sale and then removes the same amount of the void from a cash drawer?

A. The cash drawer will be in balance.

B. The cash drawer will be out of balance.

C. The cash drawer will show a cash overage.

D. The cash drawer will show a cash shortage.

4. What will be the result if a guest owes an operation $10 and pays with a $20 bill, but the cashier mistakenly gives the customer change back from a $50 bill?

A. The cash drawer will show a cash overage of $10.

B. The cash drawer will show a cash shortage of $10.

C. The cash drawer will show a cash overage of $30.

D. The cash drawer will show a cash shortage of $30.

5. What is the purpose of the guest check folder?

A. To record guest orders

B. To deliver guest orders to production staff

C. To present guest checks and return guest change

D. To ensure the accurate calculation of guest checks

6. What is a required characteristic of all professional mystery shoppers?

A. They must announce their presence.

B. They must do their work anonymously.

C. They must have previous experience as a server.

D. They must have previous management experience.

7. What is the first step in the effective management of a professional guest feedback program?

A. Reviewing guest feedback

B. Developing plans to address needed changes

C. Recognizing service employees for their good work

D. Identifying operational changes to address specific issues

8. What is a good technique managers can use in staff meetings to allow employees to practice their ability to resolve on-premise guest complaints?

A. Reading

B. Lecturing

C. Role-playing

D. Showing videos

9. What must managers always avoid when resolving on-premise customer complaints?

A. Paraphrasing the guests

B. Arguing with the guests

C. Empathizing with the guests' complaint

D. Taking ownership of the guests' complaint

10. What should managers include first when preparing their written response to a negative restaurant review about their operation that has been posted online?

A. An apology to the reviewer

B. A thank you to the reviewer for the posting

C. A summary of what happened to the reviewer

D. An invitation to the reviewer to come back again

FIELD **PROJECT**

Get a copy of the credit or debit card payment procedure at a local restaurant or foodservice establishment, or review the procedure with the manager.

On a separate sheet of paper, write a summary of the procedure and then make suggestions for improvements. Talk to other students in your class to compare and contrast the different credit card and debit card payment procedures that were obtained.

Complete this activity by creating a model credit card and debit card payment procedure you could use in an establishment you will manage in the future.

8 Marketing the Positive Guest Service Experience

INSIDE THIS CHAPTER

- Commitment to Service
- Marketing a Commitment to Service
- Off-Premise Communication of Service Commitment
- On-Premise Communication of Service Commitment
- Frequent Diner Programs
- Management Assessment of Service Quality
- Ensuring Ongoing Quality Service

CHAPTER LEARNING OBJECTIVES

After completing this chapter, you should be able to:

- Explain the importance of high-quality customer service to the marketing of a restaurant or foodservice operation.

- Summarize the advantages of using a systems management approach when operating a business.

- Describe the tools managers can use to communicate their service commitment to off-premise customers.

- List the steps required to develop and execute an effective on-premise suggestive selling program.

- Explain the importance of service recovery to the successful management of a restaurant or foodservice operation.

- Discuss the impact of high-quality customer service on the success of frequent diner programs.

- Explain the steps used to objectively measure service quality in a restaurant or foodservice operation.

KEY TERMS

advertising, p. 191

cross-functional issues, p. 187

cross-training, p. 189

marketing, p. 191

objective measure, p. 202

personal selling, p. 196

publicity, p. 194

public relations (PR), p. 195

sales promotions, p. 193

subjective measure, p. 204

supportive processes, p. 188

systems management approach, p. 186

VIP, p. 201

CASE STUDY

"What are you working on?" asked Rick, the chef at Luca's. Luca's is an Italian restaurant known for its brick oven–baked pizzas and freshly made salads.

Rick was talking to Maureen, the restaurant's new general manager, who was working in her office.

"I'm working on an ad for the local paper that I want to run this weekend," Maureen replied.

"That sounds good," Rick said. "How's it going?"

"Well, I'm not sure," Maureen said. "I want to create an ad that will draw new customers to our restaurant. All of our past ads have featured our oven-baked pizzas, and that's good. But we've been doing that for a long time and I want to try something new. Something that will make people who have not been here before stop in and give us a try."

"Well, if you don't want to feature our pizza, what do you want to highlight in the ad?" Rick asked.

"Actually, I'm thinking of featuring you," Maureen said, "and our outstanding staff."

1. Do you think guests seek out excellent service as well as good food when they consider their dining-out options? Explain your answer.

2. What do you think Maureen could say in her ad that could encourage guests seeking outstanding service levels to give her operation a try?

Exhibit 8.1

COMMITMENT TO SERVICE

An objective of every business should be to satisfy customers by providing high-quality customer service. There is a lot more to creating customer satisfaction than serving food at the right temperature in an appealing environment.

High-quality customer service means consistently exceeding customers' expectations for products and services. It requires personal attention and interaction during the delivery of service. Personal attention and interaction creates value for the customer and profit for the operation (see *Exhibit 8.1*). There are four main parts required for the delivery of high-quality service:

- Identifying customer expectations
- Consistently exceeding customer expectations
- Providing products and services that create value for the customer
- Creating profit for the organization

These four parts of high-quality customer service cannot be achieved automatically or easily. To successfully provide quality customer service, managers must develop, implement, and manage a high-quality customer service system that addresses all four parts (see *Exhibit 8.2*). In the restaurant and foodservice industry, this is most effectively accomplished via a systems management approach.

Exhibit 8.2

ACHIEVING HIGH-QUALITY CUSTOMER SERVICE

Create profits

Identify customer expectations

Design, implement, and manage a system to:

Provide products and services

Exceed customer expectations

Systems Management Approach

A **systems management approach** looks at the activities in an operation as a group of different processes. Each process is made up of tasks that work together to meet the objectives of each process and the whole operation. Effective restaurant and foodservice establishments use many different processes every day. Each process consists of specific tasks that are done to the operation's standards to achieve the desired results. There are many examples of specific processes used in an operation:

- Reservation management
- Dining-room management
- Purchasing
- Inventory management
- Food preparation
- Service management

The tasks that make up processes are usually the activities completed by an operation's staff members. For example, a typical task in a reservation management process is to record a reservation. Properly performing each task helps operations meet the goals of each individual process. To effectively manage a high-quality customer service system, managers must understand several things:

- How the system works

- All of the steps in the process

- The ways processes depend on each other

- How each task contributes to its process

- The expectations of customers

- What happens if customers are dissatisfied and do not perceive value in the dining experience

- Worker needs, because ignoring these needs may result in a loss of productivity or excessive employee turnover

The goal of a high-quality customer service system is to consistently exceed customer expectations. Therefore, the processes in that system must also include the four parts required for the delivery of high-quality customer service that were identified previously. A key characteristic of systems management is that processes affect each other. In most cases, managers have cross-functional knowledge and experience either from their own operational background or from management training. As a result, they know about the different processes and tasks in their operations and how they work. They must also understand how all the processes and their tasks depend on each other.

Knowing how cross-functional processes work together is one of the first steps needed to recognize areas in need of improvement. For example, assume a server gives an incorrect order to the kitchen, and, therefore, the wrong entrée is being prepared. As a result, the guest experiences a negative moment of truth when the server delivers the wrong meal. In a positive example of a moment of truth, assume the customer requests a rib-eye steak topped with an infrequently ordered sauce, and the kitchen prepares the dish perfectly. As a result the customer experiences a positive moment of truth when his or her flawlessly prepared rib-eye steak arrives at the table.

Managers must be able to recognize cross-functional issues to correct problems at the source. Cross-functional issues result from a breakdown in a process that can be traced to one or more interrelated employee tasks. Many problems can be traced to a breakdown in the system instead of the staff's expertise. For example, an unusually long service time may be the result of an item being under-stocked at the cook's station. The issue may not be because of the cook's skills. From a systems management view, the operation can perform well only when all of its systems function properly.

Supportive Processes and Profits

High levels of guest satisfaction lead to high profit levels. The service-profit chain in *Exhibit 8.3* shows how profit and revenue growth are linked in a high-quality customer service system. The service-profit chain shows when a business successfully implements appropriate supportive processes. Supportive processes are the elements in an establishment that impact an operation's

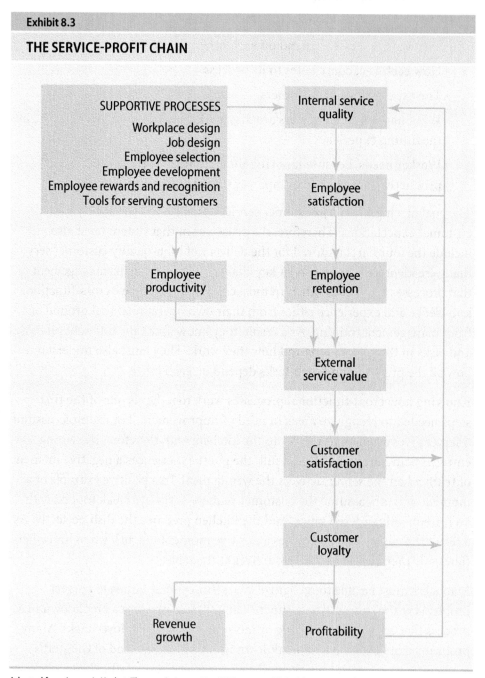

Exhibit 8.3

THE SERVICE-PROFIT CHAIN

Adapted from James L. Hasket, Thomas O. Jones, Gary W. Loveman, W. Earl Sasser Jr., and Leonard A. Schlesinger, "Putting the Service-Profit Chain to Work," *Harvard Business Review* (March–April 1994) : 166.

internal customers to help them perform their jobs well and be satisfied at work. When an operation's supportive processes work well, the result is internal service quality that leads to external service value for guests. *Exhibit 8.3* also shows some of the specific processes that support the high-quality customer service system.

There are several distinct types of supportive processes:

- **Workplace design:** Environmental conditions, safety issues, traffic flow, employee spaces such as locker rooms, restrooms, and break rooms as well as the look and feel of these back-of-the-house areas

- **Job design:** Job processes, work assignments, required tools and equipment, and detailed descriptions of each employee's work assignment

- **Employee selection and employee development:** Policies and practices for recruitment, hiring, placement, training, and employee retention

- **Employee rewards and recognition:** Wages, benefits, incentive programs, personal recognition—such as monthly birthday parties, reward certificates, and contests—and managerial practices (*Exhibit 8.4*)

- **Tools for serving customers:** Uniforms, properly maintained equipment, **cross-training** in which an employee learns how to do work normally done by someone in a different position, service skills training, and processes used to determine customers' expectations and to evaluate customer service

Exhibit 8.4

Supportive processes directly affect the internal service quality component in the service-profit chain. Internal service quality is the degree to which managers provide needed elements to keep internal customers satisfied. Higher-quality supportive processes lead to high-quality internal service quality, which increases employee satisfaction. The following are descriptions of some key components in the service-profit chain.

- **Internal service quality:** Employees are happy in their jobs when the workplace is pleasant to work in, they have the right tools, their skills and careers are developed, and they receive good rewards and recognition.

- **Employee satisfaction:** Good internal customer service, as provided by the supportive processes, leads to satisfied employees. They spend little time complaining, develop greater skills, and are able to do their jobs better.

- **Employee retention:** A satisfied employee is more productive and stays on the job longer, turning it into a career. A satisfied employee is less likely to look for alternate work. Satisfied employees are effective workers who stay and do not have to be replaced. This eliminates the costs of locating, hiring, and training new employees.

- **Employee productivity:** Productive, long-term employees provide a higher level of service at a reduced cost over time. This is because they have higher skills and interest levels than unsatisfied employees.

These four components make up the employee satisfaction portion of the chain. Managers can greatly influence and control these components in their operations.

The following additional components of the service-profit chain illustrate how satisfied employees tend to provide better service for guests. Guests then perceive more value and satisfaction in the products and services they buy, which will translate into higher profits for an operation.

- **Service value:** The higher levels of service provided by productive, long-term employees yield greater value for a business's external customers—those who buy the business's products and services. These employees have greater expertise in helping customers select food and beverage items that will provide a better dining experience because they are good at service and personal interactions. This improved dining experience will give guests more pleasure and better value.

- **Customer satisfaction:** Customers who receive better service are more satisfied. They feel more appreciated, and like the higher-quality service they receive. They also feel they are getting more for their money.

- **Customer loyalty:** Satisfied customers are more loyal. They return often to the establishment, tell others or bring them, and increase the establishment's customer base.

- **Revenue growth:** Attracting more customers means increased overall revenue.

- **Profitability:** Profitability results when the components in the service-profit chain are achieved in a cost-effective way. For example, when customer loyalty increases, some expenses, such as advertising and marketing, will decrease.

THINK ABOUT IT . . .

Have you ever visited a restaurant or foodservice operation primarily because of a specific employee who worked there? Do you think others have done the same? Why?

Satisfied employees are an important key to the consistent delivery of high-quality guest service and high levels of profitability. Having satisfied employees is so important to the success of an operation that the *Nation's Restaurant News* and National Restaurant Association Educational Foundation have established the prestigious SPIRIT Awards program, which is sponsored by The Coca-Cola Company. These annual awards honor managers who truly understand that enhancing employee satisfaction ultimately leads to guest satisfaction.

MARKETING A COMMITMENT TO SERVICE

An operation's commitment to the delivery of high-quality customer service is a powerful marketing tool. Marketing is the formal process of telling and showing potential customers how their needs and wants will be met by a business. It includes the planning and execution of the concept, price, promotion, and distribution of products or services that influence the sales and customer buying decisions while satisfying the overall objectives of a business.

Managers help ensure that their service levels are consistently high by regularly and carefully reviewing guest experiences. These include when guests arrive, when they are greeted and seated, when they are served, when they pay their bills, and when they depart. Managers must control the guests' moments of truth at each of these critical service points. Then, managers can recognize any need for additional staff training or procedural revisions that must be implemented to meet the operation's quality service goals.

Restaurant and foodservice operations sell products, but they also deliver service. An establishment's product quality may be high, its facilities attractive, and its prices perceived to be fair. Yet, poor service quality will most often result in customers not coming back or recommending the establishment to others. For that reason, a high level of professional service is needed in restaurant and foodservice operations of all types and at all price levels.

Experienced managers working in the restaurant and foodservice industry know that the top complaint is not bad food; it is poor service. As a result, managers are responsible for ensuring that guests receive the quality of service they seek. Managers know that an operation's commitment to high-quality guest service should be clearly communicated off-premise. This commitment should be communicated to those guests the business seeks to attract. It should also be communicated on-premise to those guests who are already visiting the operation.

OFF-PREMISE COMMUNICATION OF SERVICE COMMITMENT

When a manager's operation constantly delivers high-quality guest service, that fact should be communicated to the operation's target market. Advertising is one way to do that. Technically, advertising is any form of marketing message that managers must pay for. Advertisements include, for example, newspaper ads, commercials played on the radio or television, and the placement of ads on a Web site. While advertising is a powerful off-premise communication tool, it is important to recognize that it is only one of several communication tools that managers should be familiar with:

- Advertising
- Sales promotions
- Publicity
- Public relations

Advertising

Advertising is a marketing message that managers must purchase. Managers should consider advertising as part of a long-term investment in the success of an operation. Typically, people need to be exposed to an ad several times before they notice and remember it. Therefore, it sometimes may take weeks, months, or even years of advertising and marketing efforts to bring in a significant number of additional customers. Managers can use paid advertising to achieve many operational goals:

- Communicating a message to a large audience
- Generating awareness of a product or service
- Persuading customers to take action, such as visiting an operation or purchasing a product
- Strengthening existing customer loyalty
- Creating or reinforcing an image of a product or organization
- Differentiating an operation's products and services from its competitors

Managers can choose from a large number of options as they choose the places where they will advertise to customers:

Exhibit 8.5

- Television
- Radio
- Newspapers
- Phone directories
- Billboards
- On-premise and off-premise exterior signs (see *Exhibit 8.5*)
- Dining guides (print)
- Fliers and brochures

Increasingly, guests seek information about restaurant and foodservice operations from the Internet. As a result, managers can choose from a growing number of online alternatives for advertising to customers. While the specific form and nature of online advertising varies based on the type of Web sites managers choose to use, online ads should ideally allow customers to easily find key information about an operation:

- Name
- Address

- Phone number
- Driving directions
- Hours of operation
- Brief description of the operation
- Delivery information (if applicable)
- Current sales promotions
- Recent reviews or links to reviews
- Price range
- Photos
- Menus

Some managers focus their advertising messages only on the products they sell. However, managers whose operations provide excellent customer service know that effective ads can also focus on a variety of quality service–related aspects of their operations:

- Speed of service
- Friendliness of staff
- Ambience
- Exceptional social setting
- Good times
- Fair prices

In addition to sending target customers messages about available products and services, advertising can also be used to create awareness of sales promotions, to make positive publicity known, or to share information about public relations efforts. Each of these communication tools will be addressed next.

Sales Promotions

Sales promotions provide special incentives for customers to patronize an establishment. There are many types of sales promotions and different tools and materials that can be used in a sales promotion. All are designed to give customers an extra "boost" to get them into an establishment or to purchase certain items. High-quality customer service can be used as a major reason for customers taking advantage of a sales promotion.

Since sales promotions are useful only when customers know about them, they are often the focus of an establishment's advertising efforts. *Exhibit 8.6* lists a variety of sales promotions and the incentives they provide to customers.

Exhibit 8.6

TYPES OF SALES PROMOTIONS

Method	Description	Incentive to the Customer
Special pricing	Limited-time reduced prices implemented through specials, deals, coupons, or other programs	Savings on an item; low-risk opportunity to try a new item
Frequent diner programs	Gives a benefit in exchange for continuing patronage	Rewards for continued patronage (usually free meals)
Premiums	Free or reduced-price merchandise that may or may not show the name and location of the establishment, usually given away or sold for a reduced price with the purchase of a food item	Free or reduced-price merchandise
Special events	One-time or periodic occasions that provide a special incentive for the customer to patronize the establishment	Varies based on event
Samples	Free, small tastes of food items	Risk-free opportunity to try a new item
Contests and sweepstakes	Games and other programs that involve the customer and provide a prize	Chance to win a product or service

Publicity

Publicity is information about an establishment that is distributed for free but is not usually produced by the operation. A newspaper article announcing the opening of a new establishment is one example of free publicity. The main benefit of publicity is that people often find it more believable than advertising. For example, a customer reads a glowing review in a local newspaper of the service provided by an establishment. That customer might be more likely to visit the operation than if he or she merely read an advertisement for that establishment in the same paper.

Some managers wonder how they can obtain good publicity for their operations. It is not as difficult as it may seem. Consider the following examples of simple activities that would likely generate good local publicity for an establishment:

- Serving as a collection point for donations to a charity
- Offering customers a discount when they bring in a donation for charity
- Donating a portion of sales for a day to a local charity
- Offering customers a discount after they attend a game of a local sports team

Establishments do not control publicity. Managers must recognize that positive publicity is a great advantage, but negative publicity can damage the credibility of an operation. If an operation receives negative publicity, for example, through a bad food review or bad service review posted online or in print, the manager may need to take action through advertising or public relations to overcome the negative publicity.

Public Relations

Public relations (PR) is the part of an establishment's communication activities that addresses the operation's image among the community. In some cases, that community may consist of only a very small geographic area, or it may consist of an entire state or even a whole country.

Effective public relations means managing communications between an organization and its target market. Effective managers use public relations as part of a coordinated effort to shape the public's opinions about their operation. Publicity and public relations are related, but they are not synonymous. Public relations activities may lead directly to positive publicity. However, businesses may undertake PR activities simply to be contributing members of their communities. One challenge facing managers is knowing whether or not to engage in a PR activity when there is no real expectation of publicity from the activity. For example, an operation's continued willingness to encourage its staff to volunteer to serve holiday meals at a local homeless shelter may not result in sustained positive publicity.

Restaurant and foodservice managers can become involved in a variety of PR activities. Examples include assisting with the activities of local public schools, community colleges, and universities as well as homeless shelters, food banks, charities, and local volunteer organizations. Each of these options provides an opportunity for a restaurant or foodservice operation to serve the local community. If an operation is part of a chain, the chain may support one or more activities on a national level. In all cases, the good will developed through public relations activities can set an establishment apart and enhance its reputation as a good community citizen.

THINK ABOUT IT . . .

Can you recall visiting an establishment because you read something positive about it in the newspaper or online? Would you have gone if you had merely seen an ad from the same operation?

Manager's Memo

While managers cannot fully control publicity about their operations, they can sometimes influence it through good relationships with local media representatives. Managers develop these relationships by meeting regularly with local news media representatives. Good relations can significantly impact an operation's publicity efforts. Good media relations help with positive publicity, but they are just as important when an operation experiences negative publicity. The potential for negative publicity exists, for example, when there is widespread reporting of an outbreak of a foodborne illness, violence, or criminal activity in or around an establishment.

When managers have a good relationship with media professionals who shape public opinion, these managers can often provide their own view of the situation. These managers are in a good position to properly address critical events that could threaten the reputation and survival of their businesses. Especially in times of crisis, savvy managers maintain good relationships with local media representatives.

The best service-oriented managers know that communicating product-related information to guests is important. They also know that service-related information is just as important for marketing their operations' positive guest experiences. *Exhibit 8.7* summarizes the tools managers can use for the off-premise communication of their service quality commitment. It also includes a reference to **personal selling**: the presentation of a marketing message delivered by employees of a business for the purpose of making a sale. Personal selling is a powerful tool for the on-premise communication of an operation's service commitment. In some cases, such as when managers make off-premise sales calls to potential customers, personal selling can also be a powerful off-premise marketing tool.

Exhibit 8.7

TOOLS FOR COMMUNICATING SERVICE COMMITMENT

Marketing Tool	Defining Characteristic
Advertising	Marketing message content that is paid for and controlled by the business
Sales promotions	Used to give customers an extra incentive to buy
Publicity	Message content that is free and not controlled by the business; can be positive or negative
Public relations	Manages the public's perception of a business
Personal selling	Face-to-face presentation of a marketing message

ON-PREMISE COMMUNICATION OF SERVICE COMMITMENT

Personal selling is an excellent way to communicate an operation's commitment to service to each of its on-premise guests. Personal selling is the face-to-face presentation of an operation's marketing message. When personal selling is undertaken by service staff it is often referred to as suggestive selling because it takes the form of making recommendations or suggestions to guests about items the guests might be interested in buying.

To create an effective atmosphere for the on-premise communication of an operation's commitment to service quality, managers actually address two key areas: suggestive selling and service recovery.

Suggestive Selling

An effective suggestive selling program communicates an operation's commitment to service excellence because it seeks to enhance a guest's dining experience. In an effective suggestive selling program, guests benefit because servers suggest products and services they feel will make a customer's dining experience more memorable. Managers undertake specific activities when they plan and execute an effective employee suggestive selling program:

1. Develop program standards.

2. Train employees on the program.

3. Observe staff performance.

4. Evaluate program results.

5. Alter the program as needed.

Each of the above steps has a number of activities associated with it:

1. **Develop program standards:** Managers develop program standards to increase suggestive selling by employees (see *Exhibit 8.8*). As they develop their suggestive selling programs, managers address key issues that will be specific to their own operations:

Exhibit 8.8

- What specific results do we seek from our program?
- What steps should be taken to ensure our staff will be committed to the program?
- Which employees should be involved in the program? How will these employees be trained?
- How will we gather employee input as we develop our program?
- What tools, such as employee evaluation forms or service quality assessment surveys, should we develop or acquire?
- Will we provide employee performance incentives and, if so, how much money should be made available to fund the incentives?

As managers develop their programs, they can also identify a variety of specific statements that servers can make to all guests:

- Would you like fries with that?
- Would you like to upsize your order for only $1?
- Would you like to see our wine list?
- Can I suggest a pre-dinner cocktail?
- Would you care for an after-dinner coffee?

In all cases, a manager's suggestive selling program should also include methods for carefully monitoring specific numbers of items sold or measurable increases in guest check averages.

2. **Train employees on the program:** After managers have identified which employees to train in the suggestive selling program and what training method to use, they train their staff on program standards,

expectations, and sales techniques. Managers who train servers in suggestive selling often point out that it will increase the guest's check average and, as a result, the server's tip. However, suggestive selling involves more than just selling additional menu items.

When servers improve service through suggestive selling, the suggestion of an appetizer, side dish, or dessert is intended to enhance the guest's dining experience and to maximize guest satisfaction. Managers should emphasize this point in training. Doing so can be an extremely effective way to encourage staff to engage in suggestive selling. A good suggestive selling training program should meet the following criteria:

- Enhancing servers' communication skills so they can be effective when talking with customers
- Developing each server's product knowledge so he or she can vividly and accurately describe menu items to customers
- Informing servers about menu items that complement each other so these items can be suggested to customers
- Teaching servers the impact that suggestive selling has on the financial position of the operation
- Teaching servers the positive impact that suggestive selling has on their own tip income

Some employees are reluctant to attempt suggestive selling because they are shy, or they think that suggestive selling makes them too pushy, or they are uncomfortable with selling. All of these reasons for avoiding suggestive selling can be handled with proper training. Even so, it is a good practice to hire service staff with personalities that make them comfortable with the suggestive selling process.

3. **Observe staff performance:** Managers observe staff performance to determine if employees are practicing good suggestive selling and upselling techniques. Upselling is a personal selling strategy whereby the server provides guests with the opportunity to purchase related or higher-priced products that the guest wants, but also for the purpose of making a larger sale.

A common example of upselling happens when a QSR employee asks a guest who is ordering a meal, "Would you like to upsize your drink?" Suggestive selling and upselling can both be powerful personal selling strategies that significantly impact an operation's total sales, but they must be applied consistently. As they observe staff, managers can determine how often suggestive and upselling techniques are actually used. In most cases, servers who are effective at suggestive selling engage in specific activities that managers can easily observe:

- Suggesting add-on items

- Suggesting specific items; for example, asking "Would you like some iced tea on this hot day?" rather than asking "Would you like something to drink?"

- Suggesting items that servers themselves enjoy

- Suggesting the establishment's best-selling items to increase the probability that the customers will be happy with their orders

- Using visual selling aids such as dessert trays (*Exhibit 8.9*)

Exhibit 8.9

4. **Evaluate program results:** Managers continually evaluate the results of suggestive selling programs to assess program effectiveness. Managers can evaluate the effectiveness of suggestive selling programs using a variety of measurable outcomes:

- **Sales of a targeted item:** The number of sales of items specifically targeted by a suggestive selling program, for example, a specific dessert or appetizer, can be assessed to determine if the sales level met previously established goals.

- **Increased or decreased sales of targeted menu categories:** The number of sales of item groups specifically targeted by a suggestive selling program, for example, the number of all desserts or all after dinner coffee sales, can be assessed to determine if the sale of these items met previously established goals.

- **Increase in check average:** This is used to measure the overall impact on sales of effective suggestive selling programs.

- **Identification of successful sales staff:** This information can be useful when evaluating individual server performance. It is also helpful in determining if any additional training in suggestive selling must be undertaken for servers who did not sell as much.

Once the results from a suggestive selling program are known, managers can share the results. Communicating the results of an operation's suggestive selling program is important for a variety of reasons:

- Generating good feelings among staff members about their hard work

- Building teamwork

- Building morale

- Encouraging new ideas on how to improve performance

- Fostering good communication between front-of-the-house and back-of-the-house employees

Manager's Memo

In addition to taking a customer service approach to encourage suggestive selling, managers can develop incentives and contests for employees. Examples include the following:

1. Give incentives to servers who sell the most.
2. Give servers a commission for selling selected items, such as appetizers or desserts.
3. Hold contests that reward servers for selling the largest number of selected items.

Incentives of these types can work well, but managers should recognize that there can be challenges when using them. It is important to design incentives and contests that are fair to all servers on all shifts. Also, managers must be careful to avoid creating a culture in which servers do suggestive selling or upselling only when there is an incentive or other reward given for doing so.

5. **Alter the program as needed:** Suggestive selling in a restaurant or foodservice operation should maximize guest satisfaction and increase the operation's average check, resulting in increased profitability. The success of suggestive selling depends on having the right people with product knowledge, effective communication skills, and appropriate sales training. If a manager determines that these goals are not being achieved, the suggestive selling program must be altered or employees may need additional training.

In most cases, managers should make personal selling training for staff a priority and an ongoing effort. To do so, the training can be conducted formally by a manager or a designated trainer. Alternately, the topic can be an occasional agenda item for staff meetings. Managers can also set aside time at staff meetings to discuss suggestive selling best practices and challenges.

Service Recovery

Chapter 7 presented information on how managers and staff can respond to guests who have had a less than positive dining experience. Service recovery, the process of identifying the cause of a guest complaint and correcting it, is a powerful way to communicate an operation's commitment to high-quality customer service.

Customer complaints can tell managers a great deal about how their guests view their experiences in an operation. In most cases, customer complaints result from identifiable circumstances:

- The service provided was poor.
- The presentation of a product was poor.
- The price charged did not match the service levels provided.
- The price charged did not match the quality level of the product served.
- The operation did not deliver what was advertised.
- The price of a product or service was perceived to be high compared to other similar products or services.

Note that in each of these cases, guest expectations were not met. Remember that high-quality customer service means meeting and exceeding guests' expectations. Therefore, guest complaints and the opportunities they provide for service recovery give managers critical information about where operational improvements must take place. As a result, service recovery activities benefit guests who voice complaints, but they can also benefit the operation and its future customers, as well.

FREQUENT DINER PROGRAMS

Frequent diner programs, or other repeat-customer reward programs, are used to increase customers' loyalty. These programs give tangible rewards to those guests who visit an operation on a regular basis. To a large degree, the long-term success of a frequent diner program is dependent upon the quality of service the members of the program receive. These programs are designed to provide various incentives to customers who buy a specified number of meals or items or who visit an establishment a required number of times. For example, a customer may receive a free gourmet coffee after purchasing 10 similarly priced gourmet coffees over the course of multiple visits.

In most cases, frequent diner programs differ from sales promotions. Frequent diner programs require repeated visits to receive the program's rewards. Sometimes, the programs can have time limits, for example, a requirement to purchase 10 pizzas within one year to receive a free pizza.

Establishments that use frequent diner programs often distribute membership cards or punch cards to track the number of items a customer has purchased. Customers who use these cards often return to the establishments that sponsor them to build up points. In other programs, purchases are tracked online. In either case, "points" or "purchases" that program members accumulate help create customer loyalty. Managers using these programs know that repeat customers expect excellent service each time they visit an operation. Their programs will succeed if that level of service is consistently delivered.

Special Guest Status

Some managers feel it is important to treat every one of their guests "the same." The best managers, however, understand that those guests who frequent an establishment on a regular basis do not want to be treated "the same" as every other guest. These guests want to be treated in special ways that reflect their intense loyalty to the operation. In fact, these guests want to be considered VIPs, or Very Important Persons, each time they visit an operation.

VIP guests exist in most operations whether or not an operation uses a formal frequent diner program. In all operations, managers and their staff can take extra steps to recognize their operation's own VIPs:

- Greeting VIP guests by name
- Offering to seat VIPs in their favorite dining areas or at their favorite tables
- Remembering favorite beverages so that servers can please guests by asking if they will be having "the usual"

RESTAURANT TECHNOLOGY

OPEN FOR BUSINESS

Some operations grant points to their frequent diner program members based on how much the members spend during a designated time period. In these programs, the more points accumulated, the greater the benefit granted to the member. For example, in a program where each dollar spent in an operation yields 1 point, a member who accumulates 500 points might qualify for a $25 gift certificate. A member who earns 1,000 points might qualify for a $100 gift certificate.

In programs such as these, accurately tracking the actual amount spent per customer is critical. Today's modern POS systems have features that allow for the easy tracking and reporting of guest expenditures. Some of these sales tracking programs can be interfaced, or connected, to an operation's Web site. Guests with the proper password can regularly monitor their accounts to see the number of points they have earned and the rewards for which they qualify.

THINK ABOUT IT . . .

Have you ever received a complimentary menu item because you purchased a designated number of similar items from an operation over a specific time period? How did you feel when you received your free item?

- Allowing VIP guests preferred status during any hard-to-secure reservation or seating times

- Delivering complimentary items, such as a beverage or appetizer, as appropriate to demonstrate the operation's appreciation of the guests' loyalty

- Stopping by the table of VIPs by the manager to personally greet the guests and thank them for returning

- Recognizing that, in many cases, these guests value extra attention and increased personal service as much as they value the menu items they buy

MANAGEMENT ASSESSMENT OF SERVICE QUALITY

Ensuring product quality in restaurant and foodservice operations is one important step in building repeat customers. Ensuring service quality is just as important. Experienced managers know that they should regularly measure and assess the quality of service provided in their operations. Only by comparing actual performance to targeted performance can managers determine their ability to meet their customer service goals and identify areas for improvement. When managers seek to assess service quality in their operations, they choose from two types of measures: objective measures and subjective measures.

Objective Measures

An objective measure is one that can be used to evaluate real changes in data. Two or more people can use the same objective measuring tool and come to the same conclusions. For example, a manager might seek to measure customer perceptions of an operation's server friendliness. In this example, assume the manager wants at least 90 percent of all customers to rate the operation's "friendliness of server" as "excellent" during a specific time period. In this example, the manager could use guest surveys or comment cards (see chapter 7) that permit customers to assign a score to "friendliness of server" as shown in *Exhibit 8.10*.

Note that the measures in *Exhibit 8.10* are objective measures because two different managers tabulating the same data, from the same guest surveys, would get the same results. In fact, any person undertaking the measurement would get the same results. There are several reasons why objectively measuring service quality makes good sense. First, objective measures give managers an indication of the effectiveness of their service efforts. Objective measures also give managers the information they need to determine if they have achieved their service goals. Accurate objective measures of service quality also give managers the information they need to modify or improve their service delivery.

Exhibit 8.10

SAMPLE SERVICE-QUALITY SURVEY

JACK'S
FAMILY RESTAURANT

TO OUR GUESTS
We want your dining experience to be all that you hoped it would be. Please let us know how we are doing in meeting your service needs by completing this survey and returning it to the host when you leave. Thank you.

SERVICE · QUALITY
SURVEY

DATE OF VISIT

	POOR	AVERAGE	EXCELLENT
Parking lot convenience	☐	☐	☐
Parking lot cleanliness	☐	☐	☐
Valet service value for price	☐	☐	☐
Friendliness of greeter/host	☐	☐	☐
Coat check service	☐	☐	☐
Décor	☐	☐	☐
Table location	☐	☐	☐
Linens and silverware	☐	☐	☐
Helpfulness of server	☐	☐	☐
Friendliness of server	☐	☐	☐
Accuracy of meal served	☐	☐	☐
Promptness of table service	☐	☐	☐
Cleanliness of restrooms	☐	☐	☐
Cleanliness of restaurant	☐	☐	☐
Quality of private room (if utilized)	☐	☐	☐

Do you believe that you received good value for your money?   ☐ YES   ☐ NO

Is there a particular employee you would like to single out for praise?   ☐ YES   ☐ NO
If yes, please explain.

_____

_____

Would you recommend our restaurant to an aquaintance?   ☐ YES   ☐ NO

Other comments

_____

_____

Exhibit 8.11

Many managers do not have the budgets, expertise, or time to conduct detailed measurement and analysis of their service efforts. Therefore, their measurement tools and techniques should be practical ones they can easily apply. To do so, managers use specific steps:

Step 1: Identify specific and measurable service objectives where possible

When managers define specific and measurable service objectives, they can determine if they have, or have not, achieved them. The more specific the objective, the easier it is to measure it. To illustrate, consider the following two service objectives that could be used by a manager operating a fast-casual restaurant:

- Serve all guests quickly (see *Exhibit 8.11*).
- Serve all guests next week in an average time of less than three minutes.

The first objective is not easily measurable because not all managers would likely define "quickly" in the same way. The second objective is highly measurable. The number of guests served can be easily counted and the time it takes to serve them can be recorded. Note also that there is a specific time frame for achieving the objective. The best managers establish as many of their service goals as possible in an objective manner.

Step 2: Choose effective measurement tools

When managers know what they will measure, they can select appropriate measurement tools. There are a number of sources for information needed to objectively measure quality guest service:

- Comment card results
- Guest survey results
- POS sales information
  - Guests served
  - Check average
  - Average time of guest service
  - Average time to prepare orders
  - Total revenue achieved
  - Changes in revenue

Step 3: Take action

In most cases, objective measurements require managers to accumulate information during a specific time period. The data should be summarized properly, analyzed, and put to practical use. Gathered and properly analyzed, objective measures of service quality can be used to show managers where they can modify and improve service delivery in their operations.

Subjective Measures

A subjective measure is one in which two evaluators viewing the same piece of information may come to different conclusions. For example, if a manager states "guests like our service," that manager's view of "like" may or may not be consistent with another manager's view. For this reason managers should seek, whenever possible, to use objective measures of service quality. Subjective measures of service quality may have a place in an operation's overall measurement of service quality, but the actual results of subjective measures should be carefully considered before they are acted on.

ENSURING ONGOING QUALITY SERVICE

There are several methods a manager might choose to assess and improve the quality of the customer service they deliver. However, there are specific service quality–related rules all managers should follow if they are to consistently communicate, and thus market, positive guest experiences:

1. Promise only what can be consistently delivered.

2. Price products and services fairly to optimize value delivered to guests.

3. Exceed expectations by providing service at a level greater than guests normally expect.

4. Adopt a customer-centric attitude by viewing all service issues, policies, and procedures from the customer's perspective.

5. Establish an effective guest feedback system.

6. Monitor feedback to identify areas where improvements are needed by analyzing trends and patterns.

7. Respond to all on-premise or off-premise customer feedback positively and courteously.

SUMMARY

1. **Explain the importance of high-quality customer service to the marketing of a restaurant or foodservice operation.**

   Managers who deliver high-quality customer service identify customers' expectations and consistently exceed them. They provide products and services that create value for their customers, and create profits for their organizations. Since marketing is the formal process of telling and showing potential customers how their needs and wants will be met by a business, managers must ensure their operations' expected quality and service levels are consistent with their marketing efforts. They do so by reviewing guest experiences at all key points of the guests' visit. Managers control these critical service points to identify the need for additional staff training or procedure revisions required to meet their operations' quality service targets.

   Operations sell products, but they deliver service. Even if an establishment delivers quality product in an attractive setting at a fair price, poor service quality will result in customers who will not come back or recommend the establishment to others. As a result, a high level of professional service is needed to effectively market all types of restaurant and foodservice operations.

2. **Summarize the advantages of using a systems management approach when operating a business.**

   Because a systems management approach views activities in an operation as a group of interdependent processes, effective managers can analyze those processes to ensure they are working well together. Each process is made up of various tasks. When managers ensure each task is completed properly, it helps an operation

> **Manager's Memo**
>
> Consumer researchers often study specific customer behavior. A *USA Today* news article reported the findings of a ClickFox survey of 443 consumers.*
>
> The researchers found that 15 percent of customers will purchase additional products or services after receiving exceptional service. The same study found that 35 percent of customers will stop doing business with an organization after receiving poor customer service. Thus, 50 percent of all customers surveyed stated that they make their purchase decisions, in large part, based on the quality of service that they receive.
>
> Experienced restaurant and foodservice managers would not be surprised by these findings. For that reason, managers must do all they can to ensure their customers receive exceptional guest service each and every time they visit their operations.
>
> *Adapted from *USA Today*, March 6, 2012, p. B1.

meet the goals established for each individual process that directly affects guest service levels. This is so because, when an operation's processes work well, the result is internal service quality that leads to external service value for guests.

3. **Describe the tools managers can use to communicate their service commitment to off-premise customers.**

    When a manager's operation constantly delivers high-quality guest service, that fact should be communicated to the operation's target market. Managers can use advertising, sales promotions, publicity, and public relations (PR) to communicate their service commitment to off-premise customers. Advertising is any form of marketing message that managers must pay for. Sales promotions provide special incentives for customers to patronize an establishment. Publicity is information about an establishment that is distributed for free, but is not produced by the business. Public relations (PR) is the part of an establishment's communication activities that addresses the operation's image in its community.

4. **List the steps required to develop and execute an effective on-premise suggestive selling program.**

    Managers follow a five-step process in the development of an effective suggestive selling program. First, managers develop their standards for the suggestive selling program. In the second step, managers train their staff on program expectations and sales techniques. In step three, managers observe staff performance to determine if employees are practicing good suggestive selling techniques. Step four requires managers to evaluate the results of their suggestive selling programs. In the fifth step, managers make modifications, if needed, to improve the programs or to identify those areas in which employees may need additional training.

5. **Explain the importance of service recovery to the successful management of a restaurant or foodservice operation.**

    Service recovery is the process of identifying the cause of a guest complaint and correcting it. High-quality service recovery actions on the part of managers and staff are a powerful way to communicate an operation's overall commitment to high-quality customer service. Customer complaints usually result from identifiable circumstances where guest expectations were not met. As a result, guest complaints give managers important information about where improvements to their operations should be made. When improvements are made, it benefits those guests who have complained as well as the operation's future guests.

6. **Discuss the impact of high-quality customer service on the success of frequent diner programs.**

    Frequent diner programs, or other repeat-customer reward programs, are used to increase loyalty and reward customers for their loyalty. The long-term success of a frequent diner program often depends on the quality of service the members of the program receive. Frequent diner programs differ from sales promotions or other specials in that they require repeated visits to receive the program's rewards. As a result, the continual and consistent delivery of high-quality customer service is essential. Managers using these programs know that repeat customers expect excellent service each time they visit an operation and that their reward programs will succeed only if that level of service is consistently delivered to every frequent diner program member.

7. **Explain the steps used to objectively measure service quality in a restaurant or foodservice operation.**

The objective measurement of service quality gives managers the information they need to modify or improve their service delivery. To objectively measure service levels in a restaurant or foodservice operation, managers use three steps. In the first step, managers identify specific and measurable service objectives that are to be achieved within a specified time period. In the second step, managers choose effective measurement tools. In the third and final step, managers use the information they have obtained to take any actions they feel are needed to improve their operations' guest service delivery systems.

APPLICATION EXERCISE

Assume you are the manager of a fine-dining operation that features the regional cuisine in a geographic setting of your choosing. Your operation has been open for five years and its commitment to service and the quality of service it provides guests is far above average compared to its competitors. Please choose and complete any one of the marketing activities listed. Remember that the focus of the activity is to market the quality of service at your operation.

Advertising

1. Create a print advertisement suitable for placement in your local newspaper that emphasizes your operation's commitment to high-quality customer service.

2. Write a memorable radio ad (that can be read in 30 seconds) that emphasizes your operation's commitment to high-quality customer service.

Sales Promotion

1. Create a specific sales promotion that would be best communicated via off-premise paid advertising and that emphasizes the service levels of your operation.

2. Create a specific sales promotion that would be best executed via on-premises personal selling and that emphasizes the service levels of your operation.

Publicity

1. Briefly describe a special event or gathering that could be held in your operation, features products you sell, and could result in positive publicity for your business.

2. Briefly describe a special event or gathering that could be held in your operation, features your commitment to high-quality service, and could result in positive publicity for your business.

Public Relations (PR)

1. Describe in detail an off-premise PR effort that interests you as a manager and that you feel could result in positive publicity for your operation.

2. Describe in detail an off-premise PR effort that you feel your service staff would be interested in participating in and that you feel could result in positive publicity for your operation.

Personal Selling

1. Choose an item from your menu and then write a brief script that servers can recite when applying on-premise suggestive selling techniques. In the script, emphasize how the quality service provided in the delivery of the item will add to the value received by those who purchase the item.

2. Write a two-paragraph description that could be posted on your establishment's Web site that tells what customers of your operation gain by having a membership in your frequent diner program. Emphasize the service-related benefits they would receive from membership in the program.

REVIEW YOUR LEARNING

Select the best answer for each question.

1. *Marketing* is the term used to describe the
   A. set of interrelated systems that must be in place to meet profit goals.
   B. process of telling guests how a business will meet their needs and wants.
   C. way owners ensure their operations will identify the right target customers.
   D. only form of off-premise guest communication for which an operation must pay.

2. What are the final two components in the profit-service chain?
   A. Revenue growth and profitability
   B. Profitability and external service value
   C. External service value and revenue growth
   D. Customer satisfaction and external service value

3. What form of marketing communication is being used when a manager hosts, at no charge, a meeting of the local community's volunteer fire department?
   A. Publicity
   B. Advertising
   C. Sales promotion
   D. Public relations

4. What is a trait that demonstrates an operation's commitment to service quality and that could be featured in an off-premise advertisement?
   A. Perfectly cooked steaks
   B. A large and varied drink menu
   C. Fast preparation of to-go orders
   D. The use of locally grown produce

5. What is a manager's first step in the development of an effective suggestive selling program?
   A. Observe staff.
   B. Evaluate results.
   C. Train employees.
   D. Develop standards.

6. What is the impact on servers of an effective suggestive selling program?
   A. Increased tips
   B. Decreased shift lengths
   C. Increased cross-training opportunities
   D. Decreased sales of targeted menu items

7. Service recovery is the process of identifying the cause of a guest complaint and
   A. explaining it.
   B. correcting it.
   C. recording it.
   D. reporting it.

8. When using a systems management approach, managers view each of their operations' processes as
   A. cost neutral.
   B. independent.
   C. interrelated.
   D. self-reliant.

9. Which is an example of a manager's service recovery action?
   A. Greeting guests on arrival
   B. Thanking guests for coming
   C. Apologizing for an operation's slow service
   D. Explaining why a new item was chosen for the menu

10. How could a manager best measure the effectiveness of an upselling program?
    A. By measuring changes in guest counts
    B. By measuring changes in customer check averages
    C. By measuring changes in guest comment card scores
    D. By measuring changes in the number of guest complaints received

FIELD PROJECT

There are various customer service procedures used in restaurant and foodservice operations, and also various claims of providing good customer service. The goal of this project is to evaluate these procedures and claims based on the information in this book.

Assignment

1. Develop a list of the restaurant or foodservice operations in your area that have a reputation for providing excellent customer service. You should pursue several methods of determining this, such as:

   - Asking friends and family

   - Examining advertisements in newspapers and telephone books

   - Reading restaurant reviews in newspapers and online

2. Categorize the list by different industry segments (i.e., quick service, full service, fine dining, family dining, etc.).

3. Select two or three from each segment for a total of 8 to 10 operations. Depending on the size of your community, your instructor may adjust this number.

4. Arrange a one-hour interview with the owner or manager of each operation to discuss their methods of providing high-quality customer service.

5. Develop several interview questions to determine whether the standards of high-quality customer service are met by each operation. Provide a copy of the questions to the owners or managers in advance.

6. As you conduct the interview, take detailed notes. Do not hesitate to ask additional questions if you think of them.

7. Take a tour of the different operations and look for factors that might affect their ability to deliver on their claims of customer service; also keep in mind what you consider to be high-quality customer service.

8. Analyze what you have learned and draw conclusions about the following:

   - The level of customer service the restaurant or foodservice operations provide

   - The operations' ability to live up to their claims

   - Problem areas

   - Changes or improvements you would recommend

9. Prepare a report of your findings, analysis, and conclusions. Discuss the similarities and differences among operations in the same segment and also those in different segments.

GLOSSARY

Action plan A series of steps that can be taken to resolve a problem.

Advertising Any form of marketing message that managers must pay for.

Allergen An ingredient in food, usually a protein, that the body mistakes as harmful and creates a defense system (antibodies) to fight it.

Ambience The feeling or mood created by an environment.

Average sale per guest The sales achieved for a specific time period divided by the number of guests served in that time period.

Back of the house (BOH) The areas of the operation that are not typically entered into, or seen, by guests.

Beer An alcoholic beverage fermented from cereals and malts, and made with yeast and hops, which is a flower added to flavor the beverage.

Blood alcohol content (BAC) The amount of alcohol that has been absorbed into the bloodstream of a drinker.

Bounce back Another term for a **return incentive**.

Capacity The different service-related situations and outcomes that exist when establishments are busy and when they are slow.

Cash overage A situation where an operation has more cash in the drawer than the POS system or register says it should have.

Cash shortage A situation where there is not enough cash in the register to equal the amount reported in the register.

Casual restaurants Restaurants that provide table service to guests and serve moderately priced food in an informal atmosphere.

Cellar temperature The optimal temperature for serving wine, generally considered to be between 65°F and 70°F (18°C and 21°C).

Certification The confirmation that a person possesses certain skills, knowledge, or characteristics.

Check average The average amount of the bill each guest must pay for his or her menu selections.

Cleaning Removing food and other types of soil from a surface such as at tabletop or counter.

Coaching Praise and encouragement offered by managers to those employees who are achieving the operation's service standards.

Comment card A card that solicits feedback from the guests about their dining experiences.

Commercial restaurant and foodservice operations Operations that are open to the general public.

Competitive point of difference A perceived or actual difference between any two things that can be used to influence a customer's buying decision.

Condiment An edible item that enhances the flavor of food, such as ketchup.

Consistency Providing the same level of service every time a guest visits the establishment.

Controlling The term used to describe a manager's efforts to monitor performance and take corrective actions as needed.

Cross-contact The result when one food item comes into direct contact with another, causing proteins in the two items to combine.

Cross-functional issues Issues that result from a breakdown in a process that can be traced to one or more interrelated employee tasks.

Cross-training Teaching an employee how to do work normally done by someone in a different position.

Crystal Glass that contains high levels of lead and has been hand or machine cut with facets to create a "sparkle" in the glass.

Culture The attitudes, beliefs, and characteristics of a specific group.

Customer-centric service Service that is centered, or focused, on guests and their unique needs and desires.

Customer loyalty A customer's preference of one establishment to all similar establishments.

Customer service culture A culture that exists in an operation where all employees consider themselves to be in the high-quality customer service business first, and in the food and beverage business second.

Customer service plan The well-thought-out and systematic identification and recording of exactly what must be done to provide high-quality customer service.

Customer with a disability A person who has a physical or mental disability that could have been acquired for a number of reasons, including heredity, illness, accident or injury, or advancing age.

Decibel A measurement of sound.

Deuce Another term for **two-top** tables.

Directing A management function related to the leadership of others.

Dishware The reusable plates, cups, and bowls used to serve menu items.

Dress code An operation's rules regarding attire and other aspects of employees' personal appearance.

Drive-through customers Customers who place and receive their take-away food orders without leaving their cars.

Emergency plan A plan that identifies a threat to the safety or security of a property, as well as the property's planned response to it.

Employee turnover A situation where an employee leaves a job and must be replaced.

Empowerment The act of giving authority, or power, to employees to make decisions within their areas of responsibility.

External customer The end receiver of a product or service.

Facilities The grounds, building, equipment, and furnishings that combine to make up an operation's physical environment.

Fast-casual restaurants Restaurants that do not provide table service, but their food quality, overall service level, and décor is higher than that typically found in a **QSR**.

Fine-dining restaurants Restaurants that offer guests the highest-quality foods and full table service.

Flag To call special attention to an action needed to fulfill a request.

Flatware The eating utensils used by guests, also referred to as *cutlery* or *silverware.*

Food allergies Conditions that occur when the body mistakes an ingredient in food, usually a protein, as harmful and creates a defense system (antibodies) to fight it.

Foodborne illness A disease transmitted to people by food.

Food contact surface An area of an item that comes into direct contact with food.

Foot-candle A measurement of light.

Four-top A table that seats four guests.

Foyer The doorways, hallways, and lobbies that make up an operation's entrance.

Frequent diner program A program used to increase customer loyalty and provide an incentive to customers who purchase a specified number of meals or items or visit an establishment a required number of times.

Front of the house (FOH) The area of a restaurant or foodservice operation that guests have access to.

Glassware The restaurant and foodservice term for individual beverage containers.

Greeter The employee who initially welcomes guests and offers guests a smile, a pleasant attitude, direct eye contact, and a brief but sincerely offered welcoming phrase.

Grounds The plants, flowers, trees, and décor placed around the building that houses an operation.

Guest check The document that lists the amount owed by guests.

Guest check folder A folder designed for use in check presentation, payment collection, and the return of change to the customer.

Guest feedback program A formal system for receiving and analyzing customers' assessments of an operation's service and product quality.

High-quality customer service Service that consistently exceeds customers' expectations for products and services received, as well as the level of personal attention provided during the delivery.

Hospitality The manner in which services are performed, as well as the feeling that customers take with them.

Hospitality industry Businesses that provide food and lodging services to those who are away from home.

HVAC An industry term for an operation's heating, ventilating, and air-conditioning system.

Incident report A form used to document what happened and what was done in response.

Inseparability The tendency of restaurant and foodservice customers to connect the quality of service provided with the personal characteristics of the individual staff member who delivers it.

Intangible Something that cannot be seen, touched, or held before or after it is experienced.

Interface To electronically connect two systems.

Internal customer Anyone inside an operation who receives products, services, or information from someone else to complete his or her work.

Intoxication The physiological state that occurs when a person has a high level of alcohol in his or her blood.

Linens The term used to refer to tablecloths.

Maître d'hôtel A staff member specially designated and trained to greet guests, make table assignments, and manage the operation's entire service staff.

Marketing The formal process of telling and showing potential customers how their needs and wants will be met by a business.

Menu board A large visual listing of menu item descriptions or pictures that shows what is offered for sale.

Merchant copy A charge slip that is the copy for the guest to sign and leave with the operation.

Mise en place A French term that means "everything in its proper place."

Mission statement A written reminder to employees about the purpose and goals of a company, to develop their service standard expectations.

Moment of truth Any episode in which the customer comes into contact with any aspect of the organization and gets an impression of the quality of its service.

Mystery shopper A consultant or employee who visits an operation, acts as a normal guest, and secretly reports to managers on the food, service, facility, and the overall experience; also called a *secret shopper* or just *shopper*.

Noncommercial foodservice operations Operations that are not typically open to the general public.

No-show A guest who makes a reservation but does not arrive to claim it.

Objective measure A measure that can be used to evaluate real changes in data.

Organizing Arranging available resources in a way that best helps the organization achieve its goals.

Pathogen A microorganism that can cause illnesses.

Personal selling The presentation of a marketing message delivered by employees of a business for the purpose of making a sale.

Place setting All of the flatware, dishware, and glassware preset for use by one guest.

Planning The function of management that identifies goals and the strategies that will be used to achieve the goals.

Point-of-sale (POS) system The computer used to record guest orders and payments as well as other important operating information.

Pre-shift team meeting A brief team gathering held prior to the beginning of a work shift.

Process A series of operations or tasks that bring about a desired result.

Publicity Information about an establishment that is distributed for free but is not usually produced by the operation.

Public relations (PR) The part of an establishment's communication activities that addresses the operation's image among the community.

Quick-change artist A thief who seeks to confuse cashiers and steal from a business.

Quick-service restaurant (QSR) A restaurant characterized by its limited menus, fast service, and modest prices.

Reasonable accommodation provision Under Title VII of the Civil Rights Act of 1964 as amended, employers must make adjustments to an employee's dress code that will allow him or her to observe a sincerely held religious practice.

Reasonable care A legal concept that identifies the amount of care a reasonably prudent person would exercise in a specific situation.

Reconciliation The process of matching recorded sales against actual payments received.

Recruiting The search for persons who are potentially interested in an operation's vacant positions.

Return incentive A tool used to give guests a good reason to come back in the future.

Safety audit A formal and detailed examination of an operation's areas of potential threats to guest safety.

Sales promotions Activities that provide special incentives for customers to patronize an establishment (e.g., **frequent diner programs** or limited-time reduced prices).

Sanitizing Reducing the number of harmful microorganisms on a clean surface to safe levels.

Screening The process of reviewing the skills, experience, attitudes, and backgrounds of applicants to make a selection decision.

Server station The specific number and location of tables and seats assigned to each waitstaff member.

Service industry Companies that primarily earn revenue by providing products and intangible services.

Service recovery The process of identifying the cause of negative guest feedback or complaints and ensuring the circumstances that caused the dissatisfaction are corrected.

ServSafe Alcohol The name of the responsible alcohol server program developed by the National Restaurant Association.

Skill set The skills needed to properly perform a task or to complete a job.

Sommelier A restaurant or foodservice staff member who is highly trained to assist customers in selecting the wines to accompany the customer's menu choices.

Spirit An alcoholic beverage produced by distilling, or removing water from, a liquid that contains alcohol.

Standard A description of the criteria for items, tasks, behaviors, practices, and other aspects of an operation that represent the norm for the business.

Standardized recipe A set of instructions to produce and serve a food or beverage item that will help ensure that quality and quantity standards will be consistently met.

Statistical analysis system (SAS) A system used to tabulate and collate research data collected by a market research firm or consultant.

Subjective measure A situation in which two evaluators viewing the same piece of information may come to different conclusions.

Suggestive selling The recommendation of additional or different items to a customer by a server.

Supportive processes The elements in an establishment that impact an operation's internal customers to help them perform their jobs well and be satisfied at work.

System A set of standards, processes, and tasks that work together in an organized way to achieve an end result.

Systems management approach An approach that looks at the activities in an operation as a group of different processes; each process is made up of tasks that work together to meet the objectives of each process and the whole operation.

Table assignment The placement of guests at specific tables and seats in an operation.

Table management system The methods used to control the flow of guests to tables in the dining area.

Tableware The industry term used to collectively describe three categories of tabletop items: flatware, dishware, and glassware.

Task A responsibility, function, or procedure that is performed as part of a process.

Teamwork The act of cooperating and working together to complete tasks and reach common goals.

Third-party liability A legal concept in which the establishment that sold the alcohol (and, in some states, even the bartender) may be held liable if a guest who consumed the alcohol causes an accident that injures someone.

Three-top A table that holds three guests.

Training The tool managers use to improve their employees' skills, knowledge, or attitudes.

Two-top A table that seats two guests.

Uniform Any garment worn to identify the wearer as an employee of the operation.

Upselling A selling strategy where the server provides guests opportunities to purchase related or higher-priced products that the guests might want, often for the purpose of making a larger sale.

Value The difference between what customers get when they buy a product or service and what they pay to get it.

VIP (Very Important Person) A guest (such as a frequent customer) who is regarded as special each time he or she visits an establishment.

Void The situation where a cash register entry has to be corrected by canceling the entry and entering the correct item.

Wait list A record of the names of guests who have arrived at an establishment but who have not yet been escorted to their tables.

Walk-in A guest who arrives at an operation without having made a reservation in advance.

Wine An alcoholic beverage produced from grapes or other fruit.

INDEX

V

valets, 19
value, 31, 33, 48, 190
vending areas, 8
vinegar, 56
VIPs (Very Important Persons), 201–202
vision
with garnishes, 56
impairment, 43–44, 49

voids, 160
voluntary comments, 170

W

waiting areas, 19, 106, 112, 118
wait lists, 107, 112–113, 119
waitstaff, 20
walk-in, 112
weather, 64, 89
wheat, 45

wheeled cart (*gueridon*), 136
wine
bottle size, 138
definition, 137
list, 117–118
service, 138–140
stewards, 13, 20
workplace design, 189
work quality, 18
work stress, 17
wraps, 149

NOTES